Becoming a Professional Model

By the same author

The Professional Photographer

Becoming a Professional Model

Larry Goldman

BTB
BEECH TREE BOOKS
WILLIAM MORROW
New York

Library of Congress Cataloging-in-Publication Data

Goldman, Larry.
Becoming a professional model.

Includes index.
1. Models, Fashion—Vocational guidance.
2. Employment of men.   3. Women—Employment.
I. Title.
HD8039.M77G65   1985   659.1′52   85-18571
ISBN 0-688-04765-3
ISBN 0-688-06147-8 (Quill ed. : pbk.)

Printed in the United States of America

First Edition

1 2 3 4 5 6 7 8 9 10

BOOK DESIGN BY LINEY LI

BⳠB

The word "book" is said to derive from *boka*, or beech.
The beech tree has been the patron tree of writers since ancient times and
represents the flowering of literature and knowledge.

To my agent,
Michael Carlisle,
with gratitude

ACKNOWLEDGMENTS

The place to start saying thanks is with my wife, Leslie, for her monumental endurance from the time I woke up with the idea to the delivery of a final manuscript. The concerted effort of many talented people helped me to write this book. I am especially indebted to Beech Tree Book's superb staff, including Jane Meara, without whose enduring faith and thorough editing this book would have remained merely an idea. Randee Marullo monitored all the details, reviewing and then rechecking for accuracy and clarity. This volume had the extraordinary advantage of Liney Li's insightful design, which juxtaposed images and text in a manner that enhanced each. Nor could I underestimate the daring of Cheryl Asherman in every aspect of commissioning and then utilizing the unique cover art. I would also like to thank Jim Landis for creating an enlightened environment in which to publish. I then would like to acknowledge the enormous editorial guidance and support I received from John Glusman; and the assistance of Mary Broaddus, whose awesome organizational capability and humor made this book, and *The Professional Photographer*, totally bearable throughout the innumerable eighteen-hour stretches that seemed to continue over months.

I am indebted to Mary Lumet, Luna Carne-Ross, and Virginia Colton for helping to interpret and direct my thoughts. In all fairness, I must admit that *Becoming a Professional Model* would have been unmanageable without word processing.

The existence of this book is largely due to the willingness of the hundreds of people whom I interviewed for thousands of hours. Therefore, my sincerest gratitude for arranging interviews, for being conduits of the facts, and for eliminating the many misconceptions and clarifying the realities about modeling goes to: Ara Gallant, Gen Le Roy, Candy Pratts Price, George Newell, Tommy McCarthy at Zoli Theatrix, Roseanne Vecchione at Wilhelmina Men, Tishka at Ford, Jan Gonet at Elite Men, and, most of all, Terri Silvers at Elite, for her unflinching loyalty over the last two years. I am grateful to Lila Wisedom in Brooke Shields's office, Fran Crisaro in Christie Brinkley's office, Matthew Olszak in Antonio Lopez's studio, Anne Marie Rozzelli in Ralph Lauren's office, Ronn Robertson at Model's Mart, Grey Grill and Alan Mindel at Click, Laura Broaddus at *New York* magazine, my aunt Lois Beadle, Denise Shapiro, Lilith Jacobs, and Caroline Sutton.

The information in this book could not have been collected without the invaluable assistance of the reference librarians at FIT and the Donnell Library Center. Most of all, I need to thank Ed Khouri, Didi Tillson, Roberto Tamayo, and the William Morris Agency mailroom staff, who oversaw thousands of letters, releases, and valuable original artwork being transferred around New York, the United States, and the world; my gratitude for making sure each and every parcel arrived, and was returned, safely. I also wish to thank the scores of modeling agency bookers and receptionists for putting up with my interruptions, and each modeling association official who graciously allowed me to observe and talk to the contestants.

I wish to publicly thank Bert Stern for his masterful and lavish photograph of twelve Elite models. Next, to all my friends within the industry, especially: Apollonia Van Ravenstein, Zoli (for encouraging me to write the book in the first place), and Barbara Shapiro, who each helped when this was only a budding thought. The final thanks goes to Herb Wise for all his computer expertise and his advice on reproducing tear sheets.

CONTENTS

Introduction

Modeling By the Book

Any talented man or woman, teenager or young adult, who wants to break into the world of professional modeling or work more effectively within it can. *Becoming a Professional Model* guides you through all facets of fashion, live demonstration, print, and commercial advertising—introducing you to experts telling their own tales and passing along insights from their professional lives. You'll find the essentials of putting together a purposeful portfolio, details about categories of modeling work and strategies for gaining access to them, criteria for choosing the right agent, and, especially crucial for beginners, evaluating schools. You will learn what *photogenic* really means and how you can develop that quality, and how to act at a test or go-see (trade talk for job interview) and on a professional set. The book closes with very specific help in mapping out your own career: a listing of the most significant names, addresses, and telephone numbers, directories that are useful for culling a rounds list anywhere in the country, for the best place to prepare, and often begin, a professional career is in or near your own hometown.

Professional is the key word. *Becoming a Professional Model* is written for those serious enough to pursue modeling as a career—not for stargazers or those looking for fashion advice or beauty hints. If you have some potential—which the book will help you decide—this is a perfect time to begin. Never have there been so many roles for models to fill. Among the hottest current possibilities are the live situations, such as television and conventions, and demonstrating or acting as image-makers for manufacturers, retailers, and corporations.

Photography has ever-increasing sales applications; it gets a visual message across with immediacy in fashion magazines, advertising posters, billboards, public information leaflets, and catalogs. On film and video, models display—and by implication endorse—products. In the fashion arena, of course, the model really sets the pace. Every designer, wholesale manufacturer, retail merchant, and catalog producer relies on models to show his wares. Upscale advertisers—of beauty products, cigarettes, packaged foods, beverages, and the like—aren't far behind, using models to project their images to potential customers on runways, in showrooms, in product introduction, and in big-event press kits.

Models represent others to the public, and yet, in a sense, they also represent the public itself. This isn't a new concept. Models personify ideas, designs, new directions; the hope is that the public will follow. Becoming a model for others demands appealing physical attributes and a capacity to express emotion. If you have those qualities, you need only an agent or mentor to bring them out then promote you to photographers and clients within his or her "magnetic field."

ILLUSTRATIONS TO AMPLIFY THE TEXT

Though the book's text and anecdotes give a clear picture of modeling, more than 125 illustrations bring it into even sharper focus: photographs that show how to deliver a "line," project a feeling, portray a mood. Collectively, the pictures demonstrate a variety of stances and of lighting and design concepts while pointing out places for you to begin a career. One series illustrates the best way to assemble the indispensable portfolio; others demonstrate how to work in advertising, catalog, and runway.

By studying the photographs, you can broaden your sense of what photogenic can mean and how it can be projected at any age and in every category. Many of the photographs were chosen to reveal the most vital trade trick of all: how to be natural in front of a camera. Because the pictures depict established models interpreting a wide range of situations, they can teach you a lot about professional problem-solving. Photo *sources* are varied too, to show what is appropriate for many geographic areas.

CATEGORIES: KINDS OF WORK A MODEL CAN DO

The first necessity, for anyone with modeling ambitions, is to grasp the breadth of the categories, the kinds of work for which models are hired. With this knowledge a novice can more easily decide the type or types that are best for him or her. Each category has its own physical and emotional qualifications; for each, there are clues to finding employment. Not all categories exist in all markets—in most regions a model must be versatile enough to switch among the available categories—but the hiring standards remain the same.

There are three general uses for models. Both males and females are increasingly employed to sell live on a trade-convention floor or to enhance a corporate image at a booth, sometimes demonstrating products at a public-relations gathering, at other times moving through skits at corporate meetings or on live TV.

The second use for models, **advertising**—representing a salable "type" in advertisements—is the most intense form of selling by models. The themes that make up the American mix are endlessly variable; so, to no one's surprise, are the promotional types needed by Madison Avenue. Third, it is in wholesale and retail **fashion** that models most often get steady work: fitting production or samples, displaying clothes publicly on a runway or privately in a showroom.

Then, of course, there is fashion photography. Models have a choice here of areas: (a) *editorial*—fashion as news—is great for credibility, glamour, prestige, and portfolio building; (b) *catalog*—the concentrated sell—is often called the bread and butter of modeling; and (c) *commercial print* or *TV spots*—the diffused sell— is called, in industry parlance, the big payoff.

It is rare for a model to be limited to a single category or client; that happens only when there is an exclusive contract or categories are severely limited in a particular market. The same model may, for instance, work for one manufacturer trying on samples or assisting pattern makers, do a fashion illustration in another client's creation, and appear in a sportswear maker's showroom or on a couture designer's runway. One might photograph equally well as a father, a corporate officer, or a doctor in advertising. In addition, there are the specialties—no longer for Caucasian females only, this applies increasingly to all ages, ethnic groups, and sizes—such as faces, bodies, hands, legs, feet, even lips, eyes, and hairlines. Professional models are also likely to work in several different cities.

TALENT DEVELOPERS: THE ROLE OF SCHOOLS AND AGENTS

Modeling, like any profession, must be learned. Each school has its own value and probable limitations, but any bona fide modeling course should accomplish at least three things. It should: (1) sort out those who are qualified from those who aren't; (2) smooth out the rough edges and so enhance the aspiring model's chance of interesting an agent; and (3) have the contacts and know-how to place the better students on the first rung of a career ladder through an interview with a scout from a major market at a model convention. For many smaller-city hopefuls, a school is the only choice. If there is no local school, one other option is a short course often offered at retail stores.

Where it is feasible, it is better to go straight to photographers, designers, or agents for an opinion as to the chances for success. In any event, a model's first real job will come either through an agent who recommends her for free-lance hourly work, through direct hiring by a manufacturer's showroom or department store (usually full-time), or through a photographer's test.

Free-lance models must have agents, not merely to find work but also to protect their rights and to negotiate and collect fees. Each city and category functions differently. A model depends on the agent to keep abreast of her specialty in any working area. An agent's deeper role is in grooming a protégé into a professional—molding her potential, developing a personality that fits the most promising category. Your job is to get the right agent for you: Interview agents until you find one in whom you have confidence, with whom you feel compatible.

For every top market in the five largest American and the European fashion capitals, models are prepared according to their particular specialties. In the fashion-related fields, time in Europe can be desirable at an early point in development. The standards by which a model is judged are the same everywhere: a versatile portfolio that shows experience and a capacity to work with photographers; technical proficiency at selling clothes and products acquired through observation and practice; a professional attitude on rounds, on go-sees, at auditions, on the set, and on the runway; and immaculate grooming, learned from hairdressers, makeup artists, clothes stylists, and photographers.

Modeling is not a pure science, but in order to succeed you'll need to acquire skills and learn to apply them intelligently.

WHEN YOU'RE READY FOR THE REAL THING

Once the basics are mastered, it is time to start testing in a work setting, with a photographer and other professionals needed to put together a complete package. The camera reads what is there; you must invent what you want it to see. Michelangelo said, "Trifles make perfection, and perfection is no trifle." Each model, from her own combination of assets, must build her own perfection.

Proven ability to project is the common thread linking all successful models. Seek out the right photographers to test with, learn to work with them. Tests should not be rushed. Then begins a constant in your career: tracking down tear sheets and prints from photographers and blending them with existing shots so that a portfolio is always current and client-directed. A second continuing need is the search for additional clients; your hunting ground is the go-see. Go-sees are of three distinct kinds: *general rounds* (often referred to as cattle calls because no casting specification is issued); *picture submissions* (Polaroids are often taken to presort for individual characteristics); and *call-back auditions* (usually for major print work and commercials, or convention, public relations, and television modeling). It is the agency's job to prepare you to make the all-important first impression—sometimes in as little as thirty seconds. Getting a booking involves an initial interview and one or several call-backs.

As Benjamin Franklin said, "Time is money" and "Lost time is never found again." Models know what he meant. They are paid to create an effect within a specified time. To succeed—certainly to be rebooked—they must use the allotted time efficiently. They will be poked and pulled at, they will be given contradictory commands, they will have to hold poses endlessly. For this they need great patience, stamina, and perseverance. Perhaps most distressing of all is disorientation—the aftershock of slipping too often between the real and the illusory. Sound physical and emotional preparation is the only weapon against such job pressures.

Gayne de Meyer and his purportedly royal wife Olga were a fashionable London couple transplanted to New York before World War I. For Elizabeth Arden, Baron de Meyer created a turbaned Renaissance beauty with an outstretched hand gently outlining her face. All this to sell an image.

Frances Grill at Click avers that there must be a chemistry between photographer and model. That this is so is obvious from the de Meyer photograph of Berthe (left). And it is still true today. De Meyer's *Vogue* portraits made him a father of modern modeling. His use of society hostesses as models for his fashion photographs elevated both to art.

Pressures diminish, of course, as models learn what to expect and how to interact with other professionals.

There is no better teacher than exposure to those very professionals. Experienced high-fashion models know the tricks of the trade, from draping techniques to how a garment should be worn to how to create the proper aura. If any of this is to carry to the camera, direction must come from the photographer about elements to be brought in or emotion to be brought out. When characterization and pace have been determined, and a rapport established between photographer and model, the model's contribution can begin. A model's efforts are most respected in editorial fashion—a collaborative effort of editor as stylist, photographer as director, and model as subject. Catalog bookings follow another set of rules. Clothes are sold right off the page, so every detail must be crisp, yet with no loss of appeal. A model endorsing products must be precise at handling props, skilled on location, and adept at interpreting advertising layouts or sketches—more likely a casually spoken word or a thumbnail doodle than a full-blown mock-up (or storyboard, in TV). Hardest of all is to project naturalness under any and all circumstances. A knack for catching subtleties will speed the move to film work or TV commercials, where important things often go unsaid.

UNLIMITED HORIZONS

There is no telling where a wisely guided modeling career might lead. And it's never too early to begin. Very young children, particularly extroverted ones with a touch of show biz in their blood, can benefit most from the exposure. Modeling has been many a child actor's first performing experience. A child's career is very much like an adult's, with three significant differences: parent and child must work as partners; the pay scale is much lower than for adults; and rapid changes in the child can bring a career to a sudden, if temporary, halt. A teenager can start a career, or resume an earlier one sidelined by an awkward stage, as soon as he or she nears full height. When a teenager is almost ready, investigate local agents to get on their testing boards (reserved for novices), or apply to retail stores and showrooms for part-time market-week assignments. And also look into a good nearby modeling school.

It takes a combination of special physical and personality traits, developed through schooling, practice, and example, then nurtured by a mentor, to make a model. It is this book's aim to detail these various elements. Only when talents, skills, and desires come together into the world of clients does a truly professional model ready to answer their needs emerge.

PART ONE

Modeling Fields

What Modeling Is Like Today

$\blacklozenge$

*I*t was an American illustrator, Charles Dana Gibson, who first created the general image of the American woman here and abroad with his Gibson girl. A *New York World* editorial gushed in 1896: "As soon as the world saw Gibson's ideal, it bowed down in adoration, saying 'lo, at last the typical American girl."

Back in the 1930s and 1940s, when photographic modeling was getting started on a large scale, it was still considered slightly disreputable to be a paid model—an attitude not too different from an earlier one toward actresses. This began to change as fashion publications and periodicals started taking aspiring young models on tours of European couture salons. Nearly one hundred years since the status of models had gotten its initial boost from the work of Gibson, the world is still mesmerized by the American model.

The first fashion models were internationally renowned hostesses, as portrayed by Edward Steichen, Cecil Beaton, and Baron de Meyer. There was prestige, even for these illustrious ladies, in appearing on the pages of the ladies' journals. Advertisements featured illustrations of dancers and actresses drawn from poses. Photography, oddly enough, was confined to corsets and other undergarments. Photographic modeling was unheard of. A model's best option was showroom or department-store work, which was regular; few made much money at free-lance. As for the place of the American man, he always seemed to be standing in front of cars, boats, or a never-ending string of polo ponies. This has changed considerably in the last decade. Although modeling still employs many more women than men, nowadays men too can have a highly successful and lucrative modeling career. Therefore all the advice detailed in this book applies to both male and female aspirants. In addition, modeling has been a stepping-stone to acting and politics. Tom Selleck, once a model with the Joan Magnum Agency in Los Angeles, joins James Garner, Victor Mature, Gerald Ford, and Ronald Reagan as former poster boys who outgrew their britches.

Modeling has grown, from its primitive and limited beginnings, into a complex range of categories, each with its own set of standards and qualifications.

Though every modeling area imposes its own demands, certain attributes are universally desirable. Models are always "on," which calls for endless stamina and the capacity to sparkle with vitality and enthusiasm no matter how bone-tired they may be. Prosaic as it may sound, there are no substitutes, cosmetic or otherwise, for good health and fitness. A model must be expressive, which brings the eyes into prominence. Many perfectly ordinary people radiate personality when their eyes strike film. A brilliant smile is animating too—a matter, basically, of sound gums and straight teeth. With certain obvious exceptions, such as character roles, it is better to be thin-boned and tall, and have broad shoulders and narrow hips; the lens tends to distort the human frame, making it seem thicker and more squat. In any case, good proportions matter more than specific size, weight, or height. Overall, it is wiser to find niches that nature has fitted you for than to try desperately to find work in a category that is unsuitable. Average height, for one example, won't get you far in high fashion—male or female, these models tend to be taller—but it is perfect for many other modeling roles.

Certain personality and character traits are assets as well to all models. Tenacity, versatility, and determination are indispensable. After the first few tough months, you could face a few tough years—especially if you succeed! A model must be able to persist in the face of opposition and discouragement. Drive and ambition can be carried too far, however; the will to make it will be counterproductive unless tempered by thoughtfulness and tact. Cooperation is crucial to working with others, and easier if your ego is kept in balance.

MASTERING A PARTICULAR FIELD

The skills a model needs may be acquired from a school; many successful models have attended them, if only for brief periods. The second route to the requisite expertise is an agent or mentor, and

Designers need to convey many different moods and styles. It is up to the model to adapt for a client. Clotilde's embodiment of Ralph Lauren's look is used for varied purposes. The runway, the press kit, fitting a new line, informal showings, the cover of *WWD*, and variations can be used for national ads, billboards, and even hangtags. Besides an expressive face and the proper proportions, every model must bring a flexible personality and skills as a salesperson.

Ralph Lauren

"Models, especially men, have come a long way," says Joe Hunter, a high-ranking agent at Ford and one of the most respected in the industry. "They were seen and rarely heard; therefore, it was difficult to visualize their depth. Modeling has evolved out of an avocation for people who have a 'look' at the moment, and has grown into a vocation for those looking toward their future. Now more models are becoming TV sports- or newscasters, movie or commercial actors, even talk-show hosts. Dependency on looks isn't enough because next year the look is going to be different, and that is evident by scanning the magazines and runways."

Since Valentino and Yves Saint Laurent entered the menswear market during the 1968/69 collections, the male modeling experience has changed. In growing numbers men have moved onto the runway, no longer serving as mere props; everything they have on, from sunglasses to traditional underwear, is now manufactured with a designer tag. However, the three-piece suit, overcoat, and topcoat never made this transition. Men, like women, acquire confidence to work the runway by observing others. Here are nine pictures of men on the move.

a fortunate few have designers among their mentors. But models really learn to be proficient at their craft by *watching other models.* Gradually, after observing models in many kinds of action, a novice begins to gain confidence and develop a personal style. A young person first absorbs knowledge of style; second, the ability to express himself or herself.

The first practical step is exposing yourself to the field that most interests you. There are, however, two limiting factors: your qualifications, or lack of them; and whether a particular market exists in your area. There are seven basic areas within modeling: (1) *Wholesale,* consisting of designers and mass manufacturers who use models for showroom work, fitting and writing (buyers') appointments, and runway—large and small; (2) *retail,* which includes runway as well as print ads, catalog, and television; (3) *editorial* and (4) *catalog,* which are both photographic; (5) *convention,* which is live; (6) *commercial print,* which is photographic; and (7) *filmed or videotaped commercials,* which are staged to look live. The majority of modeling jobs are in fashion and for women. It is useful to remember that, whatever the category, the model is always performing as a salesperson.

CATEGORY ONE:

Wholesale—
Designers and Manufacturers

◆

---

*T*he wholesale market is the retail market's "good provider"—and what a choice it supplies! New York, with the greatest number of designers and wholesale manufacturers, is naturally the largest market for showroom, fitting, and house models, as well as a select group known as *cabine*, the models who work with couture designers. Dallas, Chicago, Los Angeles, and Atlanta all have large merchandise marts and are substantial sources of model employment. Secondary or regional markets are a somewhat different ball game. The facts about them are detailed in the out-of-town section of this chapter.

Being house model for one of New York's Seventh Avenue showrooms is a position of unique status. Broadway dress manufacturers show their lines to visiting buyers, and models try on garments in the showrooms during the various market weeks. Free-lance models join the house models for writing appointments (with buyers who write the orders). Free-lancers rotate from showroom to showroom during the different market weeks— shoes, furs, sportswear, and coats, for example, are all separate markets with individual buying sea-

sons. If a model has an especially fine figure, she may work bathing suit, lingerie, and underwear markets; one with small feet may show shoes (an excellent possibility for a petite—stockings too if she has good legs).

Even in New York City, the biggest fashion employer in the world, a model must work in more than one category to earn a decent living. Fashion City has two big seasons: fall lines, shown in April; and spring lines, which appear in October. If a model did ten runway shows each season, at $200 an hour or $4,000 per season, she would make a total of $8,000, an amount she could not live on. A model must be able to do other things—writing appointments, fittings, photography, informal showings.

Jeane Vione runs a New York agency, International Models. She prefers to work with models who have put in time getting to know the business from the inside. "For them it's great," Jeane says, "because you can earn as you learn." The garment center's numerous markets are a fertile learning field. Though each has different requirements, model selection criteria are the same for all. "A model need not be cover material for *Vogue* or *Glamour* to make a living here. A lot of those I represent aren't five-nine or five-eleven, or very experienced, but they can do in-house modeling for an informal designer show. They get four hundred dollars a week for two months, plus training and experience right in the marketplace.

"Managers who hire at the major showrooms have a model try on three garments. If they like the fit, the way she moves, and her personality, they will book her. Personality matters because the model has to be able to work with buyers. Models are in demand two weeks out of every month because each month a new market hits town. During market week, models work eight hours. For major markets, buyers come from all over to scout the manufacturers' lines. If we're doing a major show for a big department store with fifteen models, we will pull one model out for an hour to handle that. Then she'll go back to the showroom for the rest of the day."

THE EMERGENCE OF SPECIAL-SIZE MARKETS

Large and petite-size markets have blossomed in the last eight years as the industry became aware of their extraordinary potentials. Here's how Mary Duffy of Big Beauties and Little Women describes a hypothetical market week's activities for a model who falls into one of those groups: "During the shoe market, a petite model is a natural to show designer shoes, of course—at one hundred twenty-five dollars a day. She can have many clients during the day, and still break away once in a while to do photography or catalog bookings. A specialty model doesn't make most of her income during market weeks, so she must plan her time well to earn twenty-five to fifty thousand dollars a year."

The growth of special-size markets is instructive. In 1977, a New York fashion group did a study on all of them—tall, petite, and large, with emphasis on the latter. They found that, while everyone was looking the other way, the baby-boom generation had grown up.

The assumption had been that all women who loved clothes also took care to stay slim—well within average size ranges. No one dreamed we had spawned a generation of happy eaters. The manufacturers discovered there were twenty-five to thirty million good-sized women, with money to spend, who wore bowling shirts and Norma Kamali floats—because they had nothing else to buy. At least nothing that seemed to them to make sense. A large woman won't pay four hundred dollars for a coat that fits her today; tomorrow she's sure she'll fit into a size 10.

The industry did somewhat better with petites. Petite, after all, is permanent. A five-feet-two-inch woman who is a perfect size 6 is willing to invest $350 in an outfit because she knows she won't get any taller. A petite is the same as a Missy-sized customer, except that she's short—under five feet four—beyond alteration. If a suit jacket reaches your thighs instead of your hips, there is no way to alter it or, for a petite anyway, to alter yourself.

Mary Duffy continues, "A 1978 industry study showed that only twenty-five percent of large women shopped at either a specialty store like Lane Bryant or in large-size sections of department stores. So where were the other seventy-five percent? Wherever they were, they were wearing ill-fitting clothes and had to be wooed to change their buying habits. Manufacturers went into this new market with a vengeance and with remarkable results. It went from a two- to a seven-billion-dollar market in a mere five years."

THE WORK OF FITTING MODELS

A collection is the outgrowth of months of preparation; long before a model hits the runway, fitting models have been trying on the clothes over and over. Fitting models are of two types: One fits the sample that becomes a piece in the collection; the other does the duplicate pattern fittings that are to go into production. The only difference between the two is that production patterns are sized slightly larger. Jeane Vione has this to say about fitting models: "A fitting model does not have to be a perfect beauty, but does need perfect measurements for a garment. Measurements vary from size to size and also from manufacturer to manufacturer and from market to market.

Every show has its purpose. The entrance sets the tone. At that time photographers are set for the models to pose. It is that dress's first moment in the limelight. Not always will this be alone or can it be deliberate. If there is a group, an automatic tableau forms. Valentino, a Roman perennial, here lavishly displays five reflections of his theme—each one a statue to look at and admire—to excite the buyers. The other two pictures demonstrate entirely different poses. Bathing suits are often shown by black models for skin contrast in the cold Northeast. Rarely is a model alone on the runway; therefore constant harmonious interacting is essential.

"The precise physical requirements will depend on whether the garments are from a designer line or a budget line. Budget lines always fit bigger sizes—a difference of an inch to an inch and a half in the bust, waist, and hips. For instance, take budget size eight. The standard size would be thirty-five-and-a-half-inch bust, twenty-six-inch waist, and thirty-seven-inch hip. A large eight, one that will fit a ten because the clothes are cut bigger."

The duplicate pattern model does not do shows. She has the right body for translating clothes into production. A fitting model has to know construction; a regular fashion model doesn't—all she has to know is how to present a look. A fitting model has to know what's wrong with a garment and where: where it's pulling—whether the problem is at the waist, say, or in the length. She has to be able to communicate with the designer. All this knowledge is cumulative; it builds as a model works closely with many different designers.

Connie Cook free-lances through Mannequin and has been a fitting model for years, starting when she was in college. During breaks, she modeled at suburban malls and department stores. Designers who brought collections to the area liked to book her—she was right for the most expensive custom clothes. Many of them told her she should try modeling in New York, so, borrowing six thousand dollars from her parents, she went there to give it a six-month trial.

"First thing, naturally, I looked up the designers. The first few, of course, didn't remember me, but I did get a job at Geoffrey Beene for one hundred eighty-five dollars a week. There I met Bill Blass—he was in the same building—and went to work for him as a house model; this time at two hundred twenty-five dollars a week. Now they pay me two hundred fifty dollars per hour. Quite a jump!

"I worked on Seventh Avenue for about two years. The designers kept me busy and eventually I got about seventy percent of them as clients. Then the stores booked me because they saw me in the Seventh Avenue houses. Photography followed from there. Now a third of my work is photography because the designers use me. I guess you could say I've come full circle.

"Fitting for the collections involves so many hours that nobody could afford the regular rate. But I learned so much it didn't matter: how clothes are draped, what different designers know about clothes

and creating them. The model is involved in making the collection. Couture often takes five or six fittings. The designer may begin by draping on me a muslin just pinned together. A sized pattern comes later, after the original sample. It is amazing to me what I am privy to—high-level corporate meetings where the designer needs a model to express his ideas for a design he wants to push. The more experience a model has, the greater her value to the designer. With Lauren, it's a question of putting on an already made blouse and telling him that an armhole is too tight or the blouse pulls across the back. Scaasi works on an entire outfit as a concept with sketches, Halston by draping fabric. Once you have learned how all the designers work, if a client gets stuck on something, you have all that experience to draw on. Each fabric is individual too. They react differently according to whether they're bias or straight, flat or gathered."

As collection time approaches, pressures get very intense. The designer tries something and it doesn't work. Not every idea actually ends up on the line. Some work in concept but are impractical or too expensive to manufacture. This is where fitting models really pay off. A fit can be managed on a mannequin—it can be padded, pinned, whatever. But the model puts it on and she can *tell* it won't lie properly on a real body.

Two accounts are all Connie Cook can handle each season because the work is so demanding; before the collection it involves evenings and weekends. "During the season I will have six to eight bookings a day; off-season, I have four. It gets exhausting and I have to fake my way through. As in any job you must be reliable, and not fade from the top."

Travel can be strenuous as well. One Sunday, Connie left with Halston for Los Angeles, then off to Dallas early Tuesday, to Houston on Wednesday, back to New York Thursday through Saturday; then off with Blass for Oklahoma, back to New York again on Monday, Philadelphia on Tuesday, then New York once more. Eight cities in ten days (New York three times!). Not to mention the press, all the varied personalities, and the extracurricular personal appearances.

Scott Shaw is another model well schooled in fitting work. Born in New York but raised in Houston, it was in his adopted city that Bruce Cooper spotted him while scouting female models for Wil-

The models project the attitude of the designer into each article of clothing. Having objects on the stage is only one aspect of the recent changes that have taken place in runway modeling. Now models must interact with props, circular spaces, spiral staircases, and effects that take a show into its own dimensions. "Sometimes a small podium is used. Your audience will most likely be all around you," says Eileen Ford. And she advises: "Do not hesitate to stand quite still for a few seconds. To keep turning constantly looks frantic. Whatever the circumstances under which you are modeling, your function is to remain completely cool and unruffled." (*Secrets of the Model's World* [New York: Trident Press, 1970].)

Obviously, nobody is expected to wear every item, and the wings are detachable. No matter what, the model must reach the end of the runway, allowing photographers angles and action to click away at. Sometimes this requires the balance of a circus acrobat and the stamina of a marathon runner along with the grace of a jazz dancer. Even disregarding the wings, the bustle and excesses around the ankles make motion a feat.

Here are examples of the new spectacles of light, sound, and color. The model is at center stage. In a group (upper right), if a move is to be in tandem, then everyone had better move on time. In the lower right photograph is not the sort of dress everyone would wear, but it is what everyone would expect to see on a model. Here the zebra stripes move diagonally while the shape is triangular, as the model's arm movement clearly shows. No gesture is accidental and each is expressive. The designers construct an entity, from shoes, through belts and jewelry, to hats. Therefore, models have to understand accessories, from casual to formal furs, and know how each part of the body can be made to emphasize design.

helmina. After only six months' part-time modeling, Scott returned to New York. "I learned more there in six months than I would have learned in Houston in sixteen. My look is very young so I do mostly juniors—boys and girls gazing romantically at one another for cosmetic companies. I don't work for designers per se because they usually prefer older, more sophisticated types. Strangely enough, though, I now do all the fitting for Perry Ellis. I couldn't imagine why I was going on that first appointment, but he has grown into a steady client. Occasionally I work with Perry, but more often it's with people from his various men's products—sweaters, shirts, pants, suits."

Scott feels it has become much easier for each department's designers to see what garments look like on a body. "Everything has to be meticulously fitted. I am fitted in muslin if it's the first time a piece is to be manufactured, after that in fabric, redone in stages until it is right. Some things need to be fitted in each fabric; for instance, a corduroy and a worsted will need different adjustments. Or perhaps fabrics in the spring line stretch more. Some goods don't feel the same on even when the measurements are exactly the same. That is where I come in."

WRITING APPOINTMENTS

Writing appointments are two- to three-hour shows in which several models, perhaps as many as six, show the clothes to specific buyers after a designer has presented his line. A writing appointment derives its name from its purpose: Retail buyers come to the designer's showroom so that salespeople can write up their orders. Lynn Yeager of Mannequin Models knows them well. Lynn worked for designers during market weeks for many years, feeling her way and finding out which designers she would work with most comfortably.

"It took a few years to determine who I would be best for and I still work for those designers today. My first work was in-house for a swimwear company. It was that time of year. Swimwear was followed, in the funny way of fashion, by the fur market. A model who rotates according to the markets makes top dollar; there's one for every type of clothing and accessories during any year. You can learn a lot. I know I did.

"First come the formal collections, which are shown in a hotel. Then some special customer, or someone who couldn't make the show, or an editorial fashion Brahmin—say from a foreign *Vogue*, the fashion pages of *The New York Times Magazine*, or *W*—will make an appointment for a private showing, maybe of the entire collection but more often a capsule. It could be a writing appointment—buyers who have seen the whole show coming back now to order. These showings are less formal than runway presentations, but not as free-form as, let's say, a presentation at Bloomingdale's.

"In the various market areas, there are things to keep in mind. Furs must be made to look longer, thicker, and richer. That calls for more sophistication and more makeup." Lynn says, "I always pretend that I'm rich, and so you are, if you're buying a fur. With bathing suits, a model can't hold her stomach in; it should already *be* in. You must really be in good shape: perfectly groomed, toenails painted, legs shaved. If you go to a second showroom that wants more sophistication, you can add more makeup. But if it's the other way around, you have to take your face off and put it back on lighter very quickly.

"If the client wants something special, he will usually warn the models. There are rehearsals or instructions given. Very often things are extemporaneous and you just have to go with it. A buyer at a writing appointment may ask to see a garment a little closer and the rest of the models will have to wait. You have to be ready for the unexpected; that's the rule rather than the exception."

At first Lynn had to learn to juggle bookings deftly. This can be particularly hard on a beginner, who is both new in the business and usually in great need of money. Lynn recalls her struggles to hang on to one client while she courted others before signing with an agency: "While I was working for one client, they acted as if they owned me. They didn't want me to leave or go anywhere. Obviously, I had to go see the next people I was lining up. And you can't just move, in a minute, from glamorous mink coat lady to bouncy little junior. That's a big change, and not only in attitude but also in hair and makeup. Most models have spent a frantic time in a hotel bathroom, shampooing the hair spray out for the lively look of the next booking. If you're going to make it all work, you have to come to terms with constantly changing roles. In time, with me, it became tolerable."

FICKLE, FABULOUS HIGH FASHION

The collections fluctuate with the seasons and the years, with the political climate and the state of the world as interpreted by fashion designers. No one—not the designers, the models, nor the general public—knows what form fashion will take in any given season, or what makeup and hair coloring and styling will be called upon to express it. Luis Lopez, head booker for Mannequin, one of New York's leading fashion agencies, sees the fashion phenomena of the eventful seventies as typical, if not extreme, examples: "When the Vietnam War ended, there was political strife all over Italy. Milan capitalized on it by producing salable guerrilla garb: safari gear, layered activewear, baggy clothes in drab battlefield neutrals like olive, khaki, and sand. One day Yves St. Laurent sees Lena Horne live singing 'Stormy Weather'; next thing you know he and Givenchy are playing jewel colors at the cool end of the spectrum (ruby red, emerald green, sapphire blue) against a black catalyst. Sometimes designers look back in time, as St. Laurent did in updating the forties look: cinched waist with peplum emphasis changes to a drop waist, eventually working into a big flared skirt. Jewels soften to pastels and the black background to white. The spectator look of the fifties is back, complete down to the spectator pump and blond, WASP look of the Eisenhower years.

"Given such rapid-fire and unpredictable changes, it is difficult to foretell the physical demands on any model, or, indeed, what *kinds* of models will be in demand. The forties look, with its turquoises, emeralds, and rubies on black, produced a stampede to black models four to five years ago. Then there was an abrupt swing to broader shoulders and a smaller head, with close-cropped shorter hair, both thought to accentuate the waist."

During the last decade, designers have increasingly turned to models to represent their clothes to the public. Sometimes it was a model with a recognizable face. Now Broadway star Twiggy became associated with Mary Quant clothes in Lon-

The following four photographs are examples of the pure theater that fashion runway modeling has become. There is a new international style of displaying a designer's collection. Yet the show must be a publicity extravaganza; many collections have become multimedia events. In the photograph at the right, Chloé, one of Paris's favorites, uses two contrasting models to show off very similar outfits. Some costumes need to be made believable; often that happens through attitude as much as through an appropriate prop or a rakish tilt to the hat. Every show requires models to pick up on the theme while walking, climbing, or standing, whether showing separates, coats, sweaters, or a clutched bag.

In the photograph on p. 36, models are standing almost motionless to enhance the mannequinlike makeup of these new Steven Sprouses originals. With the additional dimensions of these shows came a new choreography, a new method of acting and mime. It takes a sense of self beyond physical attributes to be viewed at every angle, to have every move or gesture watched, and always in relation to the merchandise. Different stances allow the photographers to find their shots. This is a wonderful way for a novice to learn about style. Barbara Lantz of Zoli recommends "watching and practicing as the one best way." Most times the end of the runway becomes a pivotal point, surrounded by the audience.

The Japanese, schooled in the art of subtlety in the theater, apply their knowledge of accomplishing many movements. In the first photograph on p. 37, a model takes off her mask while managing to open a coat under a thick scarf, a difficult manipulation at first. With practice comes a flair with belts, gloves, and reversibles.

don's Carnaby Street era. More recently, Ralph Lauren discovered Clotilde, whose persona came to represent his entire collection, from cosmetics to accessories.

In 1977, Clotilde, of Ford, just back from the European collections, was one of some ten female models booked by Saks to be photographed with Lauren for an ad. "As far as I knew I had never seen her before," Lauren says, "but I thought she would be terrific in my new fall show. My tweedy country look was then at its height. A few weeks later, viewing tapes of the show, I was again struck by her fresh new look and decided she would be wonderful in our national ads. From the letters I received, the public thought so too."

From then on she was *the* model for Ralph Lauren fashion, cosmetics, fragrances, and skin care. Up to that time, Lauren had mostly been associated with blondes: Many saw Clotilde as a refreshing change. "Clotilde has a timeless, classic beauty, a high-quality but simple elegance. There are many moods to my clothing, and Clotilde can adapt to them all—an English hunting look, a Santa Fe prairie look, a completely contemporary cashmere look."

Models who travel in a couture designer's circle are known as his *cabine*, French for small room and taken from the cubical at the salon where they sit. They surround him at the theater, at openings, at dinner, and they represent his image on the runway. Candy Pratts, senior editor at *Harper's Bazaar* and formerly fashion coordinator for Bloomingdale's, best known for her fashion window scenarios, describes the relationship of a designer and his *cabine:* "These are the designer's team, the models who sell his name perfectly. The designer socializes with them, shows them how to eat, how to drink, how to act at a cocktail party—for a very good reason. He is giving the models the kind of life-style *that he is trying to sell.* The models are living his message; When they walk down the runway, he knows they will do it the way he has shown them."

Karen Bjornson of Ford is a veteran model, originally from Ohio, who started out working in a designer's salon. It was in New York that she found her mentor, Halston, surely one of the very best. He taught her about fashion during the two years she worked for him. Karen can't say enough about the "mentor method" of succeeding in modeling, and about Halston's invaluable help:

"I arrived in New York after winning a magazine modeling contest in Cincinnati and hadn't had any really great bookings. A friend of mine said Halston was looking for a house model. I went up and it was incredible—he tried the collection on me and everything fit! He hired me on the spot and the next day I was photographed for *Vogue* wearing Halston.

"I learned everything about fashion design; how fabric is cut and fit, color proportion, and how to show clothes to their best advantage. I showed clothes for clients and helped them get dressed. Most of them knew what they wanted, and Halston of course could guide them. It was a friendly place. There was Jackie Onassis (I modeled hot pants for Aristotle), Babe Paley, Liza Minnelli, and other private clients. It was glamorous and exciting and what Halston taught me was invaluable. Halston cared," says Karen, "enough to do what an agent might do."

ON THE RUNWAY

Center stage on the runway has gone to models with a high degree of recognition from exposure in magazine editorials and advertisements. Women with larger-than-life personalities, such as Jerry Hall, Iman, Pat Cleveland, and Apollonia, are featured by virtually every designer in every major fashion center. Designers hope that such photogenic faces and publicized personal lives will get their creations shown by the media. The models understandably demand, and get, top rates for their work. Few models have the exact body measurements required for fitting, and most who had previously worked only photographically, have, over the past decade, also learned to participate on a runway.

The presentation of seasonal collections in the design capitals—New York, Paris, and Milan—has become the clothing designers' opportunity to break into the media. Once the audiences at collections were mainly buyers for American and foreign department stores or boutiques, plus a few loyal customers of the designer. The designs were rendered by illustrators and distributed to newspapers and magazines. Today the collections are of general interest and so are covered by television news and weekly magazines as well as such trade publications as *Women's Wear Daily, W, Fashions of the*

Runway modeling would be a simple task if only the surface was being sold. But that is rarely the case. Clothes are more often layered: Under every coat there is a dress; under many a top is yet another top. Removing one gracefully and with simple movements to display the other is hard. Each item comes off differently and each movement must be learned and then practiced until it is perfect. Pat Cleveland (left and following page right) plays with the garment before setting foot onto a runway. She knows from experience that it is not enough to throw it on or off.

Every part of a garment has a better side. It is the model's responsibility to sense which it is and to show it off to full advantage.

Once the garment is removed it must be kept with you. It is not disposable. Whether it is tied at the waist, draped on a shoulder, or, very occasionally, pulled along is dictated in large part by the model's ability and feeling for style.

Along with attitude come gestures and expressions. In the upper left photograph, a girlish glance matches the outfit; the hands at the waist emphasize this. The size of the movement is implied by the space—the larger the arena, the more generous the gesture—but it must always be appropriate for the outfit. Arms and legs form the direction a dress has taken and graphically show off the shape and dimension of a garment. This is true whether for high-fashion Yves Saint Laurent or the casual look of the girl next door in Connecticut. Elegant, slim designs require more restraint and definition. Sportier looks need a genuine sense of casualness, swinging freely along. Models are selected by the coordinator because of their affinity toward a style. They spend 90 percent of their time on the runway, walking. It is therefore one of the two most important things to do well. The other is to assume stances that flow. There are only two choices: move or pose. While walking, the hand placement, very often into pockets, has to be done deftly. It has to tell what kind of pockets and where they are. From the lower three photographs this becomes quite clear. The hands are expressive instruments, used to point out the notable features of an outfit.

Times, and, for men, the *Daily News Record.* The model is still the centerpiece and many presentations now have the support crew of a Broadway musical: lighting and set designers, choreographers and sound engineers, all hired to turn these one-time events into unique and promotable spectaculars. Recently in Paris, Tierry Mugler charged the general public an admission fee.

The difficulties of becoming a runway model are well known to Barbara Lantz, president of Zoli, Inc., who ran the runway division of Zoli at one time. Barbara was in charge when photographers' models were doing an unprecedented thing: going into runway work. Here are some of her observations:

"Runway is very hard work that requires a lot of energy, technique, and skills. Beginning models aren't immediately asked to do shows because there is so much to learn. It takes practice to look graceful and relaxed and not fall on your face. A girl has to get into the runway frame of mind very fast because the time element is crucial. A model has to rush into the clothes, move onto the runway, and get buyers interested in what she is wearing before she gets off. The best way to learn is to watch other models and then go home and play around with a garment in front of the mirror . . . move around until you feel comfortable showing it and have the confidence to do so.

"A runway model should be between five feet eight and a half and five feet ten with good physical proportions. Facial beauty doesn't matter as much as general appearance. Runway is a great way to begin a career. It's stimulating and you have the most fabulous makeup and hair and extraordinary clothes to inspire you—the freshest things of the year. The clothes are photographed later, but the runway man or woman is the first to be seen in the outfit."

Ellen Harth, an adept manager of fashion models for runway shows in New York, outlines what a high-fashion model is expected to know: "There are no longer the once-typical coat designers who only make coats. Designers now have collections that include many kinds of garments, so models must be able to show a variety of clothes and vary the mood as the clothes require. If you go from jeans to a magnificent suit, or walk first in sneakers and then in heels, you have to know how to handle all of them. You must know how to cope with short, tight skirts or full ones; the legs are dominant in a tight skirt. A well-rounded model will know how to show all of these things."

Bazaar's Candy Pratts, for many years a top fashion stylist, describes her approach to selecting models for particular designers: "The first thing I try to decide is what *category* a model fits into: sportswear, very Norell-looking glamour, and so on. A model cannot be something she is not. I take into account how easily she could assume the role of the merchandise. After all, there is definitely a star model who can step onto a bare raised platform and sell you a potato sack. I personally can carry many different designers' clothes, but I can sell them a lot better when I believe in the style. If I live it. The same is true for a model on the runway. She can do all of the designers for the money, but she can't do them all equally well."

Karen Bjornson, in Candy's eyes, epitomizes the Halston woman: youthful and well bred. Pat Cleveland, who couldn't be less like her, often stands next to her on the runway. "It works," says Candy. "Somehow they're smart, zippy, and successful together. Diane de Witt and Alva Chin are another inspired pair: They are both pretty, perky, bright, and peppy. It isn't just the hair, eyes, and skin color; it's how they carry themselves."

A runway model must be objective about her strengths and weaknesses and compensate for the in-between. Nowadays she has to be able to do print as well as shows. There used to be good runway models who didn't photograph well, and photogenic models who were rotten on the runway. It has become more integrated; today's high-fashion model does it all—men and women alike.

An Armani ensemble could often be considered difficult to carry off. The mannishness of this Armani is a contrast to the usual sexuality of evening wear. Whatever else the current international runway style requires, there must be an innate sophistication, control, and energy. The model above, Cheryl Stevens, is a German schoolgirl, but she carries off the design with originality and places it perfectly within the context of the fashion of her times.

There seem to be never-ending variations to men and women showing clothes. The four models in the two photographs on p. 44 are complementary contrasts, whether two women or a man and woman. Occasionally they walk side by side, but much more frequently in single file. Walking, an activity everyone does once out of infancy, is not easy when the pace is set by music and while also projecting an attitude, turning, and demonstrating. In the photograph at the left are Iman of Elite and Karen Bjornson of Ford, two of the world-class runway models. With equal beauty they gracefully cross-reference this Calvin Klein classic V-neck dress. Men always walk with assurance, almost never alone. When matched with a woman, the possibilities for expanded interchange and a friendlier, warmer, or more vulnerable side can be shown along with the detail. Each pass down the runway must remain within the character set by the designer. Depending on the number of pieces to be shown and the variation of the garments, the music tempo, lighting effects, or other theatrical devices will allow the shaping of a new personality style to fit the clothes.

CATEGORY TWO:

Retail—
Stores and Boutiques

◆

*W*hen wholesale fashions are ready for the public, promoting and advertising them becomes the job of retailers. Department stores use models to display not only their new clothes lines but also to give demonstrations of makeup and other products. Models of all shapes and ages, both female and male, are in demand. For fashion, the criteria are identical to those in other categories: Models must be right for the clothes they will wear, and must have the ability to sell these clothes. A model may have to do runway, or walk among the aisles at a teatime showing, or even make quick changes at cocktail-hour charity previews. Therefore she will need, in addition to the physical qualifications, a pleasant, outgoing personality. Helen O'Hagan, director of special events for Saks Fifth Avenue, uses various criteria to pick models for the live shows that are put on throughout that retailer's entire chain. "If we give a girl a dress that's very hard to sell, unattractive, she has to know how to 'milk' it. I look for a very professional model who is positive and doesn't have a temper. If they can't handle their own hair and makeup and look like a million dollars, we don't rebook them. Runway models are very

well paid and *should* be able to do a lot. Along with being relatively tall and well proportioned, a runway model needs good shoulders. And she can't have big hips: Samples are size eight made on models who are five feet eight or five feet nine. Legs need to be shapely and the knee cap well placed. Foot sizes are larger than they used to be: eight and a half to ten."

A NATIONWIDE MODELING MARKET

Retail is one of the best springboards to a modeling career because it is an unlimited market. Stores everywhere hire models to attract potential customers. Even small ones in small towns advertise regularly. Across the nation, store mailing pieces go monthly to active customers; catalogs are sent seasonally and sometimes for special events. Any aspiring model can quickly judge her potential by whether she reflects a specific store's image. In most large markets, models represent retailers in sophisticated TV campaigns (a diminishing practice

Traditionally, a couture runway finale is the wedding gown. This is the creation that is to leave the lasting impression, but at every show there is a showstopper. Brooke Shields took her first twirl for a Saks Fifth Avenue remodeled children's department. Her mother, Terry, remembers her as being "so damned cute." Above: The woman who made the entire-runway-length twirl a mainstay of her repertoire, Pat Cleveland. Next page: Amalia demonstrates the show-stopping twirl. Whether a child understands is immaterial, but a pro needs to know exactly what she is doing, and no novice will just walk off the street and onto a runway without witnessing plenty of shows first.

as individual stores' geographic areas shrink); for the most part, though, the media for models are local or national publications, billboards, display cards, and sales tags. Models tend to work for only one store—a form of exclusivity stores do not pay for. There is compensation, however, in the prestige of being selected to display a product or project a store's image.

Bill Berta, a Saks Fifth Avenue senior vice-president, is responsible for maintaining a consistent Saks image nationwide. "A store's image is presented primarily through daily and Sunday newspapers and magazines. Merchandise and model selection is specific to the various medium. Not all of our models are high fashion, nor should they be. For *Town & Country*, we will select a designer who would appeal to *T&C* readers and a very elegant, understated model; for *Vogue*, the merchandise will be fashion-forward with a high-fashion model; for *Mademoiselle*, with its younger and broader-based audience, the look is updated contemporary in the clothes and in the model."

Sak's efforts may be more sophisticated than those of smaller retailers, but basically their aims are the same. At Saks, says Bill Berta, "We try our best to target our merchandising efforts. We'll do, for instance, limited mailings featuring a particular designer who has an identifiable audience. We select likely buyers from our customer list—those who have already bought that designer and those we think are good prospects. If a designer appeals to a slightly older, more conservative customer, we will select a model with that look. For career dressing, we'll avoid models who are too well known (eliminating immediate identification) and pick someone who looks like a middle-management or entry-level executive. If we run an ad campaign to expand our contemporary, updated merchandise, we will want a younger model who will attract a younger, trendier market. It all starts with the merchandise. The right model is the one whose look is most likely to get the customer to see herself in the clothes."

A DEMAND FOR EVERY TYPE: AGE, SEX, AND COLORING

Retailers have to appeal to all types of people. The models they need are therefore of all ages, sizes,

The information that a model learns during a designer's collection is useful all season long. The marketing process includes models at almost every phase. There is constant coordination between department stores nationally and the model agencies for designer shows. The same dress, though not necessarily the same model, is then photographed for advertisements and catalog sales. Often models who showed the garments are needed for road trips in order to re-create what the designer envisioned for regional markets.

Before leaving a stage there is one last opportunity to let the dress take its final bow. Whatever the best feature or however it is unique, this is the moment to display it. Here Margret Donahoe of Mannequin exits in a manner that calls attention to the back of a showstopper.

Salvatore Ferragamo knows the art of strewing men at your feet. The pump, meant for appreciation, for adoration. Gilded with an ornament. Taupe, brown or black calf, from Italy and ours alone, $54. Shoe Salon.

SAKS-JANDEL

The ultimate fashion statement in mink...the newly defined shoulder lends elegance to a softly belted classic.

SAKS-JANDEL   Chevy Chase   Washington,DC

Saks, for its fiftieth anniversary, had Deborah Turbeville photograph Jack Alexander as a man selling not only his formal attire but also a luxurious Art Deco silk pump (left). More men are being used to sell retail than ever before, either with a hint from an unseen woman, with a trendy strong female presence, or merely alone. Kim Alexis (above) is gracefully at her most photogenic self for a Washington, D.C., department store. All types and ages are needed to put across a national department-store campaign through Sunday sale ads, catalogs, monthly invoice enclosures, and even TV spots. Regional department-store ads will try to play off known national (and international) campaigns. This is true at both ends of the scale: for carriage trade specialty shops and for large, high-volume stores.

and races—not only high-fashion models. The larger chains see models all the time to be sure that they have an ample supply on tap. TV producer Kathy O'Grady also supervises and directs the video studio at Saks. "I watch the magazines closely to see if there's anyone interesting. I've noticed that the criteria for modeling have changed. Ten years ago, the beautiful woman was a classic beauty. Now, any woman with something extraordinary can be a model."

The last few years have seen increased concern with image among department chains. Many carry the same designer lines; therefore the problem becomes one of maintaining each chain's individual identity. Model selection is crucial in that context. Department-store executives target their audiences. Bill Berta tells how Saks tackles it: "Merchants present their merchandise and explain what they are trying to project and who they feel their customer is. Our response, by now, is almost immediate; we know where the appeal will be strongest."

As executive art director at Saks, Gary Lowe is responsible for producing all daily newspaper and national magazine ads. Along with operation, he has to maintain the famous Saks continuity: A customer flipping through a newspaper or magazine has to know *instantly* that an ad is a Saks ad. Gary makes final decisions about models very close to the time of shooting. This, he explains, is because no choice can be made until the merchandise is selected.

"On Monday mornings, the creative department looks at all the merchandise. Afterward we decide who will shoot what, where, and when. Then we work floor by floor matching models to the merchandise. For instance, if it's a third-floor designer, we will probably need a specific model, one already associated with his line, or at least she must be a certain type. The same targeting idea applies to men, kids, grandmas, or any other types of people who buy in our store."

The best way to enter retail modeling is through the wholesale or editorial route. The experience gained from working with designers or learning to wear clothes to their best advantage in front of a camera is invaluable at the retail level.

But model selection isn't only a matter of rightness; there is also the question of availability. Models know, though, that department stores can be very

Because every town, village, and hamlet has them, retail stores are the largest single users of models' services. And they back their models well, putting all their creative resources behind them—for their benefit, certainly, but for the models' as well. But there is a problem that inhibits a retailer's choice of models. It might be called a split personality problem in that certain models project two contradictory images. Cosmetics lines or certain designers can sign up models for exclusive use—Karen Graham for Estee Lauder, or Lauren Hutton for Ultima II. They personify the look. Department stores don't have that luxury. But they must create and maintain an individual identity. With Saks it's high fashion, with K mart it's high volume, with Bergdorf's it's high class.

Models can't go back and forth between high-volume and high-fashion retail advertising or promotion. You can't be a high-fashion model for Saks today and a sale model for Gimbels tomorrow. A store's image depends largely on the image of the models who promote its merchandise. Saks Fifth Avenue aims at its individual impression; so, on a smaller scale, does every retailer in the country. A split modeling personality can do damage to both.

And while there are different types of stores—from glossy down to the polyester slacks level—the media, especially TV, keep the general public highly aware of current trends. The models hired will have to reflect this awareness. The Sears model's makeup and hairdo may not be as sophisticated as the Saks model's, but both will have to know how to move with ease, wear their clothes with natural self-confidence, and, most of all, make the customer want to buy what they are showing.

good clients. They book a great many models for all different media every day, all year long. They don't have much control, of course, over whether a model works for their competitors. Retail stores can't afford exclusive contracts. But if a model works for too many competing stores, some will start to look elsewhere.

CATEGORY THREE:

Editorial—

Fashion Publications

Most periodicals—except for some special-interest or trade journals—use models extensively to illustrate their articles and on their covers. But although America is an enormous market for models, very little of it is for fashion editorial—where fashions are not seen as advertisements but for their news value. Editorial work is largely a publicity forum that enables a model to expose her talents. It is not, however, a full-time career; it is only one part of the wholesaler to retailer to consumer cycle. Fashion editorial publications are a well-funded, elite turnstile and are geared to soft-sell the facts about wearing each season's new styles. This is always done through the models. For the model, however, there is keen competition for being selected because the demand for these jobs is very high and the supply very low. There are only a handful of fashion magazines of any editorial stature.

Though they fly the editorial banner, essentially these magazines are lavish—no-expense-spared promotional vehicles for the garment industry. The tear sheets (pages on which a model appears) are used by the model's agency to generate lucrative advertising clients. Only a select few—*Harper's Bazaar, Vogue, Glamour, Mademoiselle, Seventeen, Self,* and *Cosmopolitan* (the latter mostly for the cover; there are few inside fashion pages)—have any real impact on a model's career. Occasionally there will be an important spread in *New York* magazine or *Sports Illustrated;* the most desirable tear sheets are from the special Sunday fashion supplement, produced biannually by *The New York Times,* and editorial coverage of the American and European collections in any of the major publications. The total number of pages devoted to fashion editorial is under one hundred a month—and those are monopolized by a tiny percentage of the thousands of models available. A mere fifteen models suffice for the meager work of magazines specializing in fashion.

Barbara Shapiro is, to put it succinctly, Cheryl Tiegs's office. Her overview of Cheryl's bookings gives her a keen perception of the editorial environment. "In editorial fashion, the editor is central. She decides on the models, picks the fashion and a range of possible accessories. She knows the layout—whether it's horizontal or vertical, how many pictures will be used, and how big each will run. It's her job to make sure an outfit looks correct; she will even help the model put it on. From the bags of fashions her assistants bring in containing forty pairs of shoes or fifty-six pairs of earrings, the editor makes the choices. She is the client. There's always someone to do hair and makeup, a stylist, photographer, and assistants—that's the smallest group of people that can handle all aspects of a fashion shoot."

The editorial page is selling the *mood* of the clothes. A reader doesn't have to know whether a garment is belted or pleated; it's the general look and feeling of the clothes that the editor tries to capture. This freedom from specifics gives the model the chance to show her versatility, her inventiveness and spontaneity. If the shot is on a beach, the model can use the sand, the rocks, the water, whatever. The picture's final form emerges from the model's creativity and the direction given it by the photographer, the editor, and the fashions themselves.

John Casablancas founded the Elite Model Agency in Paris before moving his headquarters to New York in 1977. He had built a formidable reputation for developing top fashion editorial material through his Paris office. Elite now has offices worldwide that are used to shuttle models wherever there is editorial action. John feels that the poorer quality and quantity of American editorial pages is the reason American models go abroad. Once a model has Milan or Paris exposure, she is deluged with bookings when she returns to New York.

For models to break into editorial and get the tear sheets that make the difference between a professional and an amateurish portfolio, John says they have to go to Europe. "Milan alone has more fashion tear sheets per month than all of the United States. There is Italian *Bazaar* and *Vogue, Linea, Cosmopolitan, Amica, Grazia, Bella, Joya, Donna.* And look at France: *Elle, Marie-Claire, Vingt-Ans, Vogue, L'Officiel, La Sante.* England has *Honey, Over Twenty-One, Tattler, Harper's and Queen, Vogue;* the Germans have *Der Stern, Brigitte,* and *Vogue.* Together these magazines represent an absolute mass of editorial possibility.

"Also, European formats are different. In America, twenty to thirty editorial pages have models on them; the rest is advertising. Europe, on the other hand, not only has quantity but there is also qual-

ity. American fashion editorial pages, although frequently excellent, are often a refined version of advertising or catalog. That's why magazines look so much alike. All followers and no leaders, no innovators. American magazines have a clean look that is good for selling models, but a model learns her trade in Europe in a much more interesting and looser way. There is pressure in America to make models look like working women. Pretty soon all the pictures look like catalog shots, which can burn out an editorial model mighty fast. She loses the sparkle and that special fire that editorial demands."

American photographers tell John Casablancas they love to work with models who have trained in Europe. They make better models. To make sure they go right on improving, practically every top model in America continues to work regularly with European photographers and magazines.

Editors rarely pick a total novice for their spreads. They need models who have experience to wear garments with dash, to work well with professionals, and to be comfortable with photographers. They look for new people at wholesale shows, investigate a designer or a photographer's latest personal preferences, and, of course, they are deluged with submissions (photographs and personal visits) from agents eager to have their clients appear in an editorial spread of a prestigious fashion periodical.

Ara Gallant started as a hair stylist and has become an acclaimed fashion photographer. A friend and confidant of models for three decades, Ara has seen the effects of editorial pages on other areas of a model's career. "Editorial has become a valuable endorsement. The models who do it are picked up by advertisers and catalog houses. But then the magazines lose interest and won't use them anymore. If a model has been seen in too many ads, unless she becomes a movie star or celebrity, fashion editors don't want her. The model may not mind; she has moved along and is making much more money. Some are disappointed because they liked the glory of editorial work."

Many models manage to keep two careers going: one here and one in Europe. They fly there to do the collections and editorial beauty in European magazines. New York, though, is still the modeling hub. Europe is more than aware of what is happening here. Europeans look at American magazines, know who is doing what. A model doing a lot of editorial here, if she is also an advertising model, usually doesn't get editorial work in Europe. They prefer new faces.

The type of model chosen by the editors depends very much on the type of fashion that is current—the more sophisticated the clothes, the more that look has to be matched by the model's face, aura, makeup, and hairstyle. The trend, however, is less toward the exotic and more toward the pretty. This has always been the case. Ara Gallant illustrates this with the experience of Verushka, extensively used and heralded by several magazines as the most beautiful woman in the world many times during her stellar career. "Oddly enough, Verushka never did any beauty advertising. Even during American advertising's golden days and its most creative period. She was considered too strange-looking. A Catherine Deneuve is acceptable; she has a safely perfect face. Verushka is just too interestingly gorgeous."

Unlike Verushka, most models use their editorial exposure as a stepping-stone and learning experience for advertisers and catalog work. These are the more lucrative areas of modeling. Retail and wholesale are high-volume work, editorial is good exposure, but catalog and advertisements pay large fees.

Monique Pillard is executive vice-president of *Elite* and overall director of the New York office. "I'd do anything for my girls, America's top editorial models," she says, "because most people can never understand the demands and unique situation they are placed in: traveling all the time, living out of suitcases, one day London and the next Tokyo, often no place to call home." As an originator of the Elite modeling agency, Monique appreciates the snowball effect this heady editorial world can have on a model's desirability. "Top-notch editorial can pay quick dividends, sometimes so fast it's astonishing. You are seen widely in a magazine and the small manufacturers and catalogs will begin to use you immediately. Carol Alt and Nancy Donahue, for example, started with American editorial and their success, anyone can tell you, was instant. They were the right faces at the right time. Everybody picked up on them. I also make them understand that to achieve success and eventual stardom they must learn to act responsibly toward both their clients and their agency."

MODEL SELECTION:
THE UNCERTAIN SCIENCE

Although editors have a large number of candidates to choose from, the decision about models is the last to be made—first comes clothes, layout, and other details. By the time an editor is ready to select her models, the better-known ones may already be booked on other assignments. The model editor has to see who is free. If the photographer is well known and there are other favorable conditions, such as closeups or a cover try, then even the hottest model of the moment would consider the booking, no matter her schedule.

Sarah Foley, formerly model editor at *Vogue* before booking at Wilhelmina and then Name, looks at fashion editorial from a model's vantage point: "Some models want to know who the photographer will be and who is to do the hair and makeup. Some photographers take eight hours, and the models don't like to work that way. The editorial day rate is very low compared to advertising or catalog; an experienced model wants good exposure, a larger portfolio, in exchange for accepting a lower fee. Then there are models who don't want to work *fast*; they'd rather each picture be a showpiece, and that can take time. So the model editor has to juggle and be a good diplomat. There is a constant flow of models at *Vogue*, five to ten seen every day. If there should be someone superb and suitable, which doesn't happen too often, she would be sent first to Grace Mirabella, the editor, and then to the editorial departments—fashion, beauty, accessories, shoes, et cetera. If there's a photographer about to start on a portfolio (a series of pictures for a magazine), and the model editor feels he might be able to use that look, the model is sent right over to the studio. It's a two-way street; the photographers do the same for editors."

Deborah Turbeville is a *Vogue* photographer in both New York and Europe whose entrée into the business was modeling for Claire McCardell, America's first sportswear designer. Before taking up her camera, Deborah had been special-projects editor of *Harper's Bazaar* and photography editor of *Mademoiselle*. Having watched modeling trends from these many angles, she has this to say about them: "Magazines like *Harper's Bazaar* and *Vogue*, in the forties and fifties, were full of incredibly chic, sophisticated women. No one thought about whether they should be young; the editors just wanted them elegant. Then magazine audiences changed—more and more younger women were becoming readers. In those early days, only very rich women of that certain age could afford the clothes or, for that matter, saw copies of *Vogue*. The less-than-rich loved thinking that women over thirty could look that good.

"Now the psychology has changed. The beauty business, with its so-called improvements, lets women look so much younger than they once could that they don't want to look even thirty anymore. They want girls in the magazines to make them feel that by wearing those clothes they could look a sophisticated twenty.

"I look at the people clients choose for commercials and I wonder why. They seem to be stuck in one particular groove. You can just hear the casting office saying, 'We want Lucia to look about thirty. That girl's too young and that one's too old.' The advertising world has gone overboard with this age thing lately. The only consideration seems to be, How is it going to market? Which to them means, How old should the person look?"

A COVER ILLUSTRATES
THE MAGAZINE'S CONTENT

Obviously the look for fashion publications changes with each new season. For covers, the need to express each dimension of the American mix is never ending. Outside the dictates of fashion there is every possible characterization. Here is a look at the selection process and what it takes to be on two very different, but very successful, magazine covers. The successful magazine is the one that finds its readership and gives them what they expect. *Cosmopolitan* has done this spectacularly well, using beautiful women and a clear philosophy about them, to sell millions of copies each month. Helen Gurley Brown, surely the best-known name among female magazine editors, relates the ways women have changed to the *Cosmo* philosophy.

"I think many verities do not change for women. We love, as women have always loved; we feel insanely jealous when our men betray us. But today women are freer—to go to another man or seek

satisfaction from a great job. We can get divorces, support ourselves, and start over again. It is *Cosmopolitan*'s overriding philosophy that a woman should develop her own potential and not depend on a man for her livelihood or her total identity. At its worse, that's being a parasite. You should do something that will make you feel fulfilled and that is productive. That way you can choose a man you want to be with—not just someone who can support you. This philosophy really liberates men; they don't have to be totally, everlastingly responsible—financially and emotionally—for what happens to women."

As art director of *Cosmopolitan*, Linda Cox assigns articles and stories for photographic illustration. The themes are always in sync with the editorial overview. Linda, through working on four or five such illustrations each month, has learned that by including models at the concept stage, she gets better results.

According to Jerry Ford of Ford Talent, Inc., "There is an internationalism about editorial fashion magazines, which means a beginning model is not totally dependent on the New York magazines discovering her. Models go to Europe for work training. The fashion editors get involved, for the most part, in the early part of a career. They are in a position of helping, not managing, a model. By the nature of the fashion business, everything must change pretty fast, and that includes models. So editorially there is always a quick turnover."

To be selected for the cover of any magazine anytime during a modeling career is good exposure and the highest editorial compliment. Although not a top-dollar job, it can be converted into work regionally or in related modeling fields. Helen Gurley Brown's tenure at *Cosmo* has produced some striking covers. "They are there to be admired rather than aspired to," she says.

COSMOPOLITAN

February 1983 • $1.75

Bed and <u>Bore</u>d. Getting the Zing of a Fling Back Into Your Marriage

Jack Nicholson, a Star as Hot as the Sun

Why Men Need You More Than You Need Them

How Unmarried Couples Can Protect Their Rights and Property— When the Law Doesn't

Sex Addicts. Why Some Girls Can't Help Loving That Man— <u>A</u>ny Man

Be Bigger and Firmer. Excerpt From the New Book, <u>30 Days to a Better Bust</u>

A <u>Split</u> Personality May Explain the Things You Do That Are Not <u>You</u>

Overeaters Anonymous Helped This "Binger" Overcome Her Lust for Food

<u>Modern Love.</u> "It Could" Happen to You. A New Novel by Leslie Glass

Plus <u>One-Night Stand</u>, by Jeffrey Archer

NEW YORK

How Good Is Your Bank?

—And How Well Does It Treat You?

Seven Beauties Prince 〇 Charles Missed

Esquire

JUNE 1981 · PRICE $2.00 　　　MAN AT HIS BEST

What Do Women Really Think About Men's Bodies?

Boy, Have We Got News For You!

Body Parts
by Priscilla Flood

Some other extreme uses of models, not always in a pleasant way, help to illustrate *New York* magazine cover concepts. Jordan Schaps, scenario spinner supreme, turns a benign and simple process into something sinister (and won an award doing it). The *Esquire* cover tries to express the contents: he-man image with a barbell. Male models rarely make fashion-magazine cover material. Alone on the newsstand, a male model can't sell out an issue; even *GQ* has gone to using actors, directors, couples, even fashion designers and writers in their places.

"One time I had to set up a situation—a couple—on the subject of men in love where there is a new phenomenon afoot: He is backing off from a perfect match, she adores him, and they have lots in common. At first we posed the couple as we had in other pictures and we knew it was going to look like the same old thing. So the photographer talked to the models about this new feeling, and something started to happen—something right for the emotional change. Models are getting smarter, better educated, and more sophisticated: They have to understand the feelings you want from the pictures.

"Our cover, on the other hand, is a logo, which requires the women to be direct with a very modern face. On each cover of *Cosmo*, one part of the model is always overtly sexy: eyes, lips, whatever we see to pull out. The model must have enough personality and experience to form her own body into 'covershape.' To do that, she has to feel great about herself, like the way she looks when she walks out. Most of all she has to feel a part of it all. Sean M. Byrnes styles all the covers with Francesco Scavullo. We change the color every month, so each cover girl has to match the mood of that month's color. When I have decided what the color will be, Sean looks for something—someone—in that range."

Helen Gurley Brown sees the selection process a little differently. She is only half joking when she says that *selection* simply means that Francesco Scavullo does whatever pleases him. "He has great taste in models and in women, knows who will photograph well and who excites him. I wouldn't dream of telling him anything. I have never suggested a cover possibility to him and he has never failed me.

"The most beautiful young women in the world are on the *Cosmo* covers. They are there because I think they are pleasurable to look at . . . to be admired rather than aspired to. I would rather see a beautiful woman than an ordinary one, and I think most people would. Everyone knows that models have the maximum, not the minimum, and that they do the maximum with it. With help, of course, from sensational makeup artists, hairdressers, and stylists.

"Face it. There is a difference being born Christie Brinkley or Carol Alt and being born anyone else. We ordinary souls can never catch up. Jog every morning for thirty years and it won't happen! So let's not be ridiculous about what beauties we can

all become. If you're very successful, people soon start forgetting about how you look. They just listen to how you sound. That's not to say that looking good isn't worthwhile. It's worth every effort you can put into it to look as good as you can and to improve."

Jordan Schaps, photographic editor at *New York* magazine, describes how he conceives cover-story illustrations. As in advertising print, they are calculated for split-second attention catching and then retaining that attention. "When I hire models I have expectations. I expect them to understand the situation or to at least be willing to find out what I am going for.

"No picture, at least no good magazine cover, is just a picture of something . . . it's a moment in a scenario or a relationship. For a cover on 'What Your Shrink Really Thinks of You,' my initial concept was simple: get a shrink model, a patient model, and minimally suggest an office-visit situation. It doesn't end there however. What I wanted to achieve was the encapsulation of a specific instant in a specific professional/patient relationship that anyone could recognize and also one that would be fun. So in the studio with two fitted models, I asked for and was rewarded with terrific character vignettes. I wanted the woman patient to be complaining in the most obnoxious way—dramatizing to the death about her near fatal hangnail, and to play off that I wanted the psychiatrist (or psychologist) to be giving her, almost literally, a curled lip—sort of 'you creep, people are starving and dying all over the world and you're anguishing over your hangnail.' Well, no conceptualizing, no directing, no explaining in the world could bring this off if the models were not tremendously gifted professionals, bright conceptual thinking people, and good, free-spirited sports in front of the camera. The result of that shooting was a terrifically vivid scene, accessible in a twenty-thousandth of a second.

When Jordon works with models, he conveys to them the concept he is after so that they can express it to the camera. But he then expects *more*. He expects them to surprise him:

"There is a crucial difference between character and fashion modeling. For fashion pages, if you have a good editor, photographer, and stylists, and decent clothes, you can spin a story, create a mood around a model. It needn't be even vaguely connected to anything. The photographer can mix the light beautifully and the reader will think it is sensational. Who knows what the model was actually thinking? She is only part of the tapestry. It is much different with a conceptual situation; there the idea depends on the model having that certain savvy and expressiveness to make the concept read."

Models can make it big without an editorial push behind them, but getting a few of those prestigious jobs usually means the difference between a fairly good career and a topnotch one. Likewise, the equivalent in the cosmetic field is the magazine cover. This is why models (and their agents) will court the hard work of editorial exposure. The periodicals have managed to keep the pay down but the value to models up.

A female model can sell out an issue of a fashion magazine. Here, Wanakee of Elite offers an unusual angle to the camera for *Essence*. On the following page, Kim Coleman at Kim Dawson in Dallas stares down the range in a *Town & Country* cover photograph. The *Seventeen* cover (p. 63) is the ultimate teen dream. No magazine, not even *National Geographic*, has a head on its cover without intense eye contact.

34725 • JANUARY 1983 $1.25

ESSENCE

MOVING FORWARD!

All the facts you need for radiant skin, fabulous hair, body confidence and a winning attitude for '83!

How to Get What You Want

Exclusive Interview

The Pain and Healing of Marvin Gaye

How a Family of Four Saved Over $500 a Month on Food

TOWN & COUNTRY

SEPTEMBER 1979/$2.00

An Entire
Issue on

TEXAS
The State We
Can't Do Without

**An In-Depth Look at the
Brilliant, Beautiful Women
And Dynamic, Powerful
Men Who Shape Its
Special Role in
America's Culture
And Economy**

PLUS

**T&C's Own List of the
125 Individuals and
Families Who Are
The Richest Texans**

Kim Coleman
And 6666's
Wagon Boss
Murry Rodgers:
Ranching Texas Style

YOUNG AMERICA'S FAVORITE MAGAZINE   SEPTEMBER 1980 $1

Seventeen

FALL FASHION FAVORITES
New coats, dresses, sweaters

BEAUTY MAKEOVERS
for 3 of our readers

QUIZ:
Do you understand yourself?

TOO THIN? TOO FAT?
Chart your own way to fitness

SHY GUY
How to catch his eye

Catalog—
Thematics, Manufacturers, and Department and Specialty Stores

*C*atalog is where the broadest range of types and the greatest opportunities lie for a model. However, it has the stiffest rules to master. Catalog is the fastest-paced, most no-nonsense arena of modeling. The idea is to get on with the job; there is little spare time for out-of-place jokes or moody sulking. A model must be extremely steady and reliable. No home runs here, just constant plugging away to get all the necessary shots churned out by the end of the day. The volume of catalog work is huge, across this country and in Germany and Japan as well.

A model almost always has to be prepared to cope, unaided, with requests for particular makeup and hairstyles. Only 15 to 20 percent of catalogs are budgeted for hair and makeup artists, or for elaborate location shoots, unlike more lavishly funded editorial.

As always, a model's physical appearance is geared to the type of clothes she or he is selling. In catalog more than elsewhere, the child, the large-size model, the more matronly woman, and the elegant mature man are in demand. Catalog is

straight, direct selling. The prospective buyer has to be able to identify with the person in the picture. Therefore, in most cases, the model must be attractive without being stunning. This is true at least for the strictly high-fashion or particularly upper-class audience.

Models are expected to know what they're doing, to do it well, and to do it right. This category prefers experience. Joan Severance, an Elite star catalog model who became well-known in editorial modeling, describes the catalog for the model: "*Vogue* is prestige pictures; for catalog you're paid money from walk-in to walk-out. Catalog people are very straightforward, all business. They want you to arrive with your hair and makeup done. You have twenty different outfits in every variation: singles, doubles, triples, quads, and beauty (cover only) and three-quarters cropped. The lighting never changes. If you don't look good in that light, tough. They're interested in how the clothes look, and think the model should look good in any light, which is, naturally, not always true."

On a catalog shoot, the photographer must get

his picture in two rolls of film—there is no going over budget. Therefore the pace is also brisk, the atmosphere businesslike. A model has to know what is expected of her without being told, because conversation wastes time and money. She must have a combination of acquired and instinctive knowledge about what makes a garment look good—how to be demure, or whatever the clothes call for.

The model's function is to show clothes to their best advantage, giving them life by featuring the best parts of her body. For that she is paid in the higher range of the day rate, unlike editorial, which pays at the low end.

Jamie Simpson, a top New York stylist, has watched many veterans on catalog shoots, and he sees catalog modeling for men as Joan does for women: The model is very much on his own. "By the time a model puts on the garment, all the details have been worked out. He's the last to know. By the time he does, it's late in the game, and his reactions must be instinctive. To animate the merchandise, both men and women must be sensitive to the clothes and move in a way that draws atten-

Catalog is often put into the bread-and-butter category for a model. The fact is it's hard work. The object is to show the merchandise and be quick about it. Catalogs have become part of our visual vernacular. Correct model selection is a crucial element in every successful catalog. It is age range and coloring as well as attitude that lets the buyers know they are shopping through the right book. A versatile female model will vary her looks according to the dictates of fashion, but in male model selection the norm is still typecasting. For men, the rumpled look at the left could only be possible in an active sportswear catalog. In the second photograph is Cheryl Tiegs, America's best-known model, wearing her own line for a Sears catalog cover. Her image in the catalog smashed every Sears, Roebuck record. Her pages sold more merchandise than any before. Even at this level a model needs to remain flexible, diplomatic, and personable. To remain at the top in New York, Cheryl Tiegs must be "on"—whenever and wherever she is seen. Cheryl has spearheaded another modeling first with her own clothing line.

tion to them. Men also have the often awesome task of keeping clothes wrinkle-free. Items in a catalog are shot for *sale;* nothing that is not for sale is ever displayed. Beauty, in this category, is less important than intelligent responses—and of course an air of confidence and vitality, classy or bouncy, depending on the clothing."

CATALOG PREPARATION

In working with Cheryl Tiegs's line of clothing for Sears, Roebuck, Barbara Shapiro has sat in on the initial stages of putting together merchandise for a catalog, or, as catalog professionals call it, preparing the book. It helps, she says, with preparation of the layouts, "based on what each department needs to have shown in its section of the catalog. Those who buy the merchandise know which details of the garments should be featured. There is no fuzziness or guesswork. When a customer buys from a picture, he expects to see what he needs to see and get exactly what he sees, not the spirit of the thing, which is the editorial attitude."

And that is precisely what the model must be able to bring out in catalog. Jamie Simpson has styled books and magazines as well as catalogs. He sees the stylist as responsible for detail, part of a process that goes like this: "A coordinator from the catalog house supervises the merchandise, working with the client's needs on each garment and its accessories. A department store apportions space among departments and items sold in the store are used as props and accessories. In one catalog I had to feature the same earrings throughout because they had been overordered and had to be sold." Manufacturers' catalogs are often targeted a little differently—in advertising and public relations as well as in direct sales. There are thousands of specialty catalogs, from trendy sportswear to gardening gear, for the young and old alike.

A fashion coordinator gets a stylist's help in shaping the book's image. The fashion people explain their market concept and what age and style ranges have been targeted. Model selection is based on the client's suggestions, the art director's opinion, and the photographer's preference. The stylist is the go-between, balancing everyone's opinions against the available models. When the garments have been selected and the marketing plan and style particulars fleshed out, the art director prepares his layouts. "I work from those," Jamie adds. "They are a good guide—almost always detailed drawings with instructions."

In national and regional books, the client is trying to reach the broadest possible base, which is the strongest determinant in model selection. The dominant note is generally clean-cut, fair-haired, with a certain amount of diversity. In a catalog for general distribution—not targeted, that is, to any particular market—the ratio will be about 70 percent "American conventional," with the rest a mixture of one or two blacks, some Mediterranean types, perhaps a few Orientals. In political patter, a balanced ticket.

Bob Manella was a staff photographer for one of New York City's direct-mail houses, Bel-Aire. Bel-Aire has a studio but also contracts with free-lance photographers, stylists, and models for their creative services on behalf of their clients. The organization puts the details in place, has the final say in model selection, and takes responsibility for having a representative mix of types.

"Any store you are dealing with," explains Manella, "be it in Texas or in New York, has a certain look. The degree of high fashion comes straight from the consumer. A woman in Idaho, for example, won't go for severe hair and makeup styles; they don't see themselves that way. This attitude affects budget; but it doesn't mean you can't project a catalog to appeal to a more upscale customer. Common sense has to come in. We'd be crazy to show a blond, blue-eyed model to the Puerto Rican market. The catalog business is essentially very democratic, like commerce itself; most of the time, though, the proportions of model types are probably very much the same as the current census projections for the entire population.

"The catalog itself begins with a presentation to the client, our interpretation of what we feel they want," Bob continues. "The client sees it on layout boards, and we get their feedback. The client's needs are fairly specific and they help direct the model selection. We use the same twenty models ninety-five percent of the time because we know they produce—some people as many as thirty times a year. We usually book models for half-days, longer if the client wants us to. If a model's rate is two thousand dollars a day, she'll get ten thousand dollars for a full five days. If this model has a business head, she knows that that's a good client and she is very friendly."

The layouts rarely come exactly the way they're planned. Often they are made from a list of garments. "If the garment doesn't fit the way the layout shows it," Bob explains, "we need some latitude to be able to change it."

On the whole, the conservative catalog industry has had to relax as it swelled over the last decade. Now several different photographers are used in one mailer, creating a greater diversity of shots and model types. And from the models' point of view, the good news is that with computer technology, opportunity in this category will increase. Perhaps even more freedom, as well as greater creativity in direct-sales books, will come as merchandise moves on a screen rather than on a page.

Live Modeling—
Trade and Industrial Shows
and Informal Modeling

◆

*C*atalog is a natural bridge to the hard product sell at conventions, in commercial print work, and on television commercials. When models are doing direct selling or endorsing products, they are no longer just image-makers or attitude promoters. In both cases they are selling, but live direct work is far more sharply and narrowly focused.

A good demonstrator can work press conferences and sales-promotion meetings. Public-relations modeling can mean many things: handing out flyers or sample products, or acting as a mannequin, host, or demonstrator. Suitability usually comes down to resemblance to the kind of people targeted as probable buyers: a housewife with a dishwasher, a sportsman with a rifle. Often press photographs are taken at such gatherings; occasionally, if the event is significant beyond its immediate audience, news crews will attend. These shows, which is what they are, usually take place near public spaces or, when relative privacy is wanted, in a hospitality suite or luncheon setting.

A closely aligned area is television modeling. Most television work is for game shows, where a model does little more than move objects, highlight win-

ners' choices, or usher contestants to center stage. Occasionally a model who combines good diction and appearance is used as an on-camera announcer.

Many consider convention modeling the least desirable kind, yet it is very much in the modeling mainstream. Many a novice has gotten a good, and rewarding, start on the floor of Chicago's Merchandise Mart, or at conventions in Los Angeles, Dallas, or Las Vegas. Each industry gathers to promote the sale of its wares: In movies it's called a festival; in fashion, a collection; in autos, a trade show; in audio/visual electronics, a convention.

Booth modeling may be done freestyle or from a prepared script. The model is a free-lancer, hired to help represent a company to potential buyers at the booth where its product is displayed. The multiple role—as guide, intermediary, and salesperson—is crucial to marketing success; sales hinge on how well the product is presented.

Melanie B. Neal, who works through David and Lee, a top fashion-print model agency in Chicago and Cleveland, found that trade shows were the easiest source of income from modeling. "They

Jerry Ford, agent for many superstar models, including Cheryl Tiegs, says, "It takes something more than just beauty to become a model. But if you have what it takes, you'll have a good career and a good time. For the successful model I advise the same as I would for an athlete—don't let it take you over. Success in any field has to be handled with good sense; it's a lot to have thrown at you at eighteen or nineteen. The modeling business is a series of good relationships. How pleasantly you perform has a lot to do with how widely you are accepted. This affects the breadth and longevity of a career. You can always improve with training."

A model's image is connected to a product either through commercials or photographs, or by appearing live on a convention floor; therefore a model must make garments or products sell. The skill is learned through experience on the runway and at editorial sittings, and is applied on advertising, catalog, and retail assignments. What makes a magazine cover jump out at its audience also works on a national ad. A model such as Cheryl Tiegs did not wake up one morning a superstar. She worked hard in her native Pasadena, California, to understand the field. From her first fashion-magazine location job came this *Glamour* magazine cover. It was shot quickly in a Virgin Island alley, and even today Cheryl has a reputation for scoring immediate recognition on any national news or women's magazine cover. A professional model's image acts as an endorsement and helps merchandise products from car rentals, cameras, and plane tickets to shopping malls.

Cheryl's *Time* cover shows that her presence in TV spots, national ads, and catalog covers helps promote her line at every level (there are even Cheryl Tiegs mannequins and display cutouts).

"My move into clothing design was natural because I've modeled for so many years and had on just about every fabric, color, and style. When I look at clothes, I look for fabric, design, and price. These are what I sought to provide in my own line." Cheryl Tiegs's line is a fast-moving group of easy-living sports clothes. In preparation for it, Cheryl says she had a lot to learn. "I learned it all in the field: What is irritating to the skin and which colors are flattering. I was determined to disprove the notion that only high-priced sports clothes are well designed. I live a typical American life, I know what I need and like—and I wanted my customers to have my idea of the best. Everything I ever learned, in life and in modeling, I wanted to present to the American woman."

"Often I take a look at what is planned and think, *How can I take this to a higher level?*" says superstar-model Cheryl

Tiegs. "These are situations that require personality. I try to make the result as natural as possible. I try to give the impression that someone just happened to catch me holding this product instead of being posed there." She continues, on being photographed: "Every time the picture is about to be snapped I jerk or move my head. I sort of settle in at the last second. At the point when the picture is taken, our concentration is absolute. I believe there is a tunnel, an actual line connecting me and the photographer at that moment. I zero in on him and how he is reacting."

As with the other skills of modeling, practice allows a model to change the nuance of facial expressions or gestures and play to the camera. The model must learn to talk with her face and to portray liveliness. It is the right gesture that gives a pose realism. Some photographers explain and others only nod. Openness and a willingness to respond to instruction is imperative. If a model photographs within a type and can get known for it, it then becomes easy to branch out little by little.

meant instant money, which of course you need when you are starting out, especially if you don't have the temperament to be a waitress or a hostess. I did very well at conventions and had steady clients, but I couldn't figure out why people hired me. I didn't think I had the personality, nor did I know how to sell from a booth. Now I know that my clients liked me because they knew that I would do the job, that I was the low-key type who would hand out brochures and not flirt with the men.

"Convention modeling paid the rent, and left me plenty of time for test shots. I met some great people, and it got me where I wanted to be. It taught me something about the art of selling, and that's helpful whatever you do."

Shirley Hamilton's agency in Chicago works with fashion and "believable" people, booking them into conventions and industrial films. Most of the models do product photography as well as live demonstration. Here is how she sees trade-show qualifications: "Personality and overall appearance count the most. A model need not be a raving beauty, but she does need a personality that's a real sparkler. She has to be quick and intelligent to walk into a situation knowing nothing about the product she will be working with. A good convention model learns to handle a technical script so that it's a pleasure to listen to. And the better she gets, the higher she's paid.

"Fifteen years ago, people were indiscreet with models. That has mostly changed, probably because there are now many more women on convention floors. Women have a new role in the convention industry. They must be very careful who they work for. We screen every client to make sure no one expects a model to serve drinks in a hospitality suite. Models are not waiters or waitresses."

Judi Moreo is president of Universal Models, the largest agency in its field, located in Las Vegas, the world's most popular city for booking convention talent. Like Shirley Hamilton in Chicago, Judy sees a major change in the industry where models are concerned. "It's a recent change, about the last five years. People who hire convention models are looking for more professionalism. They used to want short shorts, T-shirts, sexy getups—to attract attention, period. The market today demands a more cultivated person who can attract people to a booth and keep them there—sell a product. Models must be bright enough to explain the product and to

know when to turn a prospect over to a salesperson (*turnovers*, in their lingo) from the company. Models are often used *instead* of company salespeople to save on travel expenses. Some shows are multilingual—the electronics shows have about eight languages. A model who speaks another language can really have an edge, and make more money."

TRADE AND INDUSTRIAL SHOWS

Zachs and Perrier is a production house that exclusively produces software for trade and industrial shows: sound tracks, sets, arrangements, and lighting. They use models more often for slides and films than for the live part of the presentation; that goes to actors, dancers, and singers. Industrial shows are usually a form of live theater. It's big business. The *Geographic Professional Theater Guide*, the *New York Survival Guide*, and *Show Business* lists more than one hundred other industrial show producers.

For Zachs and Perrier, Robin Silvestrie produces shows ranging from small seventeen-city tours, which companies do for publicity, to elaborate three-day meetings using motivational material that makes them talent and technological spectaculars. Robin describes her approach to model selection: "We use more real-looking people with acting experience; singers and dancers are auditioned separately. The models drop off head shots or composites for us—we keep our own casting files. If I need fashion models I call the local agency. A lot of our fashion shows travel. For BMW, the automaker, we hired fourteen local Hawaiian models to do a whole line of clothes that the dealers were going to sell in their showrooms. This was just a segment of an entire sales conference. The working conditions can be superb, and, considering the relaxation and recreation value, the salary is spectacular."

Just about everyone associated with men's fashion here and abroad puts on a week of press shows to present an upcoming season's styles. In the spring of 1976, Steven Thomas, recently signed with Wilhelmina, was back from his first trip to Europe. He was booked to do a one-week trade show at the Mount Airy Lodge in the Poconos. "It is so intense

. . . twenty to thirty shows in a week. Plus that many rehearsals. Everyone from Cardin, St. Laurent, and Pendleton to Du Pont and Celanese were there to do shows. Everything from fully choreographed musical numbers to runway to free-form modeling within a prescribed area. Skip Talbort handles model selection and would distribute guys to the exhibitors. There were a dozen to fifteen in all. Some models worked a few shows and some worked almost all. I did Pierre Cardin's show.

"People were there from his office, at his right hand to pull everything together. Each model was fully outfitted. It was like an assembly line. Cardin does it like no one else in the world. They strip you after each pass on the runway. You just stand there and they put everything on you, tie and all. At the end there is Cardin himself. He adjusts your tie and handkerchief, whispering 'This is the attitude I want you to have' or 'Do what you think best with this music.' Then he hugs and kisses you!"

There are many trade shows for out-of-town buyers. All the manufacturers—tuxedo, sportswear, activewear, outerwear—have trade shows for which models are hired to wear clothes in the booths. Some exhibitors set up very elaborate spaces with platforms and music, and may do as many as five shows a day out of their booths. There are trade shows in Paris and Milan as well, put on for American and other buyers.

The trade-show experience teaches models to carry themselves and gives them a sense of clothes. For male models in particular, the exposure leads to other jobs—for them it is similar to showroom exposure for women. According to Universal Model President Judi Moreo, the trade-show model primarily needs personality and an ability to reach out to people. She needs to have the acting ability to assume the personality of the corporate entity she represents. Looks are of course not unimportant, and models who look alert, attractive, and American are most in demand. However, an ebullient, outgoing personality is equally crucial.

"Convention models also work at the information booth," explains Moreo, "so they need to know the convention center, the city, where the attractions and the emergency health facilities are, where interpeters can be found. A person who thinks she has it for convention work should go to an agency specializing in that kind of work."

Anita Bentley, who was born in Great Britain, has lived in Las Vegas for eleven years, working originally as a dancer. Recently, she began doing full-time modeling through Universal. She found modeling a natural crossover from dancing, and Las Vegas the perfect place. An ad in the paper led her to an agent, and she started to do fashion shows and tearoom modeling, then trade shows, conventions, and industrials. Anita "promotes Las Vegas all around the country with a showgirl routine, performing in little cabaret acts at cocktail parties and other social functions.

"In Las Vegas it helps to learn to dance. It is just that kind of town. A model here has to meet and get along with many people, which means that she has to enjoy it. She must be a good talker, and know how to conduct herself. It always pays to do a little homework in convention modeling—call it a crash course. The day before you start you get a briefing on what is expected. It is advisable to brief yourself with the company's informational material. It tells you that little bit extra about the items you are going to be selling. Sometimes the job requires a narration, often accompanied by a filmstrip, slide show, or film."

INFORMAL MODELING

Informal showings, once called tearoom modeling because the practice was so popular in turn-of-the-century Parisian tea houses, aren't to be confused with runway or showroom modeling for buyers. These are casual showings, done in malls or retail establishments. Saks Fifth Avenue uses the technique to promote store openings or new lines of major designers, and in seasonal shows around the country. Helen O'Hagan, special-events director for Saks in New York, describes these minishows:

"We take them all over—to Boston, Dallas, Kansas City, Chicago, San Francisco—thirty-eight cities in all. Each store has a fashion and public-relations director. I tell her how many models I want booked—she knows the local market and I trust her judgment. Years ago everyone had house models, but no more. New York is different. There are house models on my staff who will work informally on the floor from noon to four. Very handy when a designer makes a public appearance and we want to do a minishow.

"When we opened our new children's floor, the theme was Old MacDonald, and we went all out with the farm scene—farmer, horses, and cows. We were introducing Cacharel clothes and the children were done up as adults, with horn-rimmed glasses and briefcases. The kids love it. Children are fun to work with. Brooke Shields modeled for us when she was a child. She was the sweetest thing, totally professional and wonderful to all the other children."

As a seasoned model, Lynn Yeager is no longer a "roving ambassador" at department-store promotions. She found it exhausting to be on her feet for so many hours. "You can never forget you are a surrogate for a designer or manufacturer. When I started out I did informals every Saturday from twelve to four, then once more during the week. That's eight solid hours for a beginning model. I got so spoiled I didn't want to do it unless I was asked by a big client."

It isn't only long hours that make informal modeling hard work. It's also having to spend those hours walking around a store. The model is always a salesperson, but is often asked only for sales literature. However, he or she can get customers into a conversation that may add a touch to their interest in a company's line. What a model does at such showings depends to a large extent on the type of promotion the product needs and the funds allotted to it. The range can be from choreographed musical numbers to black-and-white photocopied information sheets. Basically, he or she is responsible for representing the client and knowing how to answer questions for the customers quickly.

The rates for informal showings are lower than for other types of modeling, but the work runs from short blocks of time to full-week bookings. This is beneficial for a beginner, who, in addition to chalking up good learning experience in, for instance, showing a garment, can—even if only by handing out simple promotional material—form a selling relationship to the buying public.

Advertising— Illustration and Commercial Print Work

*E*arly advertisements featured bar girls pushing whiskey or tobacco and were on display in male hangouts, such as barbershops, or were aimed at women as the primary buyers of housewares. Women fell into two distinct classes: urban matrons or country-bred servants. Kellogg's was one of the first cereals to use women, revolutionizing the breakfast habits of millions. A Belle Epoque poster for Egyptienne cigarettes broke new ground when it associated the product with a desirable woman, in this instance a plump, childlike blonde; both model and cigarette were labeled "Absolutely Pure." Ads of the twenties began to move women into situations outside the home—romping at baseball games, taking "snapshots," modeling the latest swimsuits.

Illustrators George Petty and Alberto Vargas drew voluptuous women for advertising: Petty for Old Gold cigarettes and Jantzen swimwear; Vargas for covers for the Follies Theater, girlie calendars, and Jergens advertisements. Manufacturers sent artists on steamer trips to Europe to render the current Parisian creations and brought them back by the next boat. "It was rare that products advertised through photography at all," recalls Joe Eula, a prominent illustrator then. "From the thirties right into the fifties, *all* fashion was illustrated, as were fashion-related products and textiles by manufacturers such as Burlington or Celanese. Beautiful women were used to sell cars, cigarettes, even travel. The turnaround began with 'Fire and Ice,' a Revlon campaign. It converted people with pretty fixed habits. Before that Revlon breakthrough, Saks Fifth Avenue or Elizabeth Arden would not have been caught dead using a photograph.

"When illustration was everything, a model was positioned with a product and painting would begin. The background was filled in later, if necessary. The process could take anywhere from ten minutes to an hour, depending on how complicated the pose and how detailed the drawing. It was the model that could make the difference in it being easy. She could wear the outfit in a way that would excite the artist.

"An illustration model is the same as any other model. She takes absolutely nothing, or nothing much, and gives it an aura or an allure—something nobody else could give it, not even the person who designed the ad. If she's good, an illustration model can go on forever. Lisa Fonssagrives, Carmen, or Betsy Pickering Kaiser could still work. An illustrator is lucky in one way: He never has to get approvals from the client or an art director, as a photographer must. The model makes close to an editorial rate for illustration work."

Antonio Lopez expresses himself through his drawings of women. Growing up, he wanted to be a fashion designer. His family has been involved in fashion since the fifties, his father dressing beauty-shop and store windows with mannequins, and his half-sister Cathy Damon, a top model. Antonio went to the High School for Art and Design on New York's Upper East Side, an environment well supplied with girls to practice his fashion ideas on. After graduation he did his first illustrations for *Women's Wear Daily.* Determined and hardworking, success came quickly to Antonio and has been continuous. He was the first to include blacks and Asians in his representations. His ideas were very new, always ahead of the crowd. An innovator in all things, he is credited with discovering and transforming Jerry Hall, Pat Cleveland, Grace Jones, and Jessica Lange, a process that began with his girlfriends in high school.

Antonio explains, "In the beginning I tried to make them look like everyone else. As a kid I idealized women into dolls. Later, I got brighter and learned to encourage them to be themselves. I am one of the earliest advocates of the women's movement; I always like seeing them feel free.

"I used to make up my girlfriends, a born Pygmalion! I could always see an element that could be improved. My so-called discoveries would catch it without me having to verbalize: Do this or that. They would be able to look at my drawings and copy the way I had done the makeup, the stance. Then they'd take it a step further on their own. What I wanted them to get from me was everything they could, then just give it back. It's a pure exchange."

Antonio started to find people, he says, out of a need, meeting them in subways, clubs, schools, sometimes through agencies. "I usually know right away if there's anything there. It can be bone structure, the lifting of an arm, a certain carriage. Nonphotogenic models can be good to draw and yet not right for photography.

"The last girl I found was a Princetonian, Bonnie Berman. After I started to draw her, she went to

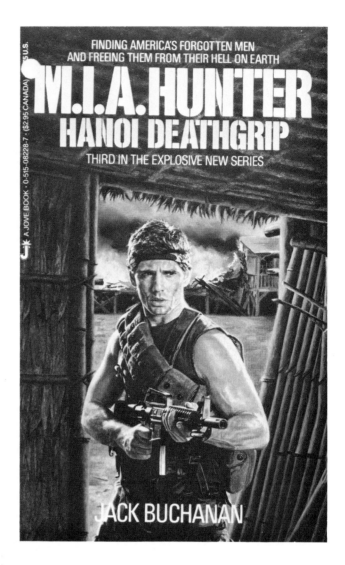

The first prestigious arena for models was fashion illustration, which included working with the society journals of the day. The only photography on live models was, ironically, for undergarments such as corsets and lingerie. These days a bonus is paid for those shots, and illustrations have taken a backseat to photographs. In these two photographs, Jason Savin, a Wilhelmina model, poses on a blank no-seam or stark-white painted photographic cyc which is then embellished by a painter to illustrate popular fiction pieces. This process takes place daily in many studios; it is where many beginners have learned tricks about photographic modeling. Often modeling requires replicating the same feeling or set of actions, even months later.

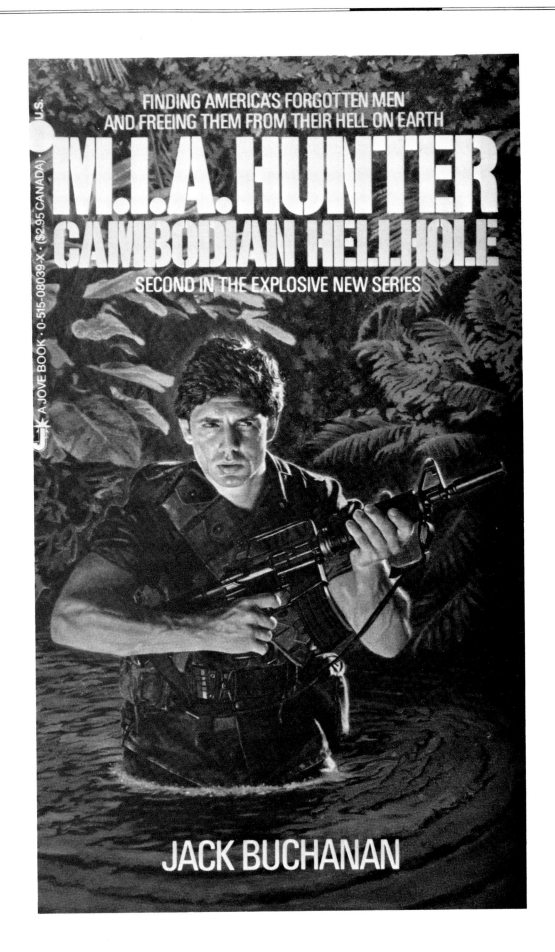

Ford. When she left them I arranged for her to meet Arthur Elgort, who loved her. She signed with Frances Grill's Click and now she's made it. Modeling is very territorial. Someone's got to feel possessive about a model, responsible for her career," Antonio concludes, "and most of all the girl herself has got to want it."

MADISON AVENUE: A DIFFERENT SET OF DEMANDS

Wallace Rogers's New York City agency specializes in product print work, different in motive and method from fashion. "What we aim for in product work," Rogers explains, "is a very attractive, almost fashion look. Our clients tend to be semi-glamour companies—cigarettes, cars, hair products, cosmetics. If you can draw that fine a line, our models look like they live in upscale Connecticut, not Middle America. We start with this kind of model and move toward fashion. There are agencies that go from Middle American toward character. My models can be generally described as pretty people no matter what age they are. The clients want a model to come in looking gorgeous and then put the glasses on and become a secretary. They don't want the reverse—a girl who comes in looking dowdy and has to manufacture gorgeous."

At Joan Magnum's agency in Los Angeles, requirements are nothing like those that would satisfy an Eileen Ford or a Gillis McGil. Ford and McGil, who both head New York high-fashion agencies, look for a size, a height, and a look for fashion—and fashion only. Joan looks for character, according to all sorts of criteria, because there are so many different types. A character model has to respond fast, "not find it strange to achieve the look of a particular profession." For instance, Joan goes on, "If I say to a model, 'You're a young lawyer,' or, 'you're going camping,' it should be understood what the requirements are. Most of the models I represent aren't strictly models. They do commercials in which they have to act and be animated. They are actors, portraying in commercial print what they would try to get across in a movie or the theater. Of course, they have to show me portfolios. An agency like mine has to know what people can do. All of them can't do everything. We help them develop their particular commercial niche, the range that they are comfortable doing."

Maureen Malone heads up the Funny Face Brigade, which is New York's largest character agency supplying models for commercial print and TV—grandmas, nerds, dads, businessmen—definitely not fashion types. "Oil of Olay and Avon are about as pretty as our accounts get. We specialize in real people and characters. A character needs a describable quality—balding, moustache, heavy, round, fat, a droopy expression, a rubbery sort of face—something to set it apart from the norm and never under a catchall beautiful.

"We work primarily with actors because most of them are used to being in front of the camera. When you get a set with a commercial photographer, a lot of what he suggests is going to be animated and require an improvisational knowledge, so you have to have a sense of acting."

Thea Krynn of Wallace Rogers is highly successful as a print model in New York. She had gone to acting school and always photographed well. Finding that she had the time to make rounds to photographers, she took on Wallace Rogers as her agent and got to work on her portfolio. "I realized the advantage of being able to look various ways. I went after things like the 'mommy' type because I was twenty-six and wanted to go for roles I was right for. It can be tough to make a living at this. You have to have a look that is wanted. It may take as long as five years to have photographers and clients know you and how you photograph. Meeting and finding congenial clients takes time too. Starting is hard, especially when you're over twenty-five. You have to be willing to be out there with your book, see photographers and chase them for pictures. It's intensely competitive because the money is so good. Only a fortunate few can really make a living at it, though. The fallout rate is high and it takes a lot of hustle to get that break.

"I didn't do a great deal of testing. Wally, my agent, sent the pictures I did have to working photographers, and I went on interviews and rounds. I had no luck the first year because people in the business were still getting to know me. Photographers have to know how you react and what kind of expression you can put into a shot. It all comes back to acting—you need the experience to draw from.

"Illustrating or modeling with products can be a fun 'up' thing if you're feeling good. You have to be alert to pick up on what the advertisers want. Often they are still sorting out their ideas, so as the model you have to approach the whole thing as a form of theater. Acting taught me to imagine and become a character. It is not intellectualizing with me but rather a natural looseness in front of the camera. Whether it's anger, happiness, or seriousness, you can think of a situation, believe in it, and convey it by using the thought. Maybe you're given simple direction, like, 'You are frustrated or anxious.' From that, you improvise agony or pain, let's say, for a pharmaceutical product. In theater, because of the time frame, you aren't usually directed all the way through. A lot of the decisions are collective. I use my intuition and background to project myself into a character.

"Modeling is more motionless, which is why poses develop. Holding positions and repeating an expression over and over gets to be a strain after a while. It's difficult to relate to the camera when you've been sustaining a pose for a very long time."

Loretta Tupper is a Funny Face model who, at seventy-seven years of age, is on her second or perhaps third career. Formerly a singing coach and a ballet pianist, it was the father of one of her students who put Loretta on the map as a grandma. He was a photographer who remembered her as a vaudeville singer. She says, "I did my first commercial one week after Sam Zaramba took my composite pictures. I went on trying to see people for voice and music, but when they saw my portfolio they would ask me to be *in* the ads. I do radio voice, print ads, and commercials. My first print ad was for a doughnut company. All I had to do was take a bite. The ad ran for eighteen months straight.

"Now I'm established and don't have to go on go-sees anymore. I get calls for spokesperson parts with auditions for the vignettes to surround me. I used to get asked to do so many calls. When you're seventy-seven, it's hard to get around. I have learned one important lesson: If you relax and enjoy what you are doing, it shows, it becomes infectious. Fun lets you get an audience or the camera in your pocket. If you relax and roll with it, the audience will come with you. I use this in all the commercials I do and also in the print ads.

"When I went to work on print fifteen months ago, I was lucky to average a commercial or two a year and a print job a week. It was the doughnut ad that got me started. I like to do cute and funny parts and I love the feisty grandma ones. The sweet grandma I just can't do anything with."

PARTS AND BEAUTY MODELING

Character modeling provides the bulk of commercial print work. Beauty and parts modeling are special categories. Parts models are those with fine feet, hands, legs, and so on; a beauty model's best part is her face. Even among the beautiful faces, advertisers make a choice depending on the product. If the eyelids are large, heavy, and prominent, liner and shadows come up clearly. A large, well-shaped mouth draws attention to lipsticks and glosses. High cheekbones dramatize blush. Shorter girls will be glad to know that a beauty model doesn't have to be tall; many of the best and most successful are under five feet six. "Female stars like Joan Crawford, Gloria Swanson, and Barbara Stanwyck were short but gave a bigger impression because they had large hands and heads," says photographer Deborah Turbeville.

"A good actor knows how to use his hands. So do good athletes and photographers themselves, and so should a good model. Jeanne Moreau comes to mind: She can steal a scene smoking a cigarette. You are riveted, watching her hands; you don't know or care what she's talking about. Very chic women know how to use their hands with a dress, in a pocket, or in a graceful gesture. When I began to photograph the parts of the body early in my career, I found I was drawn to certain bodies and I figured out why. They all had two things in common: fine shoulders and large heads. How would clothes look, I asked myself, if the shoulders weren't there to grab the fabric? What if the neck wasn't there either and the head went right into the frame? It just wouldn't work. Think of the Venus de Milo. There is nothing more beautiful in a woman than a well-formed neck, back, and shoulders."

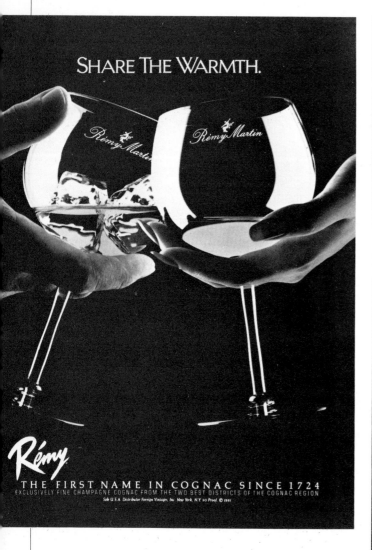

SHARE THE WARMTH.

Rémy

THE FIRST NAME IN COGNAC SINCE 1724
EXCLUSIVELY FINE CHAMPAGNE COGNAC FROM THE TWO BEST DISTRICTS OF THE COGNAC REGION

Sole U.S.A. Distributor Foreign Vintages, Inc. New York, N.Y. 80 Proof. © 1981

Sheer Energy® All Sheer.
Nothing shows but your toe

ALL SHEER
SHEER
ENERGY

Now you can wear s
that bare your toes, and
give your legs an all
massage.™ Sheer En
All Sheer pantyhose is s
clear to your toes. S
shoes like those, what
want to show sh
It comes in sizes A, B,
Queensize, all with a
pure cotton crotch p
(just like regular S
Energy). Get 'e
the L'eggs Bout

SANDBANK

In 1966 Irving Penn photographed Wilhelmina for *Vogue* with branches tucked into her bosom. The experience taught her the value of patience. Wilhelmina bore so many scratches on her neck that she canceled her next day entirely. Needless to say, modeling is not all good times. The work may seem and must look effortless, but it is often extremely taxing. Parts modeling, a useful addition to a model's repertoire, is not often by itself a provider of income. An awkward position may have to be held for a long time, a small gesture repeated endlessly. Hands are in great demand. Here too grooming and care are essential: no cuts, no bruises. It is for advertising that time under the hot lights pays off. In this business, holding a position without moving is part of being photogenic.

Advertising for shoes or stockings calls for small feet. This is where a petite model may add to her income. This Sheer Energy ad is for stockings, but also makes good use of a well-cared-for foot. The model, in this case Willy's Trish Webster, must be particularly meticulous about preening. Legs must be flawlessly smooth and hairless, feet not only small and well shaped but also impeccably groomed: No calluses or other blemishes are allowed, toenails must be perfectly cared for. A finer-boned model is always better, especially closeup.

Commercial print models in general and parts models in particular develop a strong rapport with the photographer and crew; therefore the male and female hand model and photographer may remain the same for years and for many clients handling many objects. Once reliability is established, if a team works well, the inclination for a client is to stick with it.

Lois Ross, a Funny Face character model, does hand work as a sideline. Hands are in greater demand than any other part, so this can be a good money-maker for a model, especially one who is already working. Hand models come from regular agency rosters, but some commercials require such coordination that ordinary models, no matter how extraordinary their hands, can't qualify. "It can be exhausting," Lois says, "hitting a mark or laying something down time and time again. I've been known to lose three pounds and collapse from stress doing a tabletop job. Food shots can be the toughest. Sometimes it looks easy—putting the top on a Whopper or a bottle—but believe me it isn't."

Tricia Webster became a hand, leg, and foot model after many years of editorial work through Wilhelmina. She appreciates the rewards of parts modeling, but knows all too well the strenuous physical requirements. "It's true that there are fewer ads and commercials in this area, but there are also fewer models doing them. When it all gets divided up, it's a generous living. I have many steady, long-time clients.

"An average person may seem to have pretty feet, but they may not be photogenic—the same as a very pretty woman who doesn't photograph well. Body parts, for modeling, need to be more delicate than average; arms, legs, shoulders, et cetera, can't look thick, like a football player's. Not just in general, but because the shots are up close, and the closer you come, the thicker anything looks. The finer boned the model is the better.

"When I was little, my mother says she could sit me down and I wouldn't fidget. Even then, I was calm and had a lot of patience. I am very good at holding a position without moving. In my trade, that's photogenic too!

"When I get home, my day still hasn't ended—I have to prepare for the next day. Depending on the job, I may have to shave my legs, put new polish on my toenails or fingernails. These are extra, last-minute things. Of course I keep up my basic grooming every day. I won't know what color polish I'm supposed to be wearing until the night before the booking. I also have to be ready to put on more than one color on a given day. I have the luxury of working fewer than five days a week if I want to, but even on short days those few hours may be so intense that it might as well be an all-day booking. It simply takes a different kind of concentration.

BEAUTY ADVERTISING: WHERE THE AIM AND THE IMAGE ARE ONE

Roughly 25 percent of the total budget for national beauty advertising is spent on simply getting names in front of the public. Few marketers believe that national ads even sell cosmetics; they merely establish an image in the public mind, with a face as its focal point. Even if the cosmetics and products change, that face still connects the ad to the sponsoring company. It boils down to being remembered; then come the hard sales.

Paul Wilmot is a cosmetics marketing executive formerly with Norton Simon. While he was there they marketed two lines: Max Factor and Halston. He explains how cosmetics companies decide who will get an exclusive endorsement contract: "There are research procedures that measure the percentage of people who recall an ad or even a magazine cover. Recalling a person or a face scores higher than remembering a product shot of a box. That's because a model *connects* the customer, actively and personally, to the product as desirable and useful—not just as something that is nicely packaged. It takes time to get back the total response, but pros at it know instantly when a model is a hit. No playing favorites or hunches—feedback tells you if you are right or wrong. In the cosmetics field there is no longer small-areas test marketing of new products. Advertisements must go national right away because of the competition. So everyone involved with marketing has to believe in the ad.

"Exclusivity is a logical step for a beauty advertiser who has built up an individual into a distinctive and widely recognized personality. The model then limits herself to working only for one company. Because of this restriction, companies have to pay well, so they're very careful who they sign for exclusive use. Contracts have been signed with spokeswomen at the top of their careers, only to have them start to fall. Sometimes a career can have a second high point, with benefits for both model and company. Vellum, a skin cream, uses Mary Martin and Janet Gaynor, two women looking absolutely great after having acquired their patina with age; they're perfect for the product."

Beauty advertising, of course, is far from a static thing. It is always changing with the season and with the trends. Constant change makes it even better to have one exclusive, memorable face. In the

Lips, eyes, and shoulders are also parts of the body used to sell particular products. The upper left photograph captures a perfect combination: photographer Richard Avedon's lens and superstar model Janice Dickenson's lips. They first met in their "Take Your Lips to the Maxi" series for Max Factor, creating instantaneous impact. In the lower left photograph, Sheila Johnson of Elite shows off Napier costume jewelry as though it were a million-dollar item. Model selection is exacting, particularly when casting for a neck length, eye coloring, or lip shape. Master fashion photographer Bert Stern prefers to refer to animallike qualities that are visible: lion's mane, swanlike neck, or dovelike complexion. Carrie Nygren was brought over from Paris to shoot a memorable Flex commercial: The setting was a stark desert with tall cacti, overhung with a huge blue Texan sky. For one television season Carrie jumped out to viewers, cocking a hair dryer like a gun, pulling off her cowboy hat so that her masses of hair tumbled out. The above photograph is a still national print ad pulled from the TV-spot concept.

fickle field of fragrance, Catherine Deneuve (for Chanel) and Shelley Hack (for Charlie) were the biggest names among the endorsers. Deneuve is a special case: a great personality, a consummate professional, beautiful, sophisticated, and *French*. Chanel wisely capitalized on her world-renowned charisma.

Clairol has been a big part of Robin Meyerhoff's business since she joined Wilhelmina, using her as both a part and a beauty model. The purposes are as different as the products: shampoos, cream rinses, body waves, permanents, highlights, hair coloring. Robin would think more than twice before cutting four inches off her hair; the client expects it to be very thick, very blond, and below her shoulders. "I'm afraid," she says, "I'd be chopping off some business. Luckily it grows like a weed. I need a ton of it for a picture with no face but a real mane of hair; they retouched for eighteen different colors—and my picture has run for dozens of different purposes. Heaven knows where it ended up. Last year I saw a hair shot I had done in New England on a billboard in Montmartre. I remember walking down a street in Hong Kong and seeing a picture of my hair on the back of a local Chinese magazine. In Brazil I picked up a package in a drugstore and said, 'Oh, ye gods, it's me.' "

Ara Gallant, who as a photographer has seen many, reflects on the stars of beauty advertising and how they have changed with the years: "Look at any current beauty campaign and you know the rule: No expression. Years ago, a beauty campaign had to have expression, be slightly provocative, whether it was in the raise of an eyebrow or the slant of the smile. A face today has to come as close to average as possible—nothing beyond. Marjorie Andrade, for example, works constantly, doing nothing but beauty and only for television and print, never editorial. Her face fits the 'perfect face' description: It should have planes; the cheekbones have to be high and the eyes wide-set; there must be a jawbone, good chin and hairlines, small nose, and full lips. Being blond and light helps too. The look is middle-of-the-road gorgeous.

"A model can't look like Penelope Tree or Apollonia right now." Ara concludes, "Ravishingly beautiful women like Janice Dickinson have become too risky for advertisers; clients want a glorification of the girl next door, the kind of face any woman could identify with."

"In a time when beauty models are so nearly interchangeable, stars simply aren't too likely. If you can't book one top beauty, you book another—it doesn't make much difference. Advertisers used to depend on a Jean Shrimpton or a Twiggy or a Suzy Parker because they were one of a kind. Some—a few—still do: Max Factor turned to Cristina Ferrare, Revlon to Lauren Hutton. Lauren's face is totally irregular, she's cross-eyed, wrong this, wrong that. But she's definitely got it. Christie Brinkley is another sort, the opposite sort, of exception: perfectly average, but in some way a standout. If today's beauty business has a star, Christie is it."

Every ad has a precise point of view. You know exactly what market is trying to be reached; research has suggested how it might best be accomplished. In beauty advertising particularly, model selection is pivotal. In the most literal sense, the model is your message—your point of contact with the people you want to appeal to. Sylvie Chantecaille, a vice-president of marketing at Estee Lauder, uses her company's viewpoint to illustrate corporate perspective in general. "With Prescriptives, we look for models who are extremely elegant. We try to balance this with some earthiness; a strong design, unmodified, can seem a little hard. The model's skin quality has to be sensual but not sexy. This is a skin-care line, so the quality of both skin and lighting have to be clean. We look, in our models, for excellent noses and refinement in the bone structure. We found a girl from Europe, Alexa Singer, who has an incredible profile and gives an impression of today—by which we mean having a sense of security, not too eager to please yet not haughty, unmistakably intelligent. The customers we are talking to have never really worn makeup before. They were in college studying, didn't have the time or the inclination to shop. They come to Prescriptives because they find themselves in a corporate boardroom and they figure they'd better do something. We need a woman they can relate to—one with independence, classic elegance."

Another cosmetic company might want qualities of quite a different kind. Isabella Rossellini, a top Click model, is ideal for Lancome: intriguingly European, even in her voice, which they use in the commercials because of her slight accent. She has a very modern yet rather intelligent face; her family background makes her, and her looks, all the more interesting. Isabella's face comes across as being very

A model is first and foremost a salesperson. That requires an immediate appeal, even if that appeal is not universal. A model must understand the *why* of a situation to deliver the right expression and feeling. This is true whether the product is lingerie or a bottle of liqueur. The intent of a commercial-print ad is to explain or extol, which is done through the model. A simple comparison between the two cigarette ads demonstrates a point: The casting call (except for coloring) would have been the same for both ads. The real difference lies in the motivation given to the principal male character by the photographer during the shooting. The Winston shot is a billboard for the Latin market, hence a sultry lover. On the following page is an ad for a German magazine, shot in the United States. It uses a strikingly virile man to convey that *light* cigarettes are not un-masculine.

human, and at the same time, it is comparatively well known. Upward mobility is the dream of Lancome's customers; she personifies where they want to get, and Lancome's image, to perfection.

The photographer sees all this from yet another vantage point—whether the model has what it takes to produce a good picture. If she isn't physically right for the purpose of the ad, or for the attitude it is intended to convey, the shot has to fall short of its potential. "If the model doesn't look right to me," insists master craftsman Bert Stern, "the picture won't work right for you." Star-maker Stern photographed Christie Brinkley recently for the cover of French *Vogue*, and also has an estimable list of American advertisers to his credit, among them Smirnoff, Coca-Cola, Buick, and Levi Strauss. Of fashion models as role players, he has this to say:

"There are some who can portray a character. Take Carol Alt. She can go from Miss Apple Pie to someone really wild . . . from the squarest stick to a visually exciting beauty. The right model is like insurance. If something doesn't work, it can all be taken apart and put together differently.

"This isn't true only of model selection for big pictures. For example, you might only be casting for a lip job. Even on a simple assignment like that, matching a model to a concept requires an element of knowledge, an awareness from experience—and is what an agency buys when they choose a photographer. They explain their layout in terms of a marketing approach so we are all on the same wavelength. The choice of model then narrows down. Maybe the client wants a certain model, and that's that. With any luck, they have decided the product needs a new model, and the photographer can start looking for the right one. *Look* may not be the correct word. You can look and look to come up with nothing. Then one day the right one walks in. However it happens, you find

her. If you can get agreement from the advertising agency and client (and if she's available; that's always a question), you are ready to begin.

"Some models, like Christie Brinkley, don't work unless they have an agreement or contract. A lot of beauty models are like that; they have to make hay while the sun shines. Christie is right for anything, but that can have its drawbacks. There's such a thing as overexposure, or doing the wrong things or not doing the right things well. Her greatest asset—what makes her a great model—is the way she winds up and throws aliveness at the camera like a major-league pitcher. *That's* what gets models on covers!

"Christie styles herself; she is a modern-day model—one who projects herself into the pictures and creates herself through them. Patti Hanson was the first model I ever saw do that. She transformed herself through the character she was pretending to be. Christie's situation, though, is unique. In turning herself into the American Dream Girl of the Eighties, she has also become the creation of the marketplace—the ideal girl people create in their own minds."

TV Commercials—
Advertising Spots

◆

Commercials are a staple for many models; some rely solely on commercial acting. The pay can be phenomenal: For a widely rebroadcast commercial it can accumulate to several thousand dollars or more for a day's work. Some of America's large cities—New York and Los Angeles among them—have thriving commercial production houses. New York has increasingly been recapturing business from Los Angeles and Chicago. Agents arrange the auditions, most of them with special casting agents. The most successful models, as in any category, are those who keep knocking on doors and sending out résumés. You don't need a union card to begin doing commercials, but one becomes necessary when you've done enough work to be eligible. The Screen Actors Guild recently started applying still photographic work toward eligibility. Acting in commercials does demand disciplined spontaneity and skill at improvisation, which any model willing to listen and to apply herself can very quickly learn.

Commercials are surprisingly like print work. A model with that background can have very good luck in commercials knowing little or nothing about how an actor or spokesperson goes about representing a product properly. As in other commercial categories, the most requested types are conventional: Middle American believable, and pretty. The second most favored group is character actors. Often leading men and women don't have to talk; they just have to look right for the part. The right look will get you work, just as it does in print, editorial, catalog, and runway.

Charles Selber, who teaches models how to act in commercials, says that singing or speaking lines can be dubbed; off-camera songs and narration are commonplace in the medium. The models are part of the *visual* presentation.

"It is more involved than poses because there is movement," Charles points out. "The lines, however, are fairly easy to do; a model isn't expected to audition for hard-sell delivery. The crossover from print to television is really simple for a model. A still is a single frame from a camera; television is a series of frames that all add up to movement.

"In my class we start with the body and learn about movement for motion pictures. Commercial actors get far less work than models do. When

BASILE

This ad for Basile is typical of the manufacturers' influence on the international male. The man is front center and the woman supports his role. In the photograph below is Joan Severance of Elite; although here she is in a polyester print ad, she is giving the garment an undeniable vitality and life. TV commercials often require skills developed in other arenas—skills to be carried over to film. Joan was brought to the attention of the fashion-magazine editors after she was a superstar. Joan Severance's career is an exception to the rule; she was a successful catalog model before being heralded as a darling of the *Vogues*.

Qiana excites

Jonathan Hitchcock's pleated fantastic so luxurious you'd never suspect it's practical.

Fashion of Qiana® nylon shown, available at Saks Fifth Avenue, Neiman-Marcus, and Lillie Rubin.

DU PONT

models really pursue a career in television commercials they can do fantastically well. But a commercial is more involved to land than a print job. You have to see casting directors and prepare for auditions, occasionally with a monologue. These entail homework, and you must be prepared to do it."

Barbara Lantz, overall head of Zoli's women's division, confirms the need to take classes: "Unless someone has knockout talent, we suggest a class where they learn how to read copy, how to direct their eyes to the camera, how to get in character and believe in the product they are selling. They have to convince the client that they respect the product. They must be able to deliver a personality, attractively and reliably. They must also be on time; this is a very expensive medium. A firm desire to do the work, real commitment to it, is very important. Beauty in television comes down to the eyes and an ability to sparkle. If it is a very 'up' commercial, that lift must come through in their smiles."

Charles Glaser, a Zoli model, is a twelve-year veteran. He started at twenty-eight on the advice of a friend who also started at that age. "Even if you do everything they want," says Charles, "there's no guarantee that TV will pay off. I usually make about one thousand dollars per commercial. For the past few years I've averaged ten to twelve a year. In print, I can be booked at a fifteen hundred- to two thousand-dollars-a-day rate with a bonus. For purposes of comparison, a liquor company, say, would pay three thousand dollars for a half-day romp in the country, girlfriend in hand. A commercial means working all day for three hundred dollars. After taxes and agency commission, I net one hundred eighty dollars. That says nothing about all the time spent auditioning against fifty other people. Then maybe they don't run it. There is no guarantee I will make any more.

"A New York department store buyout or flat rate will be seven hundred fifty dollars per day—exactly half the normal print rate. If the agency and client decide not to run the spot because it didn't score high on a marketing survey, I will get one hundred eighty dollars net per quarter. For that amount of money, I am prevented from working in toys, soft drinks, cars, or whatever. I am not talking about being a spokesman, like Mr. Wipple. That is a different situation. I am talking about being a simple character in a wine commercial, or insurance or beer. It's things like that that keep the average at one thousand dollars per commercial."

Tommy McCarthy, an agent with Zoli Theatrix, offers counsel on credibility, the single most important requirement of commercials and a knack any model, with effort, can develop. "Convincing the client that you're sincere is only half the battle; you must convince the *camera* that you believe in the product. That is the formula for everyone concerned. It's the guiding principle behind every decision at casting sessions, it's what motivates casting directors. If you feel differently, don't crack a smile. Don't betray it in the smallest way. This is a no-no; every commercial class will tell you that. You must be serious, whether you feel serious or not. You must get behind the product. Don't kid yourself that you can snicker underneath. It inevitably comes through to the casting people.

"On a still photographic sitting, you can have lots of fun. You can make fun of what you're doing; sometimes it is even desirable to have some humor come out in the pictures. On camera, there's no joking. Television commercials have never been, nor will they ever be, offhand or funny at the expense of the product. Those bits are carefully timed, well-acted moments. There is no innuendo either; TV also has morality clauses that everyone sticks to and takes seriously indeed."

A head shot can be enough to make a start in commercials, but a composite still is better. Some models have started primitively, from a Xerox copy, which is really underplaying it. It is a sly way of telegraphing, "I haven't been overexposed, I haven't done much . . ." Some casting directors get a personal message from that: "Here's a new one that I can discover and make into a star." "Some people love that," says Tommy. "Casting people overwhelmingly think of models as children, and love a chance to treat them accordingly."

ON THE COMMERCIAL CIRCUIT

You build a photographic personality by nursing each aspect along, and by capitalizing on the qualities you can bring to a situation. A commercial knack comes, if it can come at all, from within. It requires wit, humor, or warmth, plus a certain

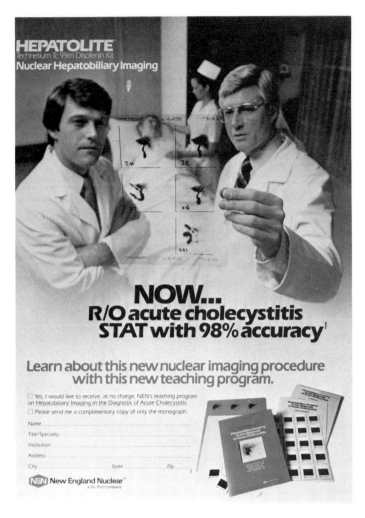

The corporate giants, such as IBM, Coca-Cola, and Bristol-Myers, often run TV spots and stills as national-print image ads with usages varying from magazine to billboard to matchbook cover. These ads depict moments from typical American lives; therefore they call for all types to be characterized. More often than not it is the same advertising concerns that demand leading ladies and leading men to add action and dialogue to a TV spot. This is the major reason why the crossover from commercial print to TV commercials is not very difficult. If you are cast for print, chances are you could be auditioned for a similar TV spot.

Every TV commercial and print ad has a message. It is the responsibility of the model to know what he or she is to convey. It is up to the director or photographer to catch that in the camera. Initially, a person's photographic range is built by nursing it along. Understanding the subtleties of projecting to the camera stems from the same ability that allows a person to get up and recite lines. It is acting.

In the photograph left, the characters act out a familiar hospital situation. The two characters are depicted as doctors by placing a few blurred props so that the photograph reads as a hospital. Doctors' offices receive literature on so many different drugs that often an illustration is required to keep the purpose of a medication easily accessible. There are many decisions to be made on how to portray an emotion or an action, even when modeling is motionless.

In a department store it would be called a hangtag, but for IBM the in-store promotions take the form of pamphlets and foldout cards (right). In this type of photograph there are less obvious interpersonal relations unfolding for the camera. Advertising is as varied as life-styles. Madison Avenue uses models of all dimensions and appearances to make its points. A TV spot or commercial-print ad can go from the most elaborate setting to the simplest, from a single model to a crowd.

A pencil acts as a pointer and a hunched shoulder reads as urgency when the subject changes to computer databases. Regardless of the situation, the commercial-print model is expected to react, or more often overreact, to highlight the product in an ad.

The more complicated the shot, the more important the coordination of efforts between the many people involved, from propmen and stylists to models and assistants. Each model has to interact with the photographer as well as with the other models. In these instances, the situation is discussed by everyone at the location.

spontaneity, a glow, and a subtle sex appeal. These are the building blocks of commercial acting.

Barbara Shapiro stresses the director's role to Cheryl Tiegs in sustaining a mood or conveying an emotion. "The boards—a series of small drawings shaped like television sets—show you the story pretty much step by step; the director will explain the mood to keep in mind, or the situation. The clothes or the product give you something to work with.

"A good director will keep bringing you back to that quality you need to sustain. He gives you the mood, and you have to take it, re-create it, then project it to the camera. It's acting, all right!

"A model has to be able to communicate and relate, while the director must know what the client is trying to achieve. That must be clearly conveyed to the model so that she or he can portray it. Subtle nuance and actions, to be done in seven seconds, must be very broad: glamour, teasing, humor, lightness, whatever is appropriate and works fast."

Commercials fall into two categories. One is a series, where the mood changes from vignette to vignette. The other is a scenario, like a little play, with a beginning, middle, and end. The director keeps you in character the whole time. You may have 15 takes and 10 different setups. That's 150 times that you have to start over again. Each time you have to get your energy level up to the original point. The director takes you back to what happened before and how that fits in with what you're doing now. That is continuity, what keeps it all looking as if it were shot as a whole.

Diane Sloves, a free-lance fashion stylist, thinks back to the elaborate scenarios devised for national cosmetics campaigns, in particular a Cover Girl effort with Cheryl Tiegs, Kelly Emberg, and Christie Brinkley called "That Face." The labor was divided three ways: Kelly was country, Christie was suburban, and Cheryl was city. The photographs were used for in-store (or point-of-purchase) displays, packaging, and billboards, along with national magazines. The print campaign came out of TV, a common advertising practice.

Diane can still see the trio playing their different parts. "Kelly was the tomboy next door who climbs trees. She wore crew-neck sweaters and bow ties and the background was an old gasoline pump and a car from the twenties—she had to look like she'd come out of the backyard to pump gas. In other scenes she was swinging on a rope or laughing in front of a picket fence. Once she was in overalls with a hose squirting her in the face. She was hysterical, having a great time.

"Christie was supposed to be a sort of Grace Kelly living on an elegant estate with her parents. She was photographed mostly on the steps wearing very tailored Anne Klein clothes. There was a lovely scene in an old-fashioned hammock: high-necked lace blouse, straw hat, and a weed in her teeth, musing about all her money in the bank.

"Cheryl was Miss New York City, all glamorous and glitzy, in a fabulous suit or sequined chiffon dress that would fall apart every time she breathed in it—all this on a rough, tough, motorcycle. One shot was on top of a building, and others with either the Brooklyn Bridge or the Manhattan skyline as a background.

COPING WITH CASTING

Jill Henry is a New York free-lance producer of television commercials, music videos, and cable-TV programs. She has conducted and filmed casting or model selection sessions, and her first advice about them is tactical: "Casting is done by type; your best move is to get to the audition early so everyone will be compared to you instead of vice versa." Behind every casting session there is a mental picture based on the client's research: of the people who buy the product, why they buy it, and how it's used, and of who watches the commercials, why they watch them, and what their responses to them have been. Says Jill, "When a model is called for the first casting session or audition, either she or the agent should find out who the people in the commercial are meant to be. If you're supposed to be a lumberjack, you don't want to show up in ballet tights. But many models with real possibilities never get beyond the suitable clothes stage. Among the first eight or ten there will be someone who measures up, and that becomes the standard for everyone else. You might have six people who can do the part and are very close visually, and all but one will be rejected because of what was seen first, and remembered.

"People, even those who are very nervous about what they're doing, do better if there is a human

A head shot that commands a second look can pay off in TV commercials. "Up" radiates through the smile while character and believability come across through the eyes. The same rules hold true for the young and the old, male and female. Each of the four examples shown here is a head shot with the punch to capture a client's attention each and every time it is seen. A model on a TV spot must deliver reliability and garner the respect of the casting director before convincing a Polaroid. After that initial phase, a model must then convince the camera and the consumer.

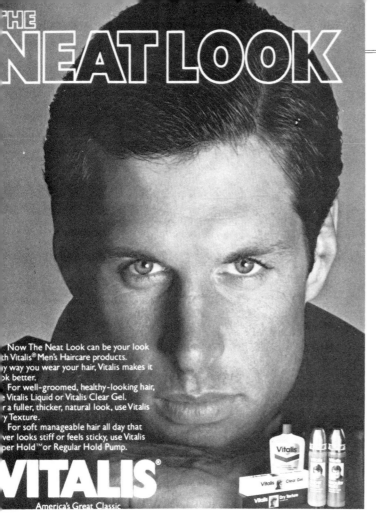

THE NEAT LOOK

Now The Neat Look can be your look
th Vitalis® Men's Haircare products.
y way you wear your hair, Vitalis makes it
ok better.
For well-groomed, healthy-looking hair,
e Vitalis Liquid or Vitalis Clear Gel.
r a fuller, thicker, natural look, use Vitalis
y Texture.
For soft manageable hair all day that
ver looks stiff or feels sticky, use Vitalis
per Hold™ or Regular Hold Pump.

VITALIS®

America's Great Classic

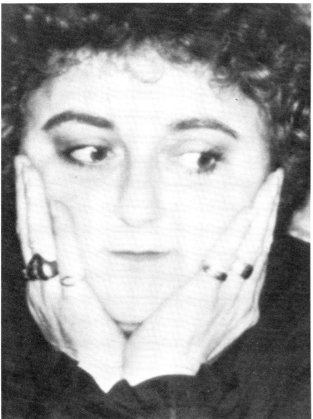

element in them for casting people to respond to. If you like someone, it's only human to want that something you're attracted to. The person who comes in 'acting' usually doesn't get such a good response. Nothing natural is coming through. Most casting is type casting—that is, nobody is made into something he's not, you only embellish what is there. So if you're the type, why not just be yourself, maybe a little more vivacious? It's what works."

Jerry Beaver, an independent casting director, conducts casting sessions, or cattle calls, where a whole mob of people comes in, gives statistics, and gets videotaped. Jerry is the last link in a long chain: Market reports suggest appropriate types, the advertising agency makes specific choices from these and passes them to the director, and the director gives them to Jerry. "A long road, but it paves the way to sound casting decisions," says Jerry. "And it's only the beginning. I round up as many as two thousand people for a casting session and put them on tape in my studio. These people are submitted by talent agents. I go through bios, résumés, and head shots and whittle it down to two hundred people. Out of those, we choose the top forty, who go to a call-back session with the director. From there we'll narrow it down to six or seven for a final call-back."

Jill Henry speaks again from the standpoint of the producer: "The director I work with, Ed Bianchi, reviews the tapes and selects a percentage from the people he and I agree could be right for the part. At the call-back session we tape them a second time. This time they have the advantage of working with the director, an advantage over just the casting director. Decisions are always by committee: the advertising agency, producer, art director, and copywriter, and the director and producer from the production company. For the model it's nerve-racking having to respond to seven people. Then, as producer, I submit the selection to the client at a preproduction meeting and hope they agree with us."

The director is the creative force. His concern is with the visual conception of the piece; his job is to bring it to visual reality. What is in the director's mind is an art director's fantasy. Ed Bianchi, formerly art director at Young and Rubicam, is a sought-after director, and one of an elite few commercial directors to have made a feature motion picture, *The Fan*, starring Lauren Bacall. In Ed's opinion, "the director gives the model her creative inspiration. He is the one who tells her who she is, what to do, and how to look. She is, in a sense, a blank canvas, especially if it's a fashion ad. The blank face gets made up and the hair gets styled, but the director's main concern is a model's acting ability.

"A director may have people do different things to see if they can take direction, or ask them to repeat the same piece of action several times with different interpretations. Some directors just suggest a situation and see what they do with it.

"Very few models have any experience and even fewer have any acting training. It's completely different from modeling. Some have natural ability and some don't. In casting, you look for the ones who can, instead of finding the right look and then giving a course in acting. Models have to be able to show up at a casting and make instant friends—convince people in ten minutes that they can do it."

Fashion Across the Country: Alternate Routes

A model's opportunities are not limited to the major cities. Every large American and European city, as well as Hong Kong and Tokyo, is a market for models. It is simple to tap into the Boston, Chicago, Phoenix, Las Vegas, Dallas, and Los Angeles markets with an on-the-spot agent to make the connections. Travel expenses can be negotiated for weekly bookings. Also, with this cross-country networking, models who begin in Portland or Salt Lake City, say, can keep their initial clients as they branch out to Seattle or Denver, then perhaps move on to Chicago or Los Angeles.

An agency in Louisville, Kentucky, or Birmingham, Alabama, can bill hundreds of thousands of dollars per year. Most cities of this size have the infrastructure in place: photography studios and labs, retail outlets, and regional advertising. There is a growing trend among catalog houses to bring in the photographer and assistants but hire models and a stylist locally, saving the high New York rates and per diem expenses of models. Smaller outlying areas are becoming more sophisticated, so that the pictures look more like those that originate in major urban centers.

SOME SIGNIFICANT OUTLYING MARKETS

BOSTON: This northeastern market has its advantages for those starting out. Each area has a different client mix that dictates which models will be most in demand, with, of course, certain exceptions. In Boston, as one would suspect, the dominant type is clean-cut and collegiate. Jo Somers of Copley Seven Talent advises young men and women "to stay in a smaller market and work professionally for a year or so before going to New York. They'll get all the learning experiences without the emotional setback. A great deal of information is coming in from all sides. It can be awesome. Most of my models are just out of high school and working their way through college. They are serious about modeling because it is their income. They can make twenty to thirty-five thousand dollars a year."

The super-high-fashion look is limited in the Boston area. That type of model won't work consistently because it is not a center of fashion editorial. The work there is more heavy-duty catalog, more Middle American conservative.

Route 128 has the largest concentration of high-tech industries in the country. There is a lot of audiovisually oriented work, but the real money is in commercial print. The models are in their mid-twenties to fifties. They have to look like computer operators or people in executive training. These are the roles being played in brochures and manuals for sales training and internal communications. "Fashion retail work in Boston is last, after television, commercial print, and high tech. But we do a lot of flyers that are mailed or passed out," Bostonian Jo Somers explains it. "Many of the local stores have branches and all the promotion and advertising is done here, which means they spend a lot of money on a consistent basis."

ATLANTA: One of the four secondary markets, Atlanta is another good place to begin because of its rapid growth rate. This market is open and quite diverse. "An out-of-towner can do quite well here," says Colin Towers of Studio One in Atlanta, "because the market is fairly loose and active. Also, there is a lot of catalog work for the major department stores: Rich's, Davison, and J. C. Penney. There are several magazines, *Atlanta* and *Contemporary Atlanta* as well as one for auto buffs. Atlanta is number three or four in conventions now that we have a large airport, so there is plenty of convention modeling. Our Apparel Mart is the hub of the South; we represent the region between here and Dallas, including Florida. There are only four or five big advertising agencies that do much print. Also, we have a certain amount of television advertising."

THE GOLD COAST: Like some other American cities, Miami attracts major clients because of its consistently good weather, but it remains a relatively small market. Mrs. Marie of Irene Marie Models in Fort Lauderdale does channel local women into other markets, but she has found that models return to work near home. "Miami–Fort Lauderdale–Palm Beach is a satellite market that has no local demand," she explains, "so not many models can make a living on local modeling. But many potential clients come here from outside to work. In the winter, especially, art directors, photographers, and commercial crews come down to shoot summer clothes when it is too cold in the Northeast and Europe. Our springlike weather is also desirable for

products like Löwenbräu. Sometimes freshness is wanted not only in the place but in the models as well. This allows models to be in catalogs for stores like Macy's, Sakowitz, Neiman Marcus, Jordan Marsh, and Bambergers. Many of my models have been in *Vogue* or *Bazaar, Seventeen, Elle, Marie Claire.* These publications also come down to shoot.

"My models' clients are more likely to be from New York, Italy, and Germany than from Florida. The clients dictate what belongs in a model's book. It doesn't make sense to show a book filled with fur coats or skiwear to someone who came here to shoot sunny bathing-suit scenes. Southern Florida has developed a standard so clients know they will find the quality they are used to working with. They choose the models from the head sheets and they won't buy the service unless the models are up to par.

"A photographer came from Milan recently to do a Valentino and Basile shoot. Each model was competing against twenty-five others. In Milan it would have been two hundred. Irene Marie uses a very personalized promotion to get models work. I am not all that territorial, but I like Florida girls because they always come back; they have family ties here. I am honest with models who have potential because at some point they'll have to leave. I try to do what's best for them. Eventually it comes back to me. The beginning is the most exciting part. When they are ready, I know they'll move on."

NEW ORLEANS: Just a few years ago this market couldn't support or develop a model. But things have changed. Dolly Dean Martinez, director of Artist's Representatives in New Orleans, claims: "Accounts that have always gone to larger markets for promotional work and catalogs no longer feel they have to import talent from Dallas or Atlanta. Sportswear companies who manufacture locally, cosmetic promotions, and informal and runway shows are being done; when Saks Fifth Avenue opened here the impact was immediate. Editorial work is done through the local newspaper and local ads are shot for the regional magazines, *New Orleans* and *Dixie.* Also, there are advertising agencies that hire for local or regional and some national ads. And there is a lot of convention work, which helps more models to do well during the slower seasons."

As in other smaller markets, New Orleans models

cannot just do fashion; they have to do television commercials as well. They also need to be able to portray different characters. About fifty really good models can support themselves in this market, but "only if they can work all parts and categories and are willing to do anything that's available," says Dolly. "Men in New Orleans find it more difficult; they must settle for part-time modeling and have some other kind of work."

DALLAS: After New York and Chicago, Dallas is the largest domestic modeling market. Before Kim Dawson began supplying models for department-store advertising, editorial and catalog work had been done in New York. The Dallas market has seen an expansion every four to five years. The men's section at the apparel mart takes up six floors; two years ago developers built a state-of-the-art film studio and the television commercial market is expanding. Dallas ranks third (again after New York and Chicago) in print, which is still the big money-maker. Runway outdistances commercials and catalog is where most of the print work is. Major stores and catalogs such as Horchow, Sakowitz, and Neiman Marcus can use forty to fifty models a day for a shooting. Consequently, there's stiff competition to get into the agencies now.

Kim Dawson now handles nearly five hundred people, "including two hundred children for whom there is almost continuous casting, mostly catalog. People are into using mostly younger models, but plenty of catalog models are older. "Models who are considered over the hill in other markets can take up a new career in Dallas," Kim says, "especially if they have market-week experience. There's a big demand for models to do fashion shows and print-advertising shootings prior to the shows. Wholesale does not pay the same high rates as advertising, retail, or catalog. Day rates in Dallas vary tremendously, even from five hundred to one thousand dollars for the same model. Hourly rates are from sixty to one hundred dollars. There is enough new business coming into Dallas to warrant it—from Chicago, Denver, Cincinnati, Louisiana, Oklahoma. We're sending out three thousand agency books to reach this wider market.

"Modeling has become very gypsy. We started a girl in Dallas, she went to Europe, came back, went to Japan, came back, and then she'll gypsy off someplace else. New York is hard for kids to take.

You would think that it would be easier, speaking the same language, but foreign working conditions seem easier to tolerate. Beginners now have a harder time in Dallas. The models all know that to compete here they have to hightail it off to some foreign market and come back with a good book. They have to go away in order to come back. A newcomer can come to Dallas and wait there to be scouted. It is great for that. Scouts come here to look for new faces. Photographic teams come from Paris to get the March sun on sportswear and naturally make some discoveries."

CHICAGO: The second largest market in the country, Chicago is mainly a product city; big advertisers like Colgate-Palmolive, Sara Lee, Bell & Howell, and Kellogg need believable people who look like the family next door. Chicago is home to an enormous still photographic industry that takes honest, no-nonsense pictures for cereal, soap, and beer companies. The Second City is also its own resource of talent, producing an abundance by acting schools and the resident theater, opera, and comedy companies. The largest department stores and catalogs are headquartered in Chicago. And McCormick Place is in constant need of convention models. The city's commercial production houses and industrial film companies, and now studios for feature films, rank a respectable third behind New York and Los Angeles. There is, however, no editorial work.

The Sears, Roebuck catalog, produced for sixty years in New York City, is now done in Chicago. Sears is the largest single catalog account in the world. Yet Sears told the New York agencies that they felt rates of $1,250 to $2,000 a day were too high and that they couldn't pay more than $800. The agencies wouldn't agree, so, over a two-year period, Sears transplanted art directors, photographers, buyers, and six studios to Chicago to do its work. For the first year and a half, New York specialists were flying back and forth, the demands being greater than the supply. But Sears was determined to stick it out and is now becoming happily entrenched in its hometown while Montgomery Ward still does half its work in New York. Models can make an annual $80,000 to $100,000 in Chicago doing catalog work almost every day. The day rate is from $750 to $1,000.

David and Lee Whitfield, the husband and wife team, opened in Chicago seven years ago, mainly to provide catalog models for the major midwestern retailers. They already had an agency in Cleveland, Ohio, where the organization began. They now operate in Detroit, Pittsburgh, Youngstown, Columbus, Cincinnati, St. Louis, Des Moines, and Minneapolis. Besides their retail advertising specialty, David and Lee supplies beautiful people for fashion or commercial print work, television commercials, and special designer runway shows. Says David Whitfield, "We started many successful models in small towns and moved them along to Chicago. New York agencies are trying to get them and can't. They want to be a big fish in a little pond. We get the top kids from St. Louis, Detroit, and Cleveland. They start in a small local market making twenty-five to thirty thousand dollars and then make their way to Chicago, where they can make one hundred thousand dollars. If they come in with pretty good books, it's not difficult to get them started.

"The smaller markets are good in the early stages because the cost of living is much more manageable. Some are married and wouldn't go into a bigger market anyway. These cities all have two or three department stores running competitive ads. At least three or four times a week they use local people at forty to sixty dollars an hour. They now are competing with I. Magnin's catalog, Marshall Field's, Carson Pirie Scott, Kaufman's. Most models in small markets have never heard of a day rate. A model can build up a clientele and leapfrog into the bigger market."

OMAHA AND KANSAS CITY: Experience with both these cities taught Nancy Bounds that it takes a comparatively large population to support a thriving model market. Omaha, where Nancy started, has only 500,000—"not enough," she tells anyone who inquires, "for all but a handful to make a living. There's just not enough work. We have perhaps five women who model full-time and make good money."

Nancy recently opened in a larger market: Kansas City. "In a city like this, there is ten times the business. Maybe fifty women and fewer men can work full-time. But they must be versatile, able to handle runway, fashion, print, and promotion. They can get along on those, without necessarily doing TV.

"We first work to get them out of this market, to New York, Europe, and Japan. Models that we have developed are working in every major fashion market in the world. Many of our graduates are in fashion magazines each month.

DENVER: The mountains make this an internationally acclaimed location. A lot of catalog, television commercial, and even big print campaigns shoot here for the scenery. Growing competition among retailers inspired Steve Vannoy to set up an exchange program with agencies around the country. "My clients appreciate a fresh face," he says, "but a change of atmosphere can also benefit a model and send her back refreshed."

The retail activity has made Denver a more sophisticated market. The lion's share is newspaper advertising for the large retail chains. They compete heavily, which has forced local stores to advertise more. The locals do so many catalogs and commercials that they've become a year-round business. "When several of the retail chains moved their headquarters to Chicago," Steve recalls, "we benefited. Denver is only a skip away. We don't have as many models but they are top quality. Now most Denver models can work full-time, which wasn't true as recently as five years ago. Now we can support seventy-five or more women, not counting models who do advertising character work."

Steve's exchange program preapproves models, who come from all over. "We look at the models' books, before they come. We want to be reasonably sure that our agency can keep them busy. Then we bring them here for a few weeks at a time. They make great money; Denver clients like new talent. We also encourage our own models to go to Europe and come back new people.

"The danger in a smaller market is overexposure. If a model is hired by the same client two or three times in several weeks, that's enough. People don't want to see the same faces over and over again. They may not use that same person for a month, which can limit a model."

Jeff Raymond now works through Wilhelmina in New York, but he remembers modeling in Denver during the late seventies: "The markets aren't that different except for their size. The selection process is the same but there aren't as many models to choose from. There aren't as many people for a model to see either. You were kept busy but there wasn't the volume to make it full-time. The only steady work is retail advertising, but it's very much like catalog work. The rates are much lower than in New York. I got sixty dollars an hour as opposed to one hundred twenty-five an hour."

PHOENIX: Helen Rogers opened Plaza Three in 1967. It has grown to a multimillion-dollar business known nationally as one of the finest smaller-market agencies. Phoenix being a resort town, Mrs. Rogers explains, "Our market is very similar to Los Angeles. There are several big department stores and we probably do more retailing than our per capita size would suggest. The resort aspect influences this. We have Saks, Sakowitz, I. Magnin, the Broadway Stores; also local stores like Goldwater's and Diamond's. There are also many fine international specialty shops in the malls. The retail outlets use illustration for daily ads and some of their catalogs are done locally. They will do retail advertisements for the local magazines. The models do editorial work too for those publications, but, as everywhere, the rates are very low; sometimes it's done just for the credit line. The magazines are a showcase but not really a market.

"Some major charity events are produced in Phoenix. Each of the major stores has a few each season. The audiences for some of these shows have numbered in the thousands. There are other big production shows built around collections. There is considerable informal modeling at lunch and tearoom places. These are simple and pleasant events for vacationing ladies—just fashion shows and not for a particular charity.

"Several local catalogs are done for the stores at Christmas time. We have work coming in from Sears and J. C. Penney. There is always work here. Catalog and print work for men and women is continuous and many national houses and stores send pages to be done. We negotiate usage, billboard, packaging fees, and point-of-purchase bonuses. Most models work in several different areas—print, runway, and television commercials, specifically—and may make forty-five to fifty thousand dollars. That's only possible if you can do all of those things. With only print and runway, you wouldn't make half as much."

LAS VEGAS: This is an unusual modeling town—nothing like New York or Los Angeles. Models do fashion shows at the hotels and local malls. Print is just beginning. Vegas slows down in the summer, which is just as well because at Universal Models, Judi Moreo's part-timers are students at the local university. Where Las Vegas is big—among the country's biggest—is in conventions and trade shows. Cities bid for conventions; Vegas is a frequent winner, with its exceptional services—exhibit space, lodging facilities, range of restaurants—and its show-biz atmosphere. Consumer electronics (computers, calculators, video games, and so on) is a big user of models for trade shows; most are hired on an annual basis, but a few every six months. These are city-to-city shows, usually going to the same city for four consecutive years. "Conventions are often nothing but meetings," says Judi, "a group of people getting together to learn about an industry. A true trade show will have exhibits on the convention floor; these shows are the market for models.

"A trade-show model can make from fifty dollars a day minimum as a soft-drink dispenser for a restaurant show to eight hundred dollars a day doing product narration, usually for automobiles." Judy sees the work as fairly strenuous, but substantial when it happens. "Models are expected to give a presentation five to fifteen times a day. They're booked for two- to four-day periods, and not just women. Men are often used, reused if they're good. Most models do this part-time; they all do something else. The university is my big source for young, attractive, well-spoken models. It pays their way through school. Las Vegas also gets a steady flow of show people working at night and willing to put in extra hours during the day."

THE PACIFIC COAST: California offers a lot of good show work, commercial print, and TV commercials. For people here, modeling is an excellent way to augment an acting income. At early stages in their careers a lot of celebrities have done it. To name a few: Raquel Welch, Farrah Fawcett, Rachel Ward, James Garner, Gerald Ford, President Reagan.

There is such a thing as a West Coast look, though it differs somewhat from south to north. The look in San Francisco is very conservative for men; for women, it's closer to New York. Sunny California, the home of the healthy, all-American outdoor look, emphasizes the more casual in design. Union costs are high in California, a fact that has benefited models from Portland: Cost-conscious clients often go where it's cheaper. Work is plentiful, though, from catalogs, which are flourishing, and from local manufacturers of bathing suits, like Jantzen, or men's clothing, like Pendleton. Models shuttle up and down the coast from Seattle to San Diego. Talent agents handle a big percentage of commercial casting because of their proximity to actors and actresses in the area.

LOS ANGELES: Mary Webb Davis, doyenne of Los Angeles fashion, remembers that city's modeling business when it was just beginning: "The most remarkable difference, between now and then, is prices. They have shot up very high and fast in only the past few years. I go back to when clients were paying ten to fifteen dollars per show. That was thirty-six years ago. At that time, the pay for photographic work was that same scale per hour."

From the start, Mary Webb tried to make her agency as nearly as possible like those in New York. Back then, the agency that found a model and gave her her first booking was the one that billed it. "I paid people right after the job, which set up an exclusive arrangement between model and agent. Now models get a check the week after they do the job, minus ten percent for fashion and fifteen percent for print. Better and more professional all around.

"Los Angeles always ran a poor second to New York. I thought, at the start, that the business would come out here. We had twenty-four couture designers who did openings as they do back East. The middy length, in 1970, killed the dress business here. People went out of business and the trade never recovered. Other things are thriving, though. Our department stores do more shows than are done in New York. European and Japanese clients flock here for the warmer weather and the light quality. Which was, after all, why the studios moved here in the 1920s."

Japanese photographers and commercial directors like to use Los Angeles models for their ads and commercials. That has been good for Joan Magnum, whose specialty is different from Mary Webb's (incidentally, Joan's first employer as a booker): "When I started seventeen years ago, I wanted to work with a totally different kind of model: funny types, character people for product shots." California was perfect for this approach. "Most of the people I represent are actors who have

been in TV shows and theatrical pieces. They're good for print because they can depict a character. A good seventy-five percent of these jobs call for an average type: husbands and wives, cute kids, standard characterizations. The market in California is not fashion-oriented. A model working in fashion has to be able to go to New York City, Chicago, or Dallas to supplement her income."

Joan's was one of the first print agencies in California. It now boasts a clientele of advertising agencies around the world. "It used to be assumed there were no people here to do advertising. If agencies came out, they brought models from New York. It was hard to break out of that mold. Men are being found right off the beaches and sent to Germany and Japan. Los Angeles now has capable people; a tremendous amount of talent, male or female, is moving back and forth between the two coasts. Many of our models work for various interests in Japan, mostly commercials. They do the work here or perhaps go there for a few days. Most of the people I handle don't want to interrupt their acting or commercial careers to go away for months at a time."

SAN FRANCISCO: "There is a market here for runway models because the department stores do quite a few shows," says Sabina Model's head booker, Marla Dell. She goes on to describe the seasonal swings: "It starts in late January and continues to the end of April. Then it slows in May and June but picks up in July when the fall shows begin. Some newer designers have established themselves here and do their own shows and print work. Print work for retail is fairly steady. Between shows and print the season continues until the end of November. Advertising for national accounts like Jacuzzi also brings in nice money."

San Francisco is a good gauge of other markets like it in size, such as Denver, Atlanta, or Boston. "Maybe thirty models earn a good living, twenty to thirty thousand dollars a year, doing photographic work," comments Gary Loftus, a San Francisco agency director. "Men may earn anywhere from twenty-five to forty thousand dollars if they are here the whole time. The few women I have had for the whole year made sixty thousand, but that is unusual. In my experience, most top models eventually get into other careers, like film, using San Francisco as a springboard."

SEATTLE: Until eight years ago, modeling here was mostly free-lance and the rates were very, very low. The market was there, but self-promotion was difficult for the individual. A visiting client can't be expected to look in the Yellow Pages. Joanne Meyers, founder of the Seattle Model's Guild, has effectively bridged that gap. About Seattle models she says, "They need to be as good as a model anywhere. Tokyo gives us a good and close money market, especially for five-feet-six and five-feet-seven models." She believes Seattle is a great place to start because scouts from all over watch it. "Our problem is that as quickly as we find models we lose them. France, Italy, and Germany are here twice a year. Photography provides the highest dollar volume. Ours is a fashion-oriented agency. We do some commercial print but there is virtually no editorial. This is definitely a catalog market. We do have sportswear manufacturers who do catalogs and are doing more national ads. They use mostly local talent.

"Television and runway are tied for second place. The Northwest is becoming a hot spot for national commercials and major TV movies. Producers prize the physical layout and using local talent saves them the high per diems.

"A model who is good in Seattle is good anywhere. She can go right from the Pacific Northwest on to an Ungaro or Galanos runway. Tokyo is terrific for the Seattle models. They can earn ten thousand dollars and up in two months doing print there, hop over to Hong Kong to renew their permits, and go right back for two more months. And the Seattle market is always waiting."

Seattle's rates are the same as European rates. Models here don't have the same shot at the really big money as top New York models. A top model who stays in Seattle and is occasionally booked in Portland or San Francisco can make thirty-five thousand dollars a year.

GUAM: "We have four good advertising agencies, a cable TV station, and a local CBS television affiliate, plus four radio stations," says Belta Perez of Agana, Guam. Describing the market for models on this thirty-two-by-ten-mile Pacific island, she says, "We now have a few select fashion designers, and a growing fashion market. We import everything. There are small fashion shows. There are twenty-eight working models here making about five to fourteen thousand dollars a year between local and Japanese accounts. Of that, eighty percent will come from Tokyo film crews that come to the island, and the rest from print work, TV commercials and live fashion shows."

And Around the World

The various fashion phenomena so familiar to-day had many, and sometimes surprising, origins. Chicago devised the raised-platform runway as a way to showcase fashion. A turn-of-the-century Marshall Field's window on State Street that displayed abbreviated underwear for men immediately altered men's fashion. From fashion magazines came the notion of American models going to Paris for the fashion seasons. Before 1920, France was first to use live models in the creation of wearing apparel. After 1920, New York started to come into its own as a fashion capital, but it wasn't until after World War II that regional American garment centers appeared.

In the beginning, modeling amounted only to part-time employment to supplement other earnings. Over time, models came to earn the income of a forty-hour week in half that time—a major leap, but less impressive when you remember that this takes no account of the time spent preparing for and getting the work, and the very low initial wages paid.

In the modeling world, although America, and New York in particular, remains central, the beginner has always gone to Europe, where the practice began. American pressures make it hard for models to develop. This pushes them toward Europe, where attitudes are more relaxed and a fashion sense can be acquired quickly. A European experience molds a young man or woman into something newer and more distinctive. The booming European editorial market offers ample and unusual work, and the promise of a more impressive portfolio.

"Going abroad is broadening in every way. Even experienced models improve technique by going overseas periodically. It also offers an opportunity for models with differing physical qualifications," says Monique Pillard at Elite. "In Europe clients don't pay as well, but there is more art put into the work, and I explain to each of my girls how important that can be for their career goals. Not every agency has international offices like ours, but a major one will have affiliates in all the primary modeling markets."

"Travel and experimentation benefit young people no matter what business they are in." John

Casablancas sees psychological as well as practical advantages. "As agents, we are dealing with very young kids who have unseasoned characters and personalities. Traveling brings them into contact with other kinds of people and situations. It gives them more confidence, style, a certain elegance.

"Time is taken more casually in Europe. It can be a pain in the neck when everybody is late and not as reliable and organized as they are here. As an agent, I'm not crazy about the way things are run in France, but, on the other hand, the feeling at the booking site is often much more interesting. Models who have trained in Europe are creative, looser, altogether better at their jobs. Ask any American photographer.

"Japan is different. There, time has *no* importance. They will work a model sixteen hours a day. They are workaholics with no concept of rest. It's a totally different mentality. American editors are very conservative, though they are opening up a little. It's still tough to get a magazine to risk using a new model just because somebody liked her. In Europe it's just the opposite. You could send a girl without one picture and she'd work every day simply because they like the way she looks. When she comes back, the editors pay attention.

"There are other reasons that are more technical. One is that heights aren't so rigid. Very tall models—about the five-feet-seven to five-feet-nine American standard—who don't do well here do just fine in Paris because Paris loves tall models. At the other extreme, a five-feet-six model can go to Japan and make twenty thousand dollars in two months. I couldn't get her started in New York. Girls with a 'German' look I can send to my German agency, and the same for England or Italy. Some girls can work everywhere but others can only work in certain places. Having agencies all over the world lets me dispatch models to the markets they correspond to. If they are very successful there, the quality of the work might help them overcome the handicap that hindered them in New York."

EUROPE: FASHION'S FOREMOST TRAINING GROUND

A further point is the perception that Europeans have a special consciousness about femininity that brings out new qualities in a young woman or man. In America, men and women tend to be chummy into their late teens. Europeans are more flirtatious and project an awareness toward pretty or handsome young adults that softens and relaxes them, actually improving their camera qualities.

Alberta Tabertzi provides a European photographer's view of the American model abroad. A former model herself, she is now one of Europe's leading female fashion photographers; her studio is in Rome. "I like American girls. There is something clean and fresh about them, without being stupid." In Alberta's eyes, "They don't have any mystery that cannot be learned. Meanwhile they are nice, and their parents straightened their teeth. A girl who comes over goes first to Paris. Paris can't use that many girls, so they send them to Milan. Chances are they'll work right away. The talent scouts are there to grab them—there is a constant need for something new. People get bored very quickly. Always having to have the Best, the Newest, and the Most Beautiful is idiotic, but it's everywhere.

"In my day, if a model was successful in New York, she was successful everywhere. Today, American magazines are not as good. They used to be onto everything that was happening in every direction. There was enormous expression and a sense of space and experiment. Now they look like catalogs but aren't even as well printed."

Lorenzo Pedrini, the director of Fashion Models in Milan, is the man who gives models their initial direction when they arrive in Italy. He was a New York model before returning to Italy; that experience is invaluable in working with Americans in Europe to strengthen their technical skills and develop salable personalities.

"Models are often sent over here after maybe fifteen days in New York. The agency didn't have time to develop or test them, so they sent them to Paris or Milan. We have thirty-three magazines and we work with the editorial outlets to give new models a new look. We do the hard job of changing the model—cutting the hair and finding the attitude. We are very successful at it.

"In Italy, a model goes on rounds. Models learn while on go-sees because most jobs are given out that way. Far too often, models come here thinking everyone will be waiting for them. It's not like that and never was. Before going to Europe, a model

Europe is the crossroads of fashion modeling and Milan is the epicenter of fashion magazines. Young people especially benefit from travel and experimentation. Agencies grab up American girls and boys because fashion operates on the axiom of rapid turnover combined with beauty and youth. Monique Pillard at Elite calls international tear sheets in a young model's portfolio "an investment—money in the bank." A pinch of continental flavoring is part of developing a successful modeling career. The photograph at the left is of Carrie Nygren, a Swede. It was photographed by Mike Reinhardt and seen in French *Vogue*. This picture epitomizes the internationalism of the modeling field. Likewise, Helen Lee (above) of Mannequin in New York is an Oriental-American photographed by a Briton, Barry Lategan, in New York for Italian *Vogue*. On p. 105 and at the left on p. 106 are two hot, New York–style photographs that ran in international fashion publications in Paris and Japan. Finally, at the right on p. 106, Farrah Fawcett displays some modern female virtues for a cover of an international *Cosmopolitan*.

Photo by LUPINO

should speak to an agency in New York. People in the business know the correct timing. Models who insist on coming find that the work has just ended or hasn't yet started. There is a definite busy and slow cycle. Also, they may not be right for the market. Sometimes when they come they're all right, but the look could change completely during the six months they're here, and they'd be all wrong.

Some models can work right away in Milan, which is strictly editorial, but not in Paris. After Milan, a model can go to the larger money markets of Europe—Germany, which is mainly catalog and requires a specific look, or France, Switzerland, or England—before returning to New York. There are no big contracts as in America, but there is great experience and prestige."

PART TWO

Becoming a Model

Schools and Agents: Getting into the Modeling Flow

If you think you may have the qualifications to be a model, it is best to see a modeling agency if one is accessible. Agencies are the most experienced at judging potential and often more objective than schools, which are interested in selling their own programs. Agencies make money only when a model does. Therefore, their training programs are more to the point.

A school is, however, the next best thing to an agency: It improves one's chances of getting an agent, and thus of becoming a model, and acts as a conduit to agency scouts. When a school recognizes potential, it will move a model right along through the agency network. At the end of a semester, for instance, local or regional conventions may be held, or the school may take its top students to national or international modeling contests. Most schools attend at least one such event.

Before looking at alternative entries to modeling, one must consider the safest: that is, through the existing system—a national network with an international arm, which permits qualified models to move anywhere in the world. The surest route into this network, for a beginner, is through a school or—a more popular and growing phenomenon—an organized contest that attracts regional, national, and worldwide scouts.

This form of talent search has recently reached new proportions with the advent of beginner model contests under the aegis of Elite, Ford, Bloomingdale's, and the *New York Post*, joining Miss Universe, Miss World, Miss USA, and Miss America. The several days of competition end with a grand finale banquet at which hundreds of prizes are awarded. Six or eight of the eight hundred entrants are offered recruitment contracts with top New York City agencies. Many contestants are scouted by other agencies for secondary markets, such as Atlanta, Denver, or San Francisco; still more are signed regionally, for places like New Orleans, Phoenix, or Guam. A model's initial agency is called the home agency because it is the first to direct and assist the individual with career development. When the novice signs up with a larger agency, the real process of development begins. Development is an agency's true function. It is in their interest to go all out for their models; this is, after all, how an agency earns its income.

SCHOOLS—A BROAD-BASED ASSESSMENT

A great many of the top United States and European models went to modeling schools because they came from small towns that offered no other access to scouts. Most small communities have modeling schools—either independent ones or franchises of established modeling schools, such as John Robert Powers, Barbizon, Patricia Stevens, or JC Modeling Centers. It is important to attend a *good* school, not just one that is conveniently located. It is the job of the school's director to route promising students to the largest potential market by putting them in contact with scouts in their region.

The essentials of a school's basic program are grooming, fashion, and makeup, with skin care and nutrition instruction when necessary. A good school will also document improvement of model skills—photography, runway, and TV—on videotape and in photographs. If students are to realize their potentials, the curriculum must be painstakingly planned and always current. Demands on the students too must be formal and strict, with regular assignments, readings, and workshops. Audiovisuals and illustrations make classwork livelier and easier to pick up. To be sure guidelines have been absorbed, progress should be reviewed periodically.

All instruction must be geared toward the highest fashion and beauty standards and the distinctive personal style that marks the professional model. Reading assignments make students aware of what will help them break into modeling, workshops stimulate self-motivation, assignments build the confidence and skills crucial to a career. Modeling is often a stepping-stone to other jobs in fashion and in related fields, such as magazine or retail styling work. Many models take art and design courses leading to careers as designers. And then there are those stellar types, like Tom Selleck or Lauren Hutton, who go from commercial performances to acting.

□ *What Some Experts Say About Schools*

Some schools have produced a bumper crop of top models. Nancy Bounds is founder and co-director of one such school in Omaha, Nebraska. She started at eighteen with nothing but a profound belief that she could bring out talent in others. Nancy advises that "just as in picking doctors, lawyers, or accountants, you must be careful who you approach first about becoming a professional model. Size is not the best criterion by which to judge a school; if you have potential, too large a class might hinder your progress. You might ask to see how they do a show at the end of a course. Ask about local clients, or to see their graduates in fashion magazines. Then ask yourself, Is that how I would want to look? The best barometer is the yearly percentage of graduates placed at agencies. There are good modeling courses everywhere. It pays to check on a school very thoroughly before enrolling."

Gillis McGill, founder of Mannequin in New York and a former star model, is more skeptical. She considers many modeling schools, at best, a form of finishing school, because they accept so many people who aren't qualified. "They don't try to discourage unqualified students or channel them into anything worthwhile, something that could benefit the person. School directors can't seem to be candid. Perhaps they can't afford to be. I guess everyone can gain *something* from it, some insight if nothing else. But success in New York takes a lot more than that."

Helen Rogers is chairman of the Plaza Three Agency in Phoenix, Arizona, which runs a widely acclaimed school. She sees more benefits: "We sign beginners who want to broaden their knowledge of runway or print. They get an understanding of techniques, and that will help any young model.

"Similarly, if a working model wants to move into a new category, such as TV commercials, we would recommend a class. The school is good for our own scouting because anyone who attends is closely scrutinized. Students are invited to attend open-interview days. If we feel we might be able to book someone, we encourage the person to sign with the agency. If we know we can't book someone, we tell the candidate why: 'We already have your type,' or 'We don't feel you are ready to be marketed,' or 'Perhaps you should try a smaller agency.'"

You don't need a college degree to get into modeling, but in today's competitive market, observes Jo Somers, president of Copley Talent in Boston, everyone can use that little bit of polish a modeling school adds. "Models perform in visual media and you won't get the job unless you are more than merely presentable. Modeling school nudges young girls to get their acts together. Most schools work with video and there's no better teacher than seeing yourself on a screen."

Fernando Casablancas, who developed a modeling school franchise under the name John Casablanca's Centers, reminds us that most models aren't too articulate on the subject of their work. They need a portfolio to *demonstrate* their abilities, something that schools can help them to start but too often do not. "Many modeling schools perpetuate the illusion that anyone with a camera and high prices can take a picture of someone who knows nothing about posing or doing her hair or makeup. Students get blowups of bad pictures and are disappointed because these don't get them an agent."

A portfolio is something you start and keep perfecting. That requires testing whether you've gone to school or not. It isn't only novices who have incomplete, evolving portfolios. Relatively established models do too, as any New York agency can tell you. Says Fernando, "To capture the most expressive moments and create the necessary variety takes several photographers, and time for the model to know herself. We develop the nucleus, but we don't claim that a student's portfolio will be complete."

Even of those predisposed in every way to modeling, some will make it and some won't. A school enhances its students' chances by making them more astute about the market and by nurturing their aptitudes. Unfortunately, too many equate modeling with New York City and the cover of *Vogue;* a small ad or mention in a less famous magazine, or simply getting that first good photograph, can be highly gratifying. And print is not the only option: There are conventions and public relations, fashion-related fields, merchandising, buying, styling, photography, and working as a photographer's assistant. A training course can be designed to explain these alternatives; a responsible school will weigh students' weaker and stronger points and direct them toward fields offering the greatest prospect of success.

Joan Koenig devised the teaching requirements for the Casablancas Centers, and she supervises every franchise to see that they are adhered to. A graduate heading for a major market, she says, must be on top of the competition and in firm command of the basic tenets of modeling. "It's hard enough being a novice. You can be at a terrible disadvantage in New York or Europe if you're unprepared. Models must know what is expected and what *they* should expect. All the basic *how-to*'s are important: conducting yourself on an interview, good manners, body language, and speech basics.

"A curriculum should go into everything: *beauty,* including skin care, hair, and makeup; *grooming,* with emphasis on exercise, diet, and nutrition; *technique,* which means posture and attitude for photography, and skills necessary for runway and commercials. There is a general umbrella course that covers what to put in your tote bag, what to do on go-sees, the different modeling markets, and how to conduct yourself on a set. Then students go on to television-commercial work: how to read a script, do a cold reading, and behave on an audition.

"After basic training," Joanne explains, "there should be preparation for an actual fashion show, conducted just like the professional ones. Rehearsal class time is spent deciding the line-up, with brief run-throughs in street clothes before the show starts—that's how it's done in real life. Everything they have studied is put into practice.

"By the end of the TV classes, students are ready to do a television commercial on video. They are given a script just as though they had walked into an office and been asked to read a script cold. It is videotaped so class members can play it back to see what they did. A 'cold' performance gives them some sense of a cattle call, and of the level of insecurity and rejection they'll be facing."

As president of the Modeling Association of America International, vice-president of John Robert Powers, and franchisee of a school in Boston, Barbara Tyler knows preparation makes all the difference: "Modeling agencies won't be interested in people who are not psychologically ready; ninety percent of our trainees wind up in other industries, or aspects of the business other than modeling. This industry, like all others, has set rules; anyone who can't or won't follow them is out the door very fast.

"Preparing students takes time. I start in January to get students ready for an April convention. They come twice a week: all day Saturday and one evening session. Much of modeling reflects feelings about yourself. I teach attitude, projection, personality, performing, and learning to like it. The more fun you are having, the better you look. It is mostly what isn't taught in high schools: self-assurance, self-esteem. If you are working in a secondary market, which is to say part-time, it's useful to know that photographers aren't always big on building self-esteem, even if you are good."

There are many aspects of a school to research before enrolling in classes. It is important that the faculty have broad professional experience. There should be ongoing contact between the director and local clients. Make sure adequate budgets are available to allow quality attention to each student. There should be good student moral—try to talk to students who are enrolled to get insiders' viewpoints. Along with the classic course of study, the school should demonstrate an ability to give extensive remedial instruction, if necessary. Last, a school's runway showings or practice video commercials should have good production values. It is important to watch the work of graduating students, then ask yourself: Is that what I want to know when I finish a modeling course?

SCOUTING—THE SEARCH FOR THE STARS

Linda Cox, art director of *Cosmopolitan* magazine, has judged modeling contests. Her hiring experience has shown her that some contest winners fail to make it because they are too young to meet the real-life demands of modeling. "A model must look fresh, as if he or she had had eight hours' sleep. Every part of the body must be carefully attended to. Models have to rise above personal problems, act like they feel marvelous and are doing exactly what they want to be doing. It's amazing to me sometimes that they can show up on time at all, but that's their job."

Appearance is only the beginning; then comes salesmanship. "For our male-centerfold contest," Linda continues, "we got thousands of entries. We finally winnowed these down to thirty, and the thirty to ten finalists. We interviewed those on the phone. One law student in Boston was particularly well spoken, so we brought him to New York. From that conversation, we felt confident that he could represent himself right away; most take time to develop."

Helen Murray was an assistant editor for *Vogue* and a publicist for Calvin Klein before becoming the scout for Wilhelmina. She knows from every angle how hard it is to find real star material, and what a minefield the search can be. Helen is constantly encountering plastic surgery: nose jobs, face lifts, eye tucks and pinnings. What schools call talent may not strike a scout the same way, and she must make decisions very fast. Helen theorizes: "What is *it*, exactly? Obviously, to be great-looking is part of it. I look first at the nose. If they pass my nose test then I really scrutinize. I look for nicely spaced eyes, good skin, good mouth and teeth. The body needn't be a traffic stopper but should be in good shape, with long legs and most of the leg between the knee and ankle.

"Noses are what keeps ninety percent of aspiring models out of the business. I will not discuss a nose job because it can be a disaster. No teenager should go to plastic surgery unless they can't get out of the bed in the morning because they literally cannot face the way they look."

Schools can do the initial screening for agencies. This is good for the agencies because though certain schools never come up to New York standards, others produce tremendous talent. Helen says, "School directors—the best of them—have a great eye and know what we're looking for. They will call and say, 'Have I got a girl for you!' If it's someone whose opinion I trust, I will get on a plane and check it out. Then again, I can visit a school that has had great people in the past and they will have nothing to speak of. It depends on the timing. Many people make fun of modeling schools, but so many top models, male and female, have gone to them that nobody can laugh any longer. It's a good place to get exposed to the industry.

"When you are scouting for quality it can be arduous. Then suddenly a young person arrives who seems to be surrounded by light, and you're not tired anymore. I spent an entire month out of town this past year. One thing that kept me going was that in two cities, after seeing about three thousand people, I found six good prospects. I get very discouraged, and then I go to the next city and find someone great. These are the odds on the road. Five or six people in your pocket after a week is pretty amazing and very rewarding.

"In my travels, I cover local beauty pageants, state fairs, and, of course, modeling-school graduations. I'm looking for one in a thousand. My job is partly public relations. I sit with each one, and, if necessary, let them know they are wasting their time. It's always possible that the aspirant I'm sitting with may have a great-looking younger sister or best friend. Can't do any harm if they remember that I was nice."

John Casablancas, who founded Elite on his ability to scout from Paris, says agents know very quickly whether the right characteristics are there. "I can sit with a model and tell what is behind the pretty face. I may see talent combined with the personality flaws that are great for modeling. Good salesmen have certain personality defects; usually they're overoptimistic, so much so that people buy. To be a good accountant you must be extremely precise and meticulous. In each profession, certain characteristics are an asset. A girl with a little spark of exhibitionism, who's a show-off or hyperreactive to certain circumstances, may be annoying to someone else, but I know that these quirks can create an extroverted, compelling personality to a camera. A more analytic person would find it hard to rationalize some of the tasks models are asked to perform. The French, who are very introspective and logical, feel silly doing certain things on a runway.

"I met a young woman the other day, and in two minutes I knew exactly what her problems were. She's fifteen, parties too much, and fantasizes about modeling. She is a little too attracted to the glitter, but she could be great. It's a question of being able to channel those fifteen-year-old energies. She could end up using those same defects and be very successful. This girl also had a weight problem and I really sounded off about it. I saw her today and she said she has lost three pounds in four days. It showed me something about her qualities and what to watch out for in her behavior.

"An agent acting as a scout should always be alert for new looks without being fooled by fads. Right now, ugly girls are working really well; I feel pressure as an agent to start looking at them. Also, the industry is reacting to years of WASP dominance, and agents are taking girls with big noses. I always stay with the classics: long legs, slim builds, good basic features—the things that are timeless."

AGENTS—AS PROMOTERS AND MANAGERS

Agents are salespeople who represent models to potential employers. Their incomes derive from 10 to 20 percent commissions from the models and 10 to 15 percent service fees on sales paid by the clients. One of the agents' responsibilities is keeping in touch with market demands; their function is to meet the buyers' needs; their goal is to sell as much as possible of their product, that is, of a model's time. Stiff competition forces the agents to seek out buyers aggressively, the scouts to search for the best talent, and the bookers to ask the highest possible fees. The marketplace constantly demands new faces, so it is up to the agents—and in their interest—to find commercially viable newcomers. Scouting is one way; contests are, increasingly, another; schools are a third.

An agent's reputation is most important. An agent must be reliable and have an excellent financial record. As a model's manager and career guide, he must account for all incoming and outgoing monies. Many states monitor the activities of talent agents who operate within their jurisdiction, certainly for minors if not in every instance for adults. It is advisable to check whether an agent belongs to local charities and organizations, is affiliated with national agents' alliances, or is chartered by an international organization. There is one very powerful New York model management group, the International Model Managers Association. Most reliable agencies are members in good standing of one organization or another. Very often, and especially outside New York City, agencies are active in the business and civic communities. A simple check into an agency's credentials will verify whether it is legitimate.

The commission that models pay to agencies gives them the responsibility and the incentive to get the models work with credit-worthy clients. An agent's office mails out a model's composites and head sheets to prospective clients on its mailing and go-see lists. They arrange for models to meet with prospective clients, work out their daily and trip schedules, and help them to organize and update portfolios and, when ready, to lay out composites.

The agency serves as an intermediary for the model with clients, but the model always has the final say. For example, you are free to turn down any job. A model is not a salaried agency employee who can be controlled. Agencies are essentially clearing houses for collecting receivables for the working models. That is one of the technical functions they perform so that models can work, and another reason why agents are paid commissions.

The agents get work by promoting models' careers. They do this by having relationships in the industry that are maintained through personal contacts and calls and through sending out the model agency promotional book of composites. To the advertising agency that sees them, those books amount to a stamp of approval. Once a career is established, work comes into an agency board because a model has acquired standing and, by this time, regular clients. But in the beginning stages of a model's career, connections must be cultivated.

It is important to bear in mind that the modeling profession is basically a service business. A model's working day is in no way like a regular nine-to-five job. Modeling is unusual in the amount of travel required and in the time pressure. It demands, above all, a good attitude toward work, not always under the best circumstances. A model must stay on top of a multitude of details during any working day. Only hard, down-to-earth effort will keep it all under control.

Modeling success does require a high profile—recognition and exposure. Any kind of positive recognition, up to a point, is beneficial. But models don't rise effortlessly to high visibility and high fees. Well-compensated models have paid their dues.

Lou Kertzberg is financial adviser and accountant for Zoli in New York City. He reinforces the service aspect of the model's role: "When the model comes on the set, all the preliminaries are out of the way: product development, market research, advertising concept. That's when he or she performs the service—instant, appropriate product representation. The product may be cosmetics, garments, automobiles, food. It doesn't matter; a good model is up for anything."

It should be remembered too that a model's career, like an athlete's, is of limited duration, because it is based on a limited asset—youth. The likely career span is ten years, "or less," Lou adds, "if you burn out under the lights. A model owes it to herself to handle this limited asset responsibly. Among other things, this is a commercial business, and there is such a thing as exploitation. Also, models should take note of the professionals *they* hire—agents, accountants, and lawyers—just as they expect the same in their line of work."

Using another professional analogy, after the first interview to determine whether you have modeling qualifications, you should get a second opinion—from another agent, or perhaps a local art director or stylist, photographer, or photographer's assistant. Agents are not infallible, and they get hundreds of inquiries every week. Luis Lopez of Mannequin in New York has this to say about the initial inquiry to an agent: "We do our immediate screening on the phone. The first fact we ask for is the person's height. If that doesn't fit in our specialization, we end the conversation. We decide whether to see the applicant by the questions the person asks and the manner of asking. If it sounds like they just got out of bed and it's four o'clock in the afternoon, we won't be too interested."

Dan Deely, director of the men's division at Wilhelmina, says he's satisfied with a snapshot as long as it's clear and in focus. "I only want to see how the person photographs. Professional pictures aren't necessary. They cost too much and are usually too portraitlike to be useful anyway. Take a picture in a very natural situation where you are comfortable. Not in the middle of the day; the sun is too high and causes shadows on the face. Shoot early, when it's low and cool, or later, when it's low and warm. Do not pose—you'll look stiff. A photographic quality is all I'm after."

Helen Murray, ex-scout at Wilhelmina, feels you need two shots to show an agent: a head shot and a body shot. "A good head shot should show what you really look like. Nothing dramatic and only a minimal amount of makeup. A good full-length shot shows your body proportions. It need not be in a bathing suit, just ordinary street clothes, with perhaps a little shorter skirt so the line of the legs can readily be seen."

□ *Choosing an Agency*

Start by making a list of all the possible agencies. While investigating each one, there are specific things to consider. Be certain, first, that you meet the director of the agency and are told that person's qualifications and how long he or she has been in business. Your second concern is the size of the sales force that will be pushing you. Third, how much you will have to invest, if anything, and for what, before you start to earn money? The fourth consideration is whether you are comfortable with the person assigned to your career. Every agency has a different style of guiding, directing, and promoting models. It is in that style that you will be represented; it must be one that will further your career goals. Fifth, make sure that the agency specializes in the area you want to enter. If it is not its speciality, then how extensively does it operate in that area? Sixth and last, two reputation questions: How well does the agency compare with others within your region? Do its references check out?

If you are to function well with an agency, it must give you a feeling of trust. An agency serves a model as agent and manager. This dual role is common in other areas of advertising and in the entertainment industry as well. The relationship is symbiotic: As the model goes, so goes the agency. The agency does all it can to promote the model and to maximize her potential. That is how the agency makes money. Without the model, there is no agency. And vice versa, of course.

Mrs. Irene Marie is the director of Irene Marie Models in Miami. Her vantage point makes it clear why models working in smaller markets need to choose their agents especially well. "Who runs or manages an agency," she warns, "makes a tremendous difference in how the models do. The director makes the agency. This is double so in satellite markets. If someone in Dallas doesn't understand that market, isn't arranging the books appropriately and assessing the model's capabilities correctly, and therefore getting her into the right clients, it doesn't matter whether or where the agency has good connections."

The time to check into those you will be working with is *before* you enter into a business arrangement. Maureen Malone of Funny Face feels strongly about this. "A beginner should sound out someone who knows the agency and its way of doing business. It's just not sensible to do otherwise. I am always more comfortable with someone who is aware of who we are and our reputation in the business." If anything about an agency seems

questionable, step back and give it some hard second thoughts.

Wally Rogers cautions against agents who may be downright disreputable. "Avoid anyone who asks you for money. Reputable managers do not take money from you until you earn something through their efforts. If someone says, 'Give me a lot of money and I'll send you to Europe and make you famous,' run. The evidence that an agent is reliable is recommendations from photographers, designers, or others who do business with agencies; best of all, from other models."

The reason so many agencies exist is that different models prefer different styles. Since no two are alike, survey the field until you find one that is congenial. David Whitfield of David and Lee in Chicago suggests attention to the size factor. "Some think an agency will work harder for them if it doesn't have hundreds of people. An agency that is very large can be a hindrance to some but a wonderful experience for others. An agency is primarily a sales force of which the model is a part. We give models leads, make sure they follow them up, and call the leads to find out what kind of impression was made."

Along with whether an agency is right for you, you must consider whether you're right for the agency. All modeling agencies have the same body of clients, generally speaking, but certain ones may be known for representing a particular look or type, or for specializing in fashion, characters, or conventions. Check with someone who knows the personalities of the various agencies you plan to approach. The best way to discover particular strengths, however, is to look at an agency's promotional book or head shot. You'll know very quickly whether you fit in or not. As a scout, Helen Murray of Wilhelmina always considered suitability. "I didn't tell a model not to go to another agency if that agency was better for models of her type than ours was. An entry-level model must be sure she is going to the right one."

Sarah Foley, also of Name in New York, sees the agency choice as an individual decision. "There is no best way to go about it," she says, "but a wise first step is to find the right mentor, a person who will help you decide for and against certain fields. It is the well-focused model who soonest acquires a specialty and reputation, and who stays longest in demand. For example, there aren't too many females who can do both catalog and editorial. A woman who concentrates effectively on these two areas should do exceedingly well."

Luis Lopez, booker at Mannequin, sees this choice as not quite so free. "Sometimes a girl will want to join an agency she's not right for because of that agency's reputation and clients." Mannequin's own client list brings them many models of this kind—fine models, but not for their purposes. "We often avoid otherwise eligible all-American girls because our clients—Galanos, Halston, Scaasi, Stravopolis, Valentino, Armani—want models who are exotic and forward-looking, a look for two years in the future, or an ultrasophisticated couture type.

□ *The Booker*

The agency handles all of a model's business appointments, basically bookings and go-sees. The booker is the person on the model board (decendant of the telephone switchboard) who manages that model's entire schedule and knows where he or she is at any time. The board also serves as a telephone answering service (all calls are screened by the agency).

The bookers on the agency phones have a schedule of each model's day—go-sees, auditions, bookings, and fittings—as well as of any bookings made for the future. Early in a model's career, while the individual is still on the testing board, the booker makes interview and go-see appointments with photographers and editors, stylists, hairdressers, and makeup artists.

The booker is on the model's side, an intermediary who has contact and clout with the client. A model's relationship with a booker should be relaxed, but also direct and businesslike. A model must be honest and open with the booker because

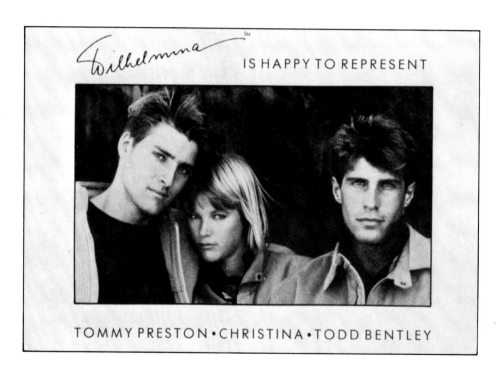

Wilhelmina IS HAPPY TO REPRESENT

TOMMY PRESTON • CHRISTINA • TODD BENTLEY

Here is a simple way to prepare personalized agency rounds lists: First, isolate nearby areas that can be reached within an hour. Next, check the industry directories and resource books or local Yellow Pages for hints. Take down the names and addresses of each agency. Call to find whom to see and when. Then draw up your schedule according to geographic proximity, always allowing plenty of time for each appointment.

One important consideration when choosing an agency is whether you can establish an easy rapport with the booker. That relationship should be comfortable yet efficient. They are the buffers, they keep you out of sticky situations. Instead of saying when late, "I've got to get out of here," tell it to the booker. She will help you. It takes unusual aggressiveness to sell oneself; a booker can put a sales push behind a model when she feels that besides beauty there is that special energy known as charisma.

Above is a mailer introducing three promising newcomers. It was prepared and sent out to clients by their agency, Wilhemina.

no one is more concerned with that model's success. After the model, bookers have the most to gain. "There's no one as important as a booker to a model's career. They know who you want to work for and who you don't, when you will work and when you won't," says veteran model Karen Bjornson of Ford. "Your booker can negotiate your rates, get you out of difficult situations, and give you good advice."

The booker is your buffer, always there if you need someone to be the bad guy. This way a model never has to be the heavy; they keep you out of sticky situations. If a booking is running over and the next client has two other models booked for a triple, you don't holler "Stop the picture" and walk off the set. You call your booker and explain the problem. She'll handle it with an explanation, an apology, whatever it takes. If the photographer always runs late, you begin to feel exploited, as if he doesn't value your time or the situation it puts you in. Instead of saying "I've got to get out of here," tell it to the booker.

The booker/model relationship depends in part on the model's reactions. The two are in touch all day every day. The booker is the model's organizer, protector, and support—not an easy role. She is often on the receiving end of frustrations: The cab driver was nsaty; it's starting to rain. A smart model knows such backing only comes from a friend and is grateful that the booker is there. As Lisa Herzog, vice-president and head of the model management board at Elite, expresses it: "The booker is a familiar voice on the other end of the phone. This provides a certain amount of stability in a most unpredictable business. When models are out there working with different clients every day, it's reassuring to them to feel there is one place where they'll know the faces, can be themselves; they know they can cry in front of you, laugh, be in a bad mood, or invite you home for dinner."

Top models require variety in their bookings. If they have editorial, they need catalog, or vice versa. If they have these, they need advertising bookings. A booker is responsible for making sure that there is a mix of work. A shrewd, well-organized booker turns a model's time into money. She may schedule a model to go from one end of the country to the other. But she makes sure it's worthwhile and she leaves enough time in between. Such carefully calculated scheduling becomes more important as a model's bookings increase. Dottie Franco at Elite explains how a booker deals with this: "It requires staying on your toes and watching and playing with the charts. You have to be aware of which models are taking what bookings and which clients will confirm what model, or which two will cancel each other out. It is constant juggling. Busy models expect and need this management from their bookers.

"A booker also recommends substitutions for heavily booked models. But we don't play games. If a client wants a particular brunette, a booker doesn't say the girl isn't available because she wants them to book someone else—though she might suggest various brunettes that she knows need work in that area. Little things can be done to promote models if you believe in them.

"It is very often qualities other than looks that top models share. Some of the real beauties don't work as often as plainer ones with genuine energy, persistence, and charisma. Often, great models don't have the aggressiveness to sell themselves. We call and tell a client someone wonderful is coming over and she gets there and does not sparkle. After we have promoted a model, it's up to her. We can only put a convincing sales push behind a model if we believe in her chance at success."

If a model feels that the booker is putting her into jobs that are wrong, she has to speak up. The model should not assume that the booker always knows how she feels; she has to let the agency know how she wants to be handled.

A good booker has a feeling about which products a model can be right for. Some will not do lingerie or nude pages, no matter how tasteful. If a booker is putting you on a job you aren't willing to do, there's something wrong with your communication. That communication must be good, with the right feedback, because it's the booker who's pitching the model to the photographers and clients.

Monique Pillard of Elite (Momo, to her models and staff) says of management in photographic fashion modeling: "It's up to the agency to capitalize on the looks and find models that fit the current look. When you stay with a really beautiful classic look, you can never go wrong. At Elite we don't take more blondes or more brunettes, we just take the best in any category." That doesn't mean that agents shouldn't be sensitive to trends, but that they should have conviction about who will respond to them. "It's not enough for an agent to believe that a model has something special," Monique goes on, "you have to know how to sell her. And the model has a part to play: She must make the photographer want to book her. The look changes all the time, just like clothes and fads. The trick is making trends work *for* you."

Monique makes a valid point about an agent's need to have a feel for trends but not be thrown by them. The agent takes a model under his wing to promote regardless of what happens to be the current trend. He doesn't have to be your best buddy, just a close partner in a relationship that works. If an agent isn't confident that you can make it, he should be handling someone else.

□ *Character Work—A Different Way of Doing Business*

Character work demands a far different selling approach from what fashion bookings do. It is mainly a part-time market; a model almost has to have another job, as well as a flexible schedule. A character agent maintains contacts with clients and photographers and sends out mailings, just as a fashion agent does. But the guidance role—toward the right go-see and well-focused composites and portfolios—is even more crucial, because the requirements are so specialized and strict. "With character work so dependent on casting, we're not in the business of soliciting calls," says Maureen Malone of Funny Face. "We have a reputation and people know what we supply. We recommend the usual kind of self-promotion to models: doing rounds, getting to know photographers, and dropping off pictures. What we do, as their agent, is make good-will calls to photographers, giving them one-to-one guidance and recommendations." Accuracy is the key in casting, Maureen explains. "Our role is to give models a sense of their casting strengths and weaknesses, what works best for them. We give wardrobe suggestions for particular casting sessions, and on wardrobe in general.

"It's our responsibility to match up compatible working relationships and to let clients know when a selection is wrong, even when it's one of our own models. When a call comes in for a model, we get precise information about how the person should look; since most casting is done with Polaroids it

is imperative the model look right for that moment. We work at keeping up their portfolios and composites. We do the regular mailings, but individual promotion comes through the castings they're sent out on. And we do follow-ups continually, not just as courtesy calls but to find out about any problems so we can relay them to the model."

Signing with an agency has legal ramifications. Before putting pen to any contract, be sure you know why you want to join that particular agency and what you are to get in return. It's always best to get some kind of legal advice; switching agencies is complicated once you are signed. If there are contractual hitches, a switch can be costly, time consuming, and an emotional drain. A first-agency contract shouldn't be so complex that you cannot easily understand it. It's your responsibility to do so; your signature signifies that you understand and agree to its terms. Even if it's just a simple form, a good agent will explain any part that puzzles you. The more money one makes, of course, the more advice one needs; therefore, a very successful model should have her own lawyer. To answer a standard legal question each agency has an attorney on retainer.

□ *The Responsibilities Spelled Out*

When a model gets on an agency board, it's time for close cooperation. There will be many methods, procedures, and details to absorb. Organization matters as never before. This orientation period doesn't go on forever; soon things will be routine and there will be no need to ask questions. Listen hard and evaluate what you are learning, but, above all, show respect to everyone you meet, until you have reason not to. You might start with your agent, suggests Tommy McCarthy, whose experience came from booking models for television commercials at Zoli. "Every model must know how to get along with the agent. An agent won't want to push you if the two of you aren't on good terms. You just don't want to think about that kind of person. Models are always asking me, 'How am I going to get television work?' A little attention would go a long way. *Know thy agent* is an important maxim. If you offend your agent or don't keep yourself in a positive, bright light in his eyes, he simply won't think of you. Why not some nice, legitimate, tax-deductible gesture like a pair of hard-to-get theater tickets? Save the ticket stub and you'll both be happy."

A model should be conscientious about keeping the agency informed—about every go-see, test, job that she goes to. A model has to stay in touch with her agency during the business day and check in at the end of it for last-minute changes. When you are not available, tell the booker. Helping your booker to stay on top of your schedule will avoid disputes and misunderstandings. Failure to do this, according to Wally at Wallace Rogers, is the most common bad habit of models. "They forget to book out with us when they are not available. This makes us crazy because when we say someone is available, people assume we know what we're talking about. That's our job. The other problem is not checking in with their service often enough. We should be able to find any model within an hour. Models don't get very far if they are not punctual and responsive. They are being paid what to everyone else seems an enormous amount. Certainly they can be on time."

□ Definitions: Copyright and Right of Privacy

Every model must understand exactly what rights are being sold. There are two kinds: *copyright*, and the *right of publicity or privacy*. The copyright is for the physical image: a photograph, videotape, or film of a model. This right is given up when a model is paid for the use of that image. The photographer and the advertising agency will get the copyright in the name of the product, but that is only part of the rights package the model agency needs for its client.

"The privacy issue is trickier," says David Blasband, legal counsel to Zoli. "You cannot use a person's likeness for purposes of trade without written consent. A model's image is taken for trade and permission for this right must be obtained. Large national advertisers want to use a model exclusively based on one-year options. If they want to prevent a model from selling her right of privacy during that year through a second picture to a competitor, or if they want to extend the length of the time period, in each case they must pay the model to forfeit that right of privacy. This holding period is negotiated either for three months, six

months, or one year.

"The holding period can hinder a model if the competitor is willing to pay more for his or her services. The modeling agency has to look out for the model's interests. Perhaps she could make more working for the second client. The result has been that models on the way up try for shorter holding periods. This restricted term lets them go, time after time, into big, high-paying campaigns for cosmetics, liquor, and cigarettes. Advertising agencies, when campaigns have run their course, are willing to release a model.

"Of course beginners rarely attract the high-paying jobs that compensate more established models for giving up this lucrative, long-term right. They are, after all, only aligned and associated with the product, which is still different from endorsing it. Either way, however, the purpose is to keep the model on hold: The client is paying to keep you on tap in case they want to continue using you. For top models, this is the central issue in their fight for higher fees. It goes back to copyright: If a second client wants to use your image, the option on the right of privacy prevents you from letting him do so."

When such a conflict arises, your booker will then negotiate the compensation, extending her power-broker role from buffer against minor unpleasantness to guardian of the model's right to privacy. Each and every model must always pay attention to what she is asked to sign. Whenever told "Sign this!" be certain that the usage is only what was agreed to by the agent. If a model signs away the right of privacy on a picture, little control can be exerted over its use.

□ Getting Top Dollar

The average income of models is dramatically higher than the norm for their respective age groups, roughly from teens to the forty-year-old range. Top models may earn as much as business executives do after twenty-year careers, but they do this for five to seven years usually. The rule of thumb used to be one thousand hours came to one hundred thousand dollars a year, and that was top echelon. Today, one hundred dollars an hour is normal. At one time the only bonus situation was lingerie; additional fees today are collected for each different usage (billboard to national ad) or for extended usage, usually after the initial six-month or quarterly option. For women, the highest-paying industries are cosmetics, including hair products, such mass-market products as soft drinks and cars, and high fees are paid, of course, for nudes and seminudes. Men's services are in demand for cigarettes, liquor, clothing, and, more recently, for male makeup and grooming lines. These contracts too carry the large-bonus possibility of exclusive use for one brand's advertisements.

Anyone wanting to know booking policy, procedures, and rates can request them from the agent. Regular customers are kept abreast of current rates and get copies of the booking policy with the promotional book. This sheet explains any additional charges—travel expenses, hairdressing, overtime, cancellations, weather permits—along with the hourly rates. It is clearly stated that any additional usages must be negotiated prior to the booking; also, whether there are hour minimums, what finance charges are imposed after thirty days, and how much will be charged as an agency service fee.

Fee negotiation can be a neat and simple process. Most markets have well-established, easy-to-follow guidelines. Since this is not permanent employment, rates are structured on either an hourly or a daily basis, determined when a job is booked. Every model should keep a detailed booking record that includes rate, usage, date and time, place, and fittings. Editorial pays a fixed and unnegotiable day rate. Catalog rate is used as a starting point for many other hourly rates; retail advertising is usually only slightly higher. Commercial print pays the most. The rates for fashion fittings and writing appointments are similar; runway shows pay more.

Work for certain advertisers carries a bonus on top of the rate. This too is negotiated when the model is definitely booked. These bonuses are tied directly to the usage. Other factors that can affect the fee are geographic distribution, type of media, whether extended to billboard, packaging, advertising displays at points of purchase (such as hangtags), even a buy-out of the rights. In fashion, personal associations or exclusive endorsements may be considerations. Beauty and fashion command the most generous fees. Each variable creates a new usage and so can involve an additional fee, often equal to the agreed per-day rate.

"In the back of my mind I am always searching for more work while I am negotiating for more money," says Dottie Franco, director of the Elite division. "I know I can book a top New York model anywhere, from Alaska to Australia, South Africa to South Carolina. They just have to let us know they are willing to follow the important jobs. There is no logic to it, but there are a few guidelines. If she is a blonde, a model will work in Germany; a dark-haired beauty will work in England or Italy. There are exceptions to every rule, however. Once a model has become established, any rate can be negotiated, based on usage and options. How high depends on how big the model is. South Africa is starting to book top women at very good rates. They pay first-class fare down and, if there is another booking to return to, the Concorde back. You have to negotiate travel time. You have to negotiate everything. Is it lingerie? Will it be nude or seminude? Those situations spell more money. Next, where will it run—worldwide, Philippines only, or any combination? Then there is usage, and options past the initial periods. When you have all this settled and you think the client is about to confirm, they say, 'Did I mention my point of purchase in Malasia and Burma?' By the time you're finished, you have negotiated, if it includes TV, maybe one hundred thousand dollars. For the agency and the model, it's worth touching every base. We might pick up an extra few thousand dollars."

Television commercials are very complex to negotiate because there are so many variables to consider. A conflict can affect the negotiator's stance, as can the possibility of residuals, or royalties, paid to a model each time a commercial airs. Tommy McCarthy at Zoli Theatrix describes how an agent weighs these factors to get the best possible deal for a model: "If the agent finds that the commercial is in a high-conflict area—that is, that the model won't be able to do a second product while this one is on the air—how much does he negotiate for? Models can only do one for a certain period of time, so they have to get enough money to hold them until they can do another. It's important to refuse a commercial if the model won't make enough to warrant agreeing to the waiver.

"There is a tremendous difference between models who are working their day rates and those accepting scale. We do have models who work for scale, of course, because national scale is good for residuals every thirteen weeks. But we try to get day rates because we never know whether a commercial will actually go from test market into national broadcast—the stuff that residuals are made of. When they do it's wonderful, like hitting the jackpot at Atlantic City, but we certainly don't know that to begin with, so we try to get the day rate, which will be applied to future residuals."

The voucher protects models from unauthorized usage of their image, and also provides the billing information for accounting. Every agency uses vouchers in one form or another, usually in triplicate: one each for the client, agency, and model. At the end of a booking, the model gets the client's signature on the form.

Usage changes are serious business. When they are brought to an agent's attention, immediate payment on the model's behalf is demanded. A novice has to understand that no work can be accepted except through the agency. Nothing starts until the rate is negotiated and the billing and financial matters are settled. An offer can usually be sweetened by the agent, who knows all the negotiable factors. They must, of course, know your career goals in order to make intelligent decisions about what bookings or fees to accept.

Photographers need a standard photographic release to protect them in case of a lawsuit. It's all right to sign provided it doesn't ask for additional usage. If you are in doubt, call your agency and clear it before signing, or merely cross out anything you are unsure of, add exactly the picture and usage information on your voucher, then initial the changes before signing the release.

Models once paid a 15 percent commission plus a 20 percent reserve to safeguard the agency against nonpaying clients. The 20 percent cushion was allowed to grow to the level of outstanding receivables. The 15 percent commission covered salaries, overhead, and profit. Models now pay 20 percent and there is no reserve. Ususally, if a model hands in a one-thousand-dollar voucher slip, eight hundred of it can go back to her the following Friday. It is the agency's obligation, no matter what the circumstances, to collect the money.

☐ *Dollars and Sense*

Some models like to be free to concentrate on their modeling and leave money management to someone else, especially models who make enough to afford the services of a professional. At any income level, an accountant can be a good investment. "Expenses incurred during the normal course of business are tax deductible," says Lou Kertzberg, tax man extraordinaire for models for two decades. "Models' expenses are different from those of other workers. Huge expenditures for photo composites—fifteen hundred to three thousand dollars depending on size and color—facials, beauty treatments, hair coloring, manicures, pedicures, waxing, dental bills, body conditioning, health-club membership; all of these are deductible.

"Professional wardrobe is looked at somewhat skeptically. It is called costumes, and if you can prove that what you had to buy for a particular job cannot be used again, then the IRS might let it go through. Or if it is unquestionably a costume, something you'd look like a fool in walking down a street. A gown or a tux that can be used continuously the IRS considers standard clothing. If a model has to go out and buy forty or fifty pairs of shoes in different styles and colors, sometimes we can uphold these deductions.

"Lessons such as acting, dancing, voice, and music all can be deducted if a model is going into these areas. For television, for instance, they'd better be able to talk, which means voice and acting lessons. Dermatologists, trichologists, all can come off. Taxis around town are deductible, but not the first and last ones to and from home—that's a regular commute.

"Then there is money spent for ordinary professional necessities: commissions, answering services, photographic prints, composites, and the agency fee for their book. The need for careful, day-to-day records can't be stressed too much."

Accidents do happen and you want to know you're protected. Like anyone else who is self-employed, models should carry their own workman's compensation, unemployment insurance, health insurance, and retirement plan. Each state has different qualifying requirements; find out about those in your state without delay.

Proper releases from subjects being photographed are essential for everyone's protection. For a picture to be reprinted, a release that is signed must accompany each copy print.

Adult Release

In consideration of my engagement as a model, and for other good and valuable consideration herein acknowledged as received, upon the terms hereinafter stated, I hereby grant _____, his legal representatives and assigns, those for whom _____ is acting, and those acting with his authority and permission, the absolute right and permission to copyright and use, re-use and publish, and republish photographic portraits or pictures of me or in which I may be included, in whole or in part, or composite or distorted in character or form, without restriction as to changes or alterations, from time to time, in conjunction with my own or a fictitious name, or reproductions thereof in color or otherwise made through any media at his studios or elsewhere for art, advertising, trade, or any other purpose whatsoever.

I also consent to the use of any printed matter in conjunction therewith.

I hereby waive any right that I may have to inspect or approve the finished product or products or the advertising copy or printed matter that may be used in connection therewith or the use to which it may be applied.

I hereby release, discharge and agree to save harmless _____, his legal representatives or assigns, and all persons acting under his permission or authority or those for whom he is acting, from any liability by virtue of any blurring, distortion, alteration, optical illusion, or use in composite form, whether intentional or otherwise, that may occur or be produced in the taking of said picture or in any subsequent processing thereof, as well as any publication thereof even though it may subject me to ridicule, scandal, reproach, scorn and indignity.

I hereby warrant that I am of full age and have every right to contract in my own name in the above regard. I state further that I have read the above authorization, release and agreement, prior to its execution, and that I am fully familiar with the contents thereof.

Dated: _____

_____

_____

_____
(Address)

_____
(Witness)

Simplified Adult Release

Dated:

For valuable consideration received, I hereby give _____ the absolute and irrevocable right and permission, with respect to the photographs that he has taken of me or in which I may be included with others:

    (a) To copyright the same in his own name or any other name that he may choose.

    (b) To use, re-use, publish and re-publish the same in whole or in part, individually or in conjunction with other photographs, in any medium and for any purpose whatsoever, including (but not by way of limitation) illustration, promotion and advertising and trade, and

    (c) To use my name in connection therewith if he so chooses.

I hereby release and discharge _____ from any and all claims and demands arising out of or in connection with the use of the photographs, including any and all claims for libel.

This authorization and release shall also enure to the benefit of the legal representatives, licensees and assigns of _____ as well as, the person(s) for whom he took the photographs.

I am over the age of twenty-one. I have read the foregoing and fully understand the contents thereof.

_____

_____
Witnessed by:

Minor Release

In consideration of the engagement as a model of the minor named below, and for other good and valuable consideration herein acknowledged as received, upon the terms hereinafter stated, I hereby grant _____, his legal representatives and assigns, those for whom _____ is acting, and those acting with his authority and permission, the absolute right and permisssion to copyright and use, re-use and publish, and republish photographic portraits or pictures of the minor or in which the minor may be included, in whole or in part, or composite or distorted in character or form, without restriction as to changes or alterations from time to time, in conjunction with the minor's own or a fictitious name, or reproductions thereof in color or otherwise made through any media at his studios or elsewhere for art, advertising, trade, or any other purpose whatsoever.

I also consent to the use of any printed matter in conjunction therewith.

I hereby waive any right that I or the minor may have to inspect or approve the finished product or products or the advertising copy or printed matter that may be used in connection therewith or the use to which it may be applied.

I hereby release, discharge and agree to save harmless _____, his legal representatives or assigns, and all persons acting under his permission or authority or those for whom he is acting, from any liability by virtue of any blurring, distortion, alteration, optical illusion, or use in composite form, whether intentional or otherwise, that may occur or be produced in the taking of said picture or in any subsequent processing thereof, as well as any publication thereof even though it may subject the minor to ridicule, scandal, reproach, scorn and indignity.

I hereby warrant that I am of full age and have every right to contract for the minor in the above regard. I state further that I have read the above authorization, release and agreement, prior to its execution, and that I am fully familiar with the contents thereof.

Dated: _____

_____   _____
(Minor's Name)   (Father) (Mother) (Guardian)

_____   _____
(Minor's Address)   (Address)

_____
(Witness)

Development: Cultivating Photographic Models

*H*igh-fashion modeling can be learned in a showroom and later moved onto a runway. Beginners can pick up techniques for TV commercials in a classroom or by doing convention work. But a photographic model must be developed: discovered, professionally packaged, and then promoted. The particulars differ from one model, one agency, one city, one country to another, but the goal is always to be a professional of such distinction that you virtually sell yourself.

Before Gillis McGil, who had been a model herself, opened her agency, Mannequin Models, she tried her hand at molding an uninitiated young girl into a lightly seasoned professional. She succeeded with Barbara Feldon. At that same time, Twiggy was thrust into the limelight by Justin de Villeneuve, Twiggy's boyfriend and mentor. Not everyone admired his tactics, but no one could say they hadn't worked. They were brilliant and bold. All models, whether man, woman, or child, need someone behind them to play star-maker in Justin's audacious style. Twiggy's wonderful one-in-a-million story offers a lesson for every agent with high ambitions.

Twiggy's entry into the business was a hype before she ever started. She was a beauty-salon shampoo girl from London's East End, and too short, five feet six, into the bargain. She only grew to the five feet eight she is today after she became famous. She could never have made it on the strength of her modeling; her look just happened to be right for the sixties—she was very skinny and the miniskirt was in. She was the perfect blend of teenager—with which everyone identified—and poor little Cockney Cinderella. Justin orchestrated it exactly right, turning her into a personality with a big publicity campaign that propelled her into magazines. By the time Twiggy got noticed as a model, she was already phenomenally well known.

BEING DISCOVERED

A model with potential will be found wherever she is—by a school, by walking directly into the right agency, or by being seen by a scout at a contest. Some are headed for other professions and model a while before becoming comediennes, actresses, or pharmacists. Joan Severance got a letter from John Casablancas after he had seen her in an ad. Many a model has been trailed by a photographer; Eileen Ford has been known to stop young women on department-store escalators or in bus-stop shelters. Isabella Rosselini's road to modeling began in New York when she was almost thirty. Her first career was as an Italian TV journalist. Lauren Bacall was introduced to Diana Vreeland and sent immediately to Louise Dahl-Wolfe; both saw her as a natural beauty not to be tampered with. For each great photographic model there has been a moment of discovery, when someone with perception and power saw potential and moved to bring it to fruition.

"Only a chosen few are exposed to fashion at a young age," says Candy Pratts, who didn't settle for sitting in the stock room of Bergdorf's taking inventory. "I went to Catholic high school and wore a blue uniform every day for twelve years. It taught me to appreciate an entrance, the ability to be special and carry an attitude. The technique of styling yourself is something that can be acquired, and must be. Great modeling takes a certain star quality. That comes from refining your look, tapping into a fantasy that takes you the way you should go. Take Suzy Parker. She was of an era when all models were glamorous; she was the *most* glamorous, never seen looking less than the star model she was. Now models show up in sweat pants and transform themselves into Oscar de la Renta runway models. That alone is two roles. When Karen Bjornson came from the Midwest, her look was right for the time and place. It took years to develop it to its peak even with a fine teacher—Halston."

THE EARLY STAGES

The management of a model's career is undertaken by the agent. Agencies devote as much attention to developing new models as they do to guiding the careers of established ones. Many models are totally inexperienced and require closer initial supervision. Others have mastered some basics and may soon move into the cultivation of a steady and growing clientele. No two situations are exactly alike; the agents' experiences equip them to decide with whom and where and how to start.

The time required for development depends on the model. Some go on the market three weeks after having tested with seven photographers. Others take six months; men average a full year. It varies with aptitude, determination, and personality. Agents are most enthusiastic about models with strong drive and initiative. For most, this development process begins when a model is signed and given a rounds list of agency sources to go and see. In a smaller agency, models are expected to make these appointments. That's when drive comes in handy. At larger New York agencies, and in Milan, the booker prearranges a model's early rounds. In Europe, every appointment is for an advertising job or an editorial assignment because of the working structure and pay rate. The development stage ends when a portfolio is ready to be seen by clients, or a model is ready to leave the test board, or the requisite working knowledge has been mastered. But learning never stops for a model.

Larger agencies in the fashion capitals do their developing during the summer months when school is out, or by arranging a trial week during a vacation period. The agency arranges everything from housing and training to testing with experienced photographers. A model can slowly learn her way around, get a feel for the market, visit magazine editors, and see the results of her tests. At the same time, the agency will be determining whether the candidate has serious modeling potential. Some New York agencies make quite elaborate housing arrangements. Elite maintains two apartments with house mothers; Eileen and Jerry Ford groom new models out of their own home; Zoli always provided a room in his house for his models; Kay Mitchell, founder of Legends, has had extra rooms in her apartment. Deborah Turbeville tells a great story of how a Parisian agent ensconced green American girls, often Texans, in palatial rooms to help them put on layers of sophistication quickly. Steve Vannoy makes a high-rise Denver apartment available for visiting models. All this accommodation is worthwhile. Settling in a new city can be traumatic for new arrivals, particularly for those aged sixteen to twenty-one. Agencies can calm parental fears by moving newcomers into apartments to share, or into junior suites in midtown hotels. New models living together can be supports for one another.

Another problem for new models is skin and

weight instability caused by stress and a change of diet. Makeup under hot lights is new and draining; so is a steady diet of fast food at photography studios. An agent cannot send an overwrought or overweight model to visit clients or be tested by photographers. The opposite too can occur: extreme weight loss brought on by homesickness. A qualified agent does his best to see that his young charges eat properly on either side of the scale, and give the same attention to their emotional well-being.

Another important early lesson is the need for discipline. Models must build up confidence while learning to handle rejection. At the start, it is tough to make judgments about oneself. The competition is fierce, so models need an honest perspective about themselves if they are to have a chance for success.

It is never easy for a model to make her own calls, but it is the only way to arrange tests and calls for organizational skills, a well-designed apointment book, and stick-to-itiveness. Debbie Egger was developed into a successful working model by Kim Dawson's agency in Dallas. Debbie found that although setting up appointments was difficult and anxiety producing, it was the only way of making client connections. "At the start of every day I had time set aside for making calls and seeing potential clients. I would force myself to call and see a set number of people per week. When I began to have a busy working schedule, coordinating my time became more difficult.

"Learning to be objective about oneself is another major hurdle. The way you look is not ordinarily a business decision. If it is hard to be sure, ask someone you trust at the agency. The color, length, and texture of one's own hair is not an impersonal matter. Not that there should be board meetings over the color of eye liner, lip gloss, and blush—just some kind of help available."

Here's how Sarah Foley, a booker at Name, describes their procedure for inexperienced models: "The first thing we do is go through a model's book. Usually the portfolio will be too tacky for New York professional people. Too often girls equate more makeup with sophistication or believe cosmetics hide flaws. We get them to wash their faces for starters. Then we clear out their books and send them off on rounds to photographers and magazines. Next comes learning how to dress and how

to buy the right clothes. Clothes for tests are always a problem. Once a book has a few usable pictures, we build from there.

"It's hard work when you're new to ask the right questions and to be open to criticism and change—not so much change as taking steps toward something better. A model must trust the agency from the start. It is usually when a novice realizes that the photographer should be able to fantasize, or knows she must enter like a fashion plate, that she approaches being ready."

Valerie Hamerton won the annual Wilhelmina Pacific Northwest Modeling Contest in 1976. The next year, she flew to New York with the one-thousand-dollar prize ticket and stayed with the head of Willy's women's division, Kay Mitchell (now director of Legends). Valerie hit the streets like everyone else. "I found it too competitive and didn't get more than a half-dozen jobs in the six months, though I did manage to get my portfolio together. Willy kept after me to hold on for another eight or nine months. 'Everything will be fine when your hair grows,' she would tell me. 'You are going to be one of my top money-makers next year. Just stick it out.' But I never seemed to be quite right for New York. The day I decided I just couldn't stay was when another model and I were up for a job, a good-sized one. The photographer called and said that she needed the other model, not me. I went to Kay and asked, 'What's wrong with me?' Kay told me that it was the old song and dance: The other model took the photographer out to dinner the night before the assignment. I really thought those things didn't happen. I couldn't play those kinds of games.

"While I was there I learned to be professional: always on time, good attitude, pleasant to the photographer, client, and crew. I always have what I need. A model, no matter how wonderful or gorgeous, cannot become a prima donna. I learned to project a salable picture with the first professionals I worked with. I came back to Seattle and worked mainly for department stores and ads for daily newspapers and regional magazines. Those contacts have carried through until today. The experience in New York taught me a lesson for a small market: Change your look every few years. It has kept me near the top for the past six years."

Preparing a model for the market entails more than setting up a hair-salon appointment or teaching her how to apply makeup or shape eyebrows.

A photographic model must be developed: discovered, professionally packaged, and then promoted. Every model needs to go through a carefully calculated developmental regime. How this period is handled varies slightly around the country, and in each branch of photographic modeling. Rounds to photographers for tests requires a discipline all its own, and it's hard work to ask questions while being open to constant criticism and change. Often the most difficult lesson is learning to be objective about aspects of oneself. Two hints: Being natural in front of a camera comes with practice; and testing with a good photographer is the best introduction for a neophyte.

Veruschka was often touted as the most beautiful woman in the world by the fashion magazines when she appeared on their pages. Her ability to give a photograph whatever the picture needs comes from a deeper understanding of light and composition, and a lack of ego on the set. She has a reputation of going to any length to help a photographer get what he wants (in this instance, two famous photographers—David Bailey on the ground acting out his role as protagonist in *Blow-Up*, and Bert Stern behind the lens). Eventually Veruschka's modeling career was put aside and replaced by acting and working as a professional photographer, and twelve years later, back from Paris, she is now modeling again. Zoli actually developed Veruschka himself, during the early 1960s.

At the Seattle Models Guild, says Joanne Meyers, "We have small compulsory group meetings and we start with the basics: go-sees, fittings, and so on. Each model has to be individually educated in handling herself with a client. Our instructors are working models who teach novices before they are even ready for tests or for the testing board. Testing—the new model's introduction to photographers—is a constant process until our models are ready. My reputation and the agency's depend on how well my models do and how high their performance levels are. That is why we take the time and care.

"We have a mandatory meeting every two months on areas we feel models are not grasping, or to tell them where they have been fabulous. We bring in professional photographers who are passing through Seattle. We work with models picking out shots from contact sheets, selecting pictures to blow up, deciding what would go best on a composite. It behooves the agent to groom the models the best he possibly can."

Each section of the country, even each city or town, has different testing methods because of variations in film, processing, and darkroom expenses. The cost should not be exorbitant, but photography is costly. An agent will steer the developing model away from undue expense and toward competent, reliable photographers in their region. Wherever there is an active advertising, editorial, or convention industry, an agent should be able to arrange a test quickly and efficiently, if not cost free. Chicago was once an easier place to test than New York because so many photographers were willing. Says David Whitfield of David and Lee, "Now a novice will have to pay one hundred dollars for a test. Photographers don't seem as willing to shoot tests anymore. It has gotten too expensive. It makes breaking into this market something of an investment. When someone is a rookie, though, photographers may want to take a roll before booking a model for an important client. They won't take a chance. If a new model comes to Chicago with a great composite and portfolio, we can go right to work with it—distributing copies and setting up appointments with people. Depending on their strengths, we'll get a new model to fashion, catalog, or beauty clients. Certain clients will be honest with us about whether they will book. If someone wants to see a model with ten pounds less or another hairstyle, we'll note it and send them back at a better time. This way we can tell in two weeks exactly who we've got."

In Columbus, Ohio, even a full-time model works part-time. The business there consists of three department stores, some national catalog-house shootings, and a smattering of advertising agencies. Connie Dease, now a model with David and Lee in Chicago, started in Cleveland before graduating to the next bigger market, Chicago. "Models came in from New York, Chicago, or Toronto; I learned how to sell the clothes by copying the style of imported models. Occasionally I worked with top models. Almost everyone was more than willing to teach me. In a smaller market your booker can make a great difference, especially when clients are looking for something new. The smaller Ohio towns depend on agency connections and models willing to move around. I paid my dues by starting off in malls and auto shows and doing extra work for scale. I moved to Chicago because I like the Midwest and I already had an agency here. At first I came for rounds and commuted back and forth to Cleveland. In Chicago, you are not discovered as you are in New York. It took a while, but I now have clients throughout the Midwest."

"Or a model can get very good training and tear sheets here in Boston," says Copley Plaza director Jo Sommers. "It is like sandlot baseball. They get ready to work with the pros but the pressures are very different. A city like Boston gives a model more time to get her head together. I get them halfway up the ladder. When an out-of-town model is well trained, all New York agencies vie for her contract. A few girls are so ready they can work on accounts here as they prepare for New York. We could always send models to Paris or Milan directly from here. European agents welcome the new, so that's always an option," she concludes.

BECOMING A PROFESSIONAL MODEL

Alberta Tabertzi's stellar ascent to modeling was in New York, but she later returned to her native Rome and photographic stardom. Alberta began inauspiciously. She was discovered in her Italian village

Sports Illustrated

FEBRUARY 4, 1980 $1.25

Islands
in the
Sun

Christie Brinkley
Brightens
The British Virgins

For a young model, New York City is still both Mecca and where the payload lies. Summer vacation is when many agencies conduct crash programs. In a short time it is possible to learn from professionals, put a portfolio together, and assess your chances of a working career. Even if being a bathing-suit model for *Sports Illustrated* isn't a high career priority, mass appeal is the reassurance designers want. Being a runway model requires a photogenic quality when showing a designer's line while the paparazzi is madly snapping away. As Veruschka was in her heyday, so is Christie Brinkley today.

Jerry Ford advises to give it a year or so. "If you find after that your family is still supporting you to keep you in carfare, then start to look for a way out." As for finding the right agent, "Go to the three or four best. If they all turn you down, then you could go to fourteen until someone says, 'I'll make you a model,' but can they? Start by making a list of all the possible agencies."

as she was finishing high school. A photographer needed someone with good legs for modeling shoes and accessories. "The editor looked at me like I was a cow and said, 'Show me your legs.' I went home," recalls Alberta, "and told my mother, 'If they call again, tell them I am not here.' What did I know about American *Vogue?* And besides, there wouldn't be a copy for me to look at in Italy. They kept insisting, so I grudgingly went to work. The pictures were supposed to be little spots, but when the magazine came out they were huge. Diana Vreeland sent for me and I was ushered into her little red office at *Bazaar.* They booked me two days a week for one year solid. I never showed anyone a portfolio. I was pushed to become a model, and *then* I became professional.

"Though I did it later, I can't stress professionalism enough. So much money depends on it, and so many people are involved." Now Italy's most successful female fashion photographer, Alberta understands what is below the busy surface. "A lot of the frantic activity here stems from the idea that a woman is old at twenty-six. It may be ridiculous, but the European modeling market is desperate for new faces, and the competition gets stiffer. Behind all of the glamour is hard work and interpersonal relationships. That requires the physical agility and flexibility of youth.

"Everyone knows what it takes; that's nothing new. The trick is to keep if it you have it. A model is like an athlete. The more you train, the better the practice makes you. You have to study yourself and discover your body's advantages and disadvantages. It's good to read because you will be associating with knowledgeable people."

Haute couture in Europe has its difficulties, but deciding to come to New York, and stay, is a big decision for a young model. For many, its fast-paced life-style is harder to adjust to than the big cities of Europe. Even in very big-time Milan and Paris, the language barrier can be easier to scale than our native high-pressure hurdles. Kathy Ireland is perhaps the quintessential small-town girl become highly qualified model. She had not quite finished Santa Barbara High School, and had gone briefly to modeling school, when a scout from Elite noticed her and asked her if she'd like to go to New York for their summer crash program. "When they first asked me," says Kathy, "I didn't really want to. I had never thought that much about becoming a

model anyway. There weren't many modeling jobs in Santa Barbara. It was more or less something to do after school.

"In New York I did some testing, and had many appointments and interviews. I remember how hot it was and what a mob of girls was at every interview. I met some nice people and some who were not so nice. I did get enough pictures to put together a portfolio, and I learned the most from watching the makeup artists who worked with me on my tests.

"I went back to California to finish my last year of high school. I thought I'd work awhile, and, when I was ready, go back to New York and try again. In January of that year, I went to Elite in Los Angeles and was introduced to a man from Paris who was a stylist/designer. He took my pictures to Europe and later brought me to a photographer friend, Peter Lindbergh." Since graduating from high school, Kathy has been traveling back and forth to and from Europe, spending a week there each time. She has no apartment in New York because in between trips she'd rather go home to California.

"My first day out of high school, Italian *Vogue* and German *Stern* flew me over to Rome for four days, then on to Paris for five, and to Milan for another four. Paris was easy for me because I never stayed more than five days at a time. One hard thing is that usually nobody speaks English on a booking. On my first assignment, a full week, the photographer was German, his assistant was Japanese, the editor was Italian, and the hair and makeup men were French. To make matters worse, some English, Italian, and French words are used interchangeably by everyone. The first day I didn't even realize they were speaking different languages. I don't think I knew what anyone was talking about.

"We were doing the collections and I didn't know one designer's name from the other, or who were good photographers. Of course, I didn't learn to speak all those languages, but I absorbed enough to get along. After eight months I was so used to the international flavor that I could even handle New York."

Joan Severance is from Houston. Like Kathy, her career eventually took her outside her home territory. Joan entered a Clairol-sponsored Long & Silky contest and won—a modeling course, not the stereo she was after. "I was no outgoing cheerleader type. I was into my grades, my room, television, and sleep.

I went to that modeling course twice. It was an eighteen-hour program and I went for two. I learned how to make cheekbones, which I already had, and to display boxes with my hands like on *Let's Make a Deal*. I told my mother I wasn't going anymore, but a woman from the school entered me in a pageant. I wanted no part of a pageant, but I did it anyway and got Fourth Runner-Up and Most Photogenic. It was so embarrassing. In retrospect, I made a total fool out of myself!

"A photographer saw me and took a picture for Saks Fifth Avenue that appeared in the local newspaper. John Casablancas saw it and wrote me a letter: 'I have a famous modeling agency and I would like you to come to Paris. Here's your ticket. Your apartment is waiting for you.' My mother said, 'You're not going to Paris. How do you know he's a real person?' Mother made me write him a letter back saying I was interested in the offer but my mother needs more information. So he sent this elaborate head sheet with Janice Dickinson, Lisa Cooper, and Lisa Taylor. I said to Mom, 'I guess I got to get to Paris'; and the next week I went. Mom made sure it was a round-trip ticket so that if I didn't like even the *airport*, I could come back on the next flight.

"I have always been comfortable with people and made friends easily; when I was a kid we lived all over America and Europe and Africa. I was always leaving friends and houses and getting used to new ones. It wasn't such a drastic change, though if you've grown up in one place I can imagine it would be hard.

"The first eighteen months in Paris I worked for German catalog clients. They paid well but didn't care what I ate or how heavy I got as long as I worked long and hard every day. I got to eat so well (too well!) and worked with Helmut Newton once. But finally I got bored and came home with a marvelous Frenchman, the model Eric Milon, and married him in Texas. Then we came to New York. When I walked into Elite, the bookers all saw me as the catalog type, so I immediately started working for big houses like Vogue-Wright, Pringle and Booth, Chelsea Studios, AGA, Warsaw. I said no three years in a row to Arthur Elgort to do the collections in Rome for American *Vogue*, but by the fourth time I had had enough of catalog exclusively, so I went. That's how my editorial career started. The look the magazines gave me is so

weirded-out, my catalog clients wouldn't have recognized me!"

Carrie Nygren started in Sweden and had worked for all the Swedish magazines for six months before going to Paris, where she worked for a few years before settling in New York. "It is easier to start in Europe because everything is smaller, more familiar, and there is less competition. Scandinavia is a limited market. There is very little work, but people aren't as reluctant to take a chance. I was very lucky in Paris. I arrived there with two Swedish magazine pages; I had never tested. My first job was twenty pages for the collections in French *Vogue*. Guy Bourdin was the photographer. I didn't know who he was. That week I did *Elle* magazine days and French *Vogue* at night. Which meant I was sleeping about three hours in the early morning.

"Though I was only seventeen then, I looked twenty-five. People assumed I was at least twenty because I looked so sophisticated. My agency was excited; they thought I was going to become a star. Guy Bourdin was very special. It seemed to me that he tried to drive his subjects a little insane right before he took their pictures. He didn't talk much to me—but he observed me a lot. It made me feel insecure of course, and nervous. I got so tired from only sleeping three hours a night that after a few days I decided modeling wasn't for me and took the plane back to Stockholm. I didn't tell anyone about it; I just left and Bourdin had a fit.

"When I got back to Sweden I realized it had really been pretty exciting after all, so when the agency asked me to come back I decided to give it another try, and Bourdin booked me again. He said he understood why I left.

"To me there is a big difference between Europe and America. In Europe I did editorial work and was never expected to be perfect. I was overweight, but they liked it. In New York you have to be skinny and have long nails and straight teeth. They retouch pictures here; that's how flawless they like it. I think Europeans think that imperfection is interesting. It's called personality there. The first day of work here I was seven minutes late. It took me a while to iron that habit out, because nobody is on time in Paris. On the other hand, you don't make nearly the money in Europe that you do here. You can do well, but not two or three thousand dollars a day."

In Europe, as in America, being discovered is not

the same for everyone. Elite's Bitten started modeling in Germany and, like Carrie, became a superstar in New York. Bitten was a baby-sitter for a Danish family—the husband a well-known furniture designer and the wife a skiwear designer. There was a Copenhagen Fashion Fair and Bitten took the children there to see their mother during a lunch hour. "I was browsing, just looking through the clothes. I was shy, with long, unkempt hair. There were plenty of genuine fashion models around. Everywhere I went, this photographer kept following me. He asked if I wanted to meet John Casablancas. I said no, I just wanted him to stop. He asked me to do an ad for milk, right then and there. The money was so good I couldn't refuse. He developed the film and the next day I went with him to Hamburg, which is only a few hours by car from Denmark. I didn't bring a suitcase because I didn't plan to stay. All I had was the one milk picture, but Dorothy Parker [of SED Agency] and her partner Sebastian promised I would be making so much money I wouldn't want for anything. They were great supports for me at the beginning, making sure I ate and slept. I lived in a pension for two months. Giorgio Palazzio of Fashion Models heard about me and came up from Milano. He convinced me to come to Italy. I was all of a sudden in Milano and

modeling. I thought the next step would be Paris. I even went there, but I never joined an agency because I decided I didn't like Paris. I went back to Italy. There I met Eileen Ford, who explained the possibilities ahead for me in New York much as Giorgio Palazzio had about Italy. It was at this point, in America, that my career took off. I imagine that's why I love America. Until then modeling was just a day-by-day business to me. In New York it is a career.

"The first day I went to see Condé Nast, Avedon, and Scavullo and got a commercial. The second morning I was on location at five A.M. to start my first booking. I was very nervous and unsure of myself in a foreign country. I was living at Eileen and Jerry Ford's home and had only had a glimpse of New York from the limousine coming in from the airport. So that morning out of a cab hops Joey Mills, the makeup man. He was very good to me; he explained all about the American market. I worked with him the next day for *Mademoiselle*, and every day after that for a year straight. I did a few tests to meet his friends, but I already had a good European book. It turned out I had come to America to follow through on a modeling career that was handed to me. I learned to take it seriously because it is a serious business."

Men at Work: The Male Model's Milieu

A developing male model often runs the same gamut as a woman. He must rely on a mentor, an agency, or perhaps a photographer. The development time varies but will undoubtedly be longer (not to learn but to earn) than for a woman. There is the same market to understand, housing and other basics to arrange, city streets and transportation to navigate. A man too has to learn style and selling, how to test with photographers and behave toward clients. Weight and skin are factors to be dealt with, but cosmetics and the displaying of clothes are nowhere near as complex as they are for a woman. Overall, a man pays about the same kind of dues as a woman, and his going can get just as rough.

Many men photograph well, but male modeling depends more on being a type that is currently in demand. Generally, it is a handsome, naturally rugged type, not too pretty. Hair and eye color don't much matter as long as he fits into a category. The men's divisions of major agencies, like the women's, see hundreds of candidates and pictures every week, but few have the current desired combination of height, size, and look. Clothing is sold on the principle that no matter what the cloth quality or how well made or designed, the product must be perfect in pictures. Men's clothing traditionally categorizes more than women's because it takes a certain type of man to wear a particular style. Use the wrong person and it can throw the entire picture off. You've got to get the face and body structure correct; the smallest nuance can alter the message.

Male fashion photography used to be very stiff, straining to bring out any detail that could be considered unique. Today, that old-fashioned, straight-laced view is loosening up. Male models are no longer mere props or clothes hangers. Nor can they be considered incidental. A cursory look at any issue of the *Women's Fashion of the Times* supplement will show men featured prominently in 50 percent of the ads. A handsome man can exude every bit as much glamour as a gorgeous female. Very few male models, though, have become stars in the same way as women, probably because the variety and the dollar volume of business are smaller. Also, few outstanding men or movie stars come from the ranks of male models. Until recently, would-be actors rarely tried modeling—occasionally TV commercials, but not fashion stills. Women get more exposure too because there are many more women's magazines. Beauty endorsements are exclusively for women. There are liquor, cologne, cigarette, and designer contracts for men, but because it's a smaller pie, the competition is rougher. For all these reasons men are developed and pushed a bit differently from women. They must themselves take control. A man cannot work in a showroom, but he can be picked up by an agency for a university pinup calendar; many men are discovered on beaches. With the women's garment-center designers' move into menswear, the presence of male models on the runway has increased. This provides a fertile training ground for men to acquire polish in wearing, displaying, and selling clothing. An old rule of thumb was that a man with no pictures would take six months or longer to develop. Some men nowadays take off with one or two shots. This is partly because of an increased demand for new faces, male as well as female. But beyond that, men at times just seem to take charge more easily than women.

"If a women is a 'born model,' there will be a place for her in one category or another. Since men are not born models, they have to work harder at kicking off a career." Acclaimed fashion photographer Ara Gallant sums up succinctly the psychological problems for male models: in a word, rejection. "Difficult for women, it goes painfully against the grain for men. It goes completely against male socialization to be rejected on a go-see for not looking right, to be told to put this on or take this off, pose like this or stand like that. Waiting to get picked is too passive for a good-looking, alert man. A man may have to go on rounds and test for months before seeing a penny from modeling. That usually means temporary jobs or other part-time work. Most men drop out before they even get close, because the momentum is tough to build and will die unless it's kept up. Like women, men have a lot to absorb at first, but the process can be much more discouraging for men. Men have to work for every picture.

"After an agency signs a man, he no longer pays outrageously for each test shot, but he still must supply a wardrobe to cover situations, things like shoes, shirts, and blazers. Men are frequently cast to accompany women in fashion shots, so a male model has to be the right height. Aside from problems with sleeve lengths or cuffs, the proportion to a taller-than-average woman will be wrong if he's not. If the model is to bring his own clothes for an ad, he can get away with being slightly under six feet."

Michel Castellano of Elite, a very successful male model and restaurateur in New York, started in Hamburg after meeting a professional model in Milano. Michel learned the value of being adaptable; also, there was an acceptable attitude for a male model much as there is for an advertising account supervisor or a retail salesman. "Male modeling requires that you be low-key, simple and nice to everyone you meet. And you are constantly meeting new people. Being low-key demands intelligence and control.

"I learned what qualities I was capable of showing. It took concentration and practice. At the beginning it is natural to be eager, to want to prove there is more to you than shows on your face. I know now that what really shows 'smarts' is understanding your limitations. The more successful models are not the most perfect but the ones who have learned to compensate for their defects. If this is how you plan to earn your living, the hardest thing to learn is not to be vain and self-centered—two unattractive qualities that the camera can pick up."

MALE STARDOM

Eric Milon must be credited with changing male modeling. His head shot on the cover of *GQ* brought him clients who wanted an unshaven, greasy-haired look, a true break with the image men had previously projected. Men's fashion magazines historically have not sold when male models were on the covers. This negative spawned the man and woman cover, the celebrity actor, director, sportsman, or even socialite cover. Not only did the cover make Eric known overnight, but it happened entirely by chance. "When the choice for the cover was that head shot, it gave me an excuse not to shave in the morning! I was surprised because on location they did the usual shot of a couple for the cover, and only a few rolls were shot of me."

Hathaway
Introduces
Evening Pastels.

"Never wear a white shirt before sundown." proclaimed Hathaway some years ago. However, Our dictum did not mean that you should wear ONLY white shirts after dark. Far from it. A solid color evening shirt can make a refreshing change, as long as it isn't too bold. Hence our introduction of five Maine Line Evening Pastels. (This is Stone Pink.) They are woven exclusively for Hathaway, from the finest Sudanese cotton, by Switzerland's famous Moos Co. (Which explains a price of about $18.00.)

For store names, and free Dictionary of Shirts & Shirtings, write C. F. Hathaway, Waterville, Maine.

A male model's career is now as varied as a woman's. But a man cannot find his niche solely as a fashion model (fitting, showroom, and runway). Therefore, a sense of fashion cannot be acquired as quickly. It takes almost a year to break in, rather than a few months, and the momentum of a male modeling career constantly needs to be reinforced by going on rounds.

While men may not earn as much as women because the volume isn't nearly as big (there are far fewer men at the top of their profession), they can, however, work for a much longer time. Men are no longer cardboard figures standing stiffly and unnaturally in their wrinkle-free suits. David Ogilvy's use of Colin Fox with an eyepatch made advertising history. The Hathaway man campaign, one of the longest-running on Madison Avenue, capitalized on the patch's sense of mystery. Men's basic casting begins with coloring and age. The age categories are young student through first employment, young married, junior executive, successful spouse and father, and contented retiree. Also, a man can break into modeling at any age.

When Eric was in school at the Sorbonne, he had a couple of friends who were models. One was Jerry Hall; through her he met illustrator Antonio Lopez. One day, walking down a Paris street, Antonio and Eric ran into a photographer who was looking for a man to shoot the next day. Antonio suggested Eric. "We did a series of shots for *L'Amour* magazine that were never published," says Eric. "Three days later I got a call from the art director to work with another photographer. This time my pictures got in the magazine. I still wasn't a model, but Antonio took some shots in different situations and that was the beginning of my portfolio. I went to an agency and approached it as I would have any job. Even if you get a little boost at the start, you have to make your own effort to get known by a few key people."

It takes a certain personality to tolerate poking, pampering, and being the focus of attention for unusually long periods of time. Not all men can put up with that. Working in close quarters is another annoying aspect of this business. A man must learn to bear with it if he is to start the ball rolling. His options are few and competition is intense. In New York, there are only one or two magazines in which exposure is valuable. As for the men's clothing industry, "Men don't make the same kind of money as women, because there isn't the activity in menswear that there is in women's." Those are the words of Frances Grill, founder of Click, who has seen the action in the garment center firsthand as a photographer's representative and now as the owner/director of Click in New York. "Another fundamental difference is that women can be manipulated in a variety of ways to project what is wanted. You can change their hair, their makeup, their clothes. A man doesn't have those possibilities. His hair is long or short. It will only grow with time and even then cannot be curled, colored, or coifed. Women are more 'convertible'; they can look different on each magazine page. Clients actually need another man if they want a different look. You don't pluck a man's eyebrows; what you can do is very limited. Whoever is young, new, and special goes to *GQ*. Once men have been seen there five times, they have become 'tired' to the readers.

"One break a man does get: His career will begin later than a woman's but can last much longer. A woman of thirty has been modeling awhile and is starting to get beyond her prime years. Men often age better for the camera. A man, as long as he is progressing and making money, can remain. Why not?"

The ultimate modeling fantasy happened to Vincent Vallarino. He did not have an agent at the time, but he knew Richard Avedon; they had worked together on a "Nastassja Kinski and Snake" poster. Vallarino marketed the idea as an art-photography project. " 'I want to test you for an upcoming campaign, the Dior Family.' When Avedon says that, you don't say, 'Come on, Dick. I don't want my picture taken.' You say what I said: 'Great. You want me to put on a chicken suit too?' " After the initial test, the Dior group tried a WASPy-looking bunch, but went back to André, Kelly, and Vincent. The highly visible campaign ran over six months and, besides being lucrative, it gave Vincent exposure within New York fashion-photography circles. "Now I find," says Vincent, "I am in the same position as any other model: I need to get an agent and start doing rounds."

Matt Norklun at Zoli is best known as the solo figure in every Perry Ellis men's ad. Matt also got into modeling by accident and did things out of the usual order. It was only after his first magazine cover that he signed with an agency. The accident happened while he was working in the Hamptons on Long Island as a lifeguard. He had always been interested in becoming a stunt man, so one day, when he saw some people shooting an ad on the side of the road, he stopped and asked if they knew anyone to contact about stunt work. The photographer's girlfriend asked if she could take his picture and at lunch gave him the names of New York agents and some photographers who would test him. Every agent he saw told him that at six feet four he was too tall. Matt did manage to meet Ken Haak, a photographer known for effective testing of male models. Matt was about to take a boat down to Florida, and Ken asked him not to shave on the trip. Matt came back three weeks later with a scruffy beard and Ken took pictures, which he sent to agencies and magazines. Coincidentally, Matt was invited to a weekend workout with the Professional Stuntman Federation. This started him in that long-desired direction, and he gave up modeling completely. Seven months later, *GQ* was looking through their files and found the picture he had sent. "I didn't know until I got there that they were calling because they needed a substitute," says Matt. "I was used for a group shot on a Shelter Island location spread. I had to kneel down behind the couch because the clothes fit so badly. I then worked a few very small jobs for foreign magazines like Italian and British *Vogue*." That was in June. In July, *GQ* called Matt to go to Sun Valley and he got his first cover. "On the way back, a Zoli model found out I had a cover but no agent, so she suggested that I speak directly to Zoli. I still get blamed for raising the height of male fashion models to over six feet, but what actually did it was Perry Ellis's fascination with designing for elongated men. It was a good thing they wanted a very serious look when I came in. I wore braces that whole year and couldn't smile. My mouth looked like a picket fence."

Todd Bentley has been with Wilhelmina quite a short time. His opener was a calendar he had done for a Jacksonville State University sorority. A cheerleader took the pictures to a local agency and they sent them to Wilhelmina. Dan Deely got interested enough to telephone Todd and invite him up for an interview. Todd Bentley hit New York Monday morning, went to Deely's office that afternoon, and started working on Tuesday morning. "My mom wasn't crazy about my coming to New York until I told her the kind of money models made in ads. Then her attitude changed because there's no way you can earn that kind of money back home in Alabama.

"For the first interview I wore a formal blue suit, but then Dan explained that I should wear jeans to my appointments. I had no clear picture of what I was supposed to be as a model. I did several small jobs, and these gave me the impression that perhaps I could do okay; working successfully with photographers gives you a basis for security. Acclimating myself to New York was kind of tough the first few weeks. I'm not used to traffic and I was always sure I was going to get run over. I walked around a lot at first—it was summer—and before long I bought myself a bicycle to get to photographers' studios.

"Learning to work on professional jobs was easier than I expected. You don't have to worry about anything—clothes, your hair, how it all looks. There are people to deal with that. First I caught some of the lingo. It doesn't all come to you right away. Then I learned to pick up on what the photographer wanted. Once I understood that, I began to relax. There are expressions for editorial, and different

ones for catalog fashion. I watched what photographers asked of others, figuring it would be pretty much the same for me. I studied at home and practiced the same as for any job."

Charlie Haugh, an established model with Elite, remembers well going to agencies like Ford and Wilhelmina. They all told him the same thing: Get a haircut and some pictures. People told him to expect a long time of walking around, doing tests with photographers, and trying to develop a book. After that, maybe he'd make some money. Turned out it wasn't that bad. "I was recommended to a photographer who took some pictures and gave me a little work before I showed my book directly to Zoli. He said, 'Get some clothes and we'll send you out to see photographers.' I still didn't get it, so I said, 'Does this mean I'm with the agency?' And he said, 'Oh, yes.' I was very happy on that subway back to Brooklyn thinking 'I'm going to be a model.' Then, as I tested and got good feedback, I would walk the streets with my book and feel quite proud. You know the feeling: 'Hey, I'm a model.'

"One day I was early for a job and I wasn't feeling too terrific. Ted Dawson was there finishing up a job for Saks, and I started watching him. He was incredible. He had all the moves down, the way he looked, the way he turned, even the way he put his hand in a pocket. After that it was my turn to get up. And I want to tell you I felt uncomfortable. At that stage in my career, to see a Ted Dawson, who was at the height of his career, made me feel mighty insecure. Afterward, when I saw my job and his, I saw the big difference between how the two of us came across. I might have been young and naïve, but I knew there was more to his standing there than simply looking pretty.

"Soon after that I met Tony Spinelli, another successful model, outside Zoli's office. Tony recommended that I go to Europe to develop. I went in and told Zoli. He laughed and said, 'Oh, that's just like Tony, he wants the competition out of town. Stay here awhile.' But I was very close to this French girl, so I followed her to Europe. In Milan, I spent two thousand dollars on clothes and began dudding up for shootings. I walked around very dressed up, always sharp, everything neat, clean, and in place. That lasted about a week. I knew that wasn't me; I only tried to pretend for a while. In the beginning I tended to be quiet and conservative on jobs. Then I decided I'd only continue modeling if I could write my own script and have fun doing it. I couldn't go on conforming my behavior to what I saw others doing. In time, my personality came out. I became adept at taking direction. You can when you're being yourself.

"When I came back to New York, *Seventeen* and *Mademoiselle* would use me to break in new models because younger ones were often uptight. I would talk to them on the set, playfully: 'You got dirty ears,' or 'How about you and me . . .' The editors felt they could depend on me to lighten up pictures. Now I had something to give to a photography session. I quickly picked up on what the photographer needed and I knew no matter what else to always relate to the camera. I would wait for the chance to act and play a character. For example, dressed up in a tuxedo I am different than I am in a suit— I look and am another personality. In a pair of jeans my attitudes and actions are different again. When the photographer catches a part of me in a photograph, there is a feeling of satisfaction and of us having worked together."

Tommy Preston is another model to break the mold. He came to New York after meeting Dan Deely at a convention where he was not even a contestant. The only thing he had to show was a calendar picture of himself in college. Tommy never did a test or editorial pages or work in Europe before being hired to work for Japanese and European designers. His story is a lot like the ones you hear about female superstars, except that Tommy started without development or testing. Dan Deely saw immediately who the right clients might be. Tommy was used and reused within a single month by four different photographers. Tommy's early life had made it easy for him to adapt to new people and circumstances. His father was in the marines, so the family traveled a lot, moving every year or so to a new part of the country, eventually to Africa. During his senior year in high school, the marines moved them to Dallas.

"My friends began to push me to try modeling. My first reaction was embarrassment, but eventually I did go see Kim Dawson. She told me I was too big and didn't look old enough, so I gave it up and went to the University of Hawaii for a year. My sophomore year, at Florida State University, I was on a calendar. I came up to New York and showed my pictures to the agencies. I was told to come back at the end of the school year. During spring break

I went to a modeling convention in Savannah, Georgia, mainly to look at girls. That was where I met Dan. I showed him my two or three pictures and he told me the same thing. When I did get to New York, Wilhelmina sent me over to the photographers who see all their new models.

"Friday of the week I arrived, I did a job for a Japanese designer. That was my first photo session, the only pictures I had done besides the calendar pictures in Florida. I worked again Monday of the next week. The crew and client on the first job were nice and understanding, and they didn't rush me. It went very smoothly and the mood was up. On the second job, for an Italian designer, I learned that clients vary. There was fighting and arguing, and it was highly disorganized. I found I could adapt to the situations and people at hand like I did when we moved around as kids. But if I am genuinely having a good time, it is easier. I worked for Tito Barbieri for British *Vogue* that first month, where I was told to 'Smile and be yourself.' That allowed me to get myself into the picture. I worked with Barry McKinley for French *Vogue* and discovered that big, good photographers are easygoing because they have a solid foundation. Also, that creativity at that level can come without struggling. It's uncomfortable for me not to act naturally, but advertising can require improvisation. I developed some special things that would work for catalog, and once the mood is set I could simply be myself in editorial."

WHAT CLIENTS LOOK FOR IN A MAN

Photogenic for a man means prominent cheekbones and a well-defined jaw line; these give planes for a photographer to light. The nose can be important but matters less than it does for a woman. Skin qualities are a consideration, but often for a picture men apply a light coat of makeup to absorb the light. The physical requirements are a 40 regular suit size, an elongated medium, with slightly broader shoulders. Body proportions are crucial. A man can be longer in the body and shorter in the leg, or the reverse, as long as the clothes will fit with minor alterations. You can do a lot with Nautilus, but a size 44 long can't be crammed into a 40 regular. The right body proportions are flexible, but

The big accounts are for department stores, liquor, cigarettes, and automobiles, along with fashion accounts (manufacturers and catalog houses). Nowadays, men also do ads for hair care, as in this striking shot for Vidal Sassoon (left). Men are used for a variety of business-oriented ads that often cover service industries such as airlines and fast food. The Lord West ad for formal attire (right) shows the male model, supported by a pretty woman, comfortably playing chess.

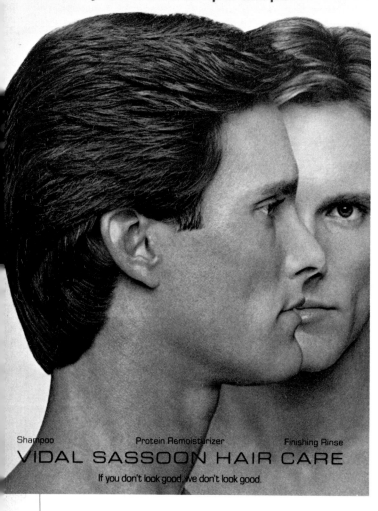

Every day
you have a new opportunity for terrific hair
in just three simple steps.

Shampoo   Protein Remoisturizer   Finishing Rinse

VIDAL SASSOON HAIR CARE

If you don't look good, we don't look good.

YOUR
NIGHT,
YOUR
MOVE.

For 65 years Lord West has tailored a single American-made product...
fine formal attire for discriminating gentlemen. Available at the finest stores.

Dress by Priscilla of Boston

LORD WEST
45 West 18th Street New York, N.Y. 10011
© 1982 Lord West Formalwear

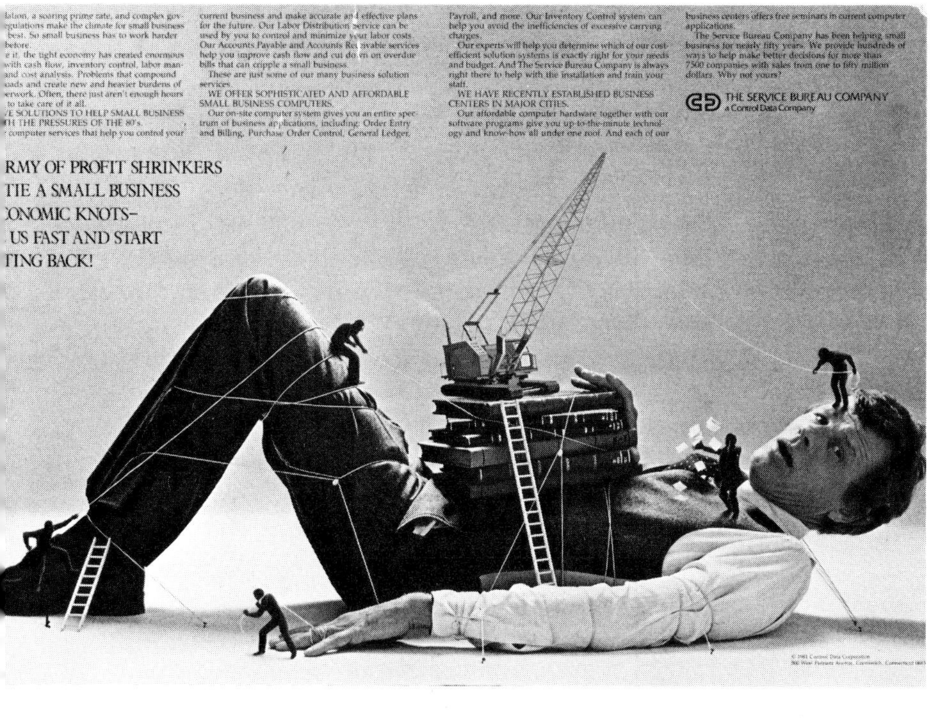

CREST MARK BY CRICKETEER®

1290 Ave. of the Americas, N.Y. 10104 A Subsidiary of Philips-Van Heusen Corp.

IT'S AN UNUSUAL PERSON WHO WOULDN'T HAVE A PROBLEM CHOOSING BETWEEN SONY'S NEW HEADPHONES.

[advertising body text not legible]

SONY
Professional Series

[The lower-left advertisement — partially cut off at the page edge — reads:]

lation, a soaring prime rate, and complex gov-
egulations make the climate for small business
best. So small business has to work harder
before.

if, the tight economy has created enormous
with cash flow, inventory control, labor man-
and cost analysis. Problems that compound
oods and create new and heavier burdens of
erwork. Often, there just aren't enough hours
to take care of it all.

E SOLUTIONS TO HELP SMALL BUSINESS
H THE PRESSURES OF THE 80's.
computer services that help you control your

**RMY OF PROFIT SHRINKERS
TIE A SMALL BUSINESS
ONOMIC KNOTS—
US FAST AND START
TING BACK!**

current business and make accurate and effective plans
for the future. Our Labor Distribution service can be
used by you to control and minimize your labor costs.
Our Accounts Payable and Accounts Receivable services
help you improve cash flow and cut down on overdue
bills that can cripple a small business.

These are just some of our many business solution
services.
    WE OFFER SOPHISTICATED AND AFFORDABLE
SMALL BUSINESS COMPUTERS.
    Our on-site computer system gives you an entire spec-
trum of business applications, including: Order Entry
and Billing, Purchase Order Control, General Ledger,

Payroll, and more. Our Inventory Control system can
help you avoid the inefficiencies of excessive carrying
charges.
    Our experts will help you determine which of our cost-
efficient solution systems is exactly right for your needs
and budget. And The Service Bureau Company is always
right there to help with the installation and train your
staff.
    WE HAVE RECENTLY ESTABLISHED BUSINESS
CENTERS IN MAJOR CITIES.
    Our affordable computer hardware together with our
software programs give you up-to-the-minute technology and know-how all under one roof. And each of our

business centers offers free seminars in current computer
applications.
    The Service Bureau Company has been helping small
business for nearly fifty years. We provide hundreds of
ways to help make better decisions for more than
7500 companies with sales from one to fifty million
dollars. Why not yours?

THE SERVICE BUREAU COMPANY
a Control Data Company

Similar juxtapositioning of a man and a woman can also be used for the traditional business suit ad (upper left). The male fashion image has gone full circle from the Ivy Leaguer in a gray flannel suit to gold chains of the jet setter, then gay and macho to punkster, and back again to a yuppie conservative value structure, which once again brings in a business situation. In the elaborate and unexpected pose for The Service Bureau Company (lower left) a male model is fit to be tied. Again men must fill roles where the requirement is a hard-working man theme.

There are thousands of situations and many more thousands of goods that need a male image for sales. The preparation for a Sony ad (upper right) took many hours more than the actual Art Kane shooting; this is an unusual circumstance for a man. A booking for a man will come in for half the time of a similar assignment for a woman because a quick change is all that is required. Men do not as a rule go through the metamorphosis of a makeup session.

only slightly: a 32 waist, a 10-inch rise (calculated by subtracting the inseam from the outseam), a 40–42 chest (sometimes 38–40, depending on height), a 15 or 15½ neck, a 33 or 34 sleeve, and a height of 6 feet to 6 feet 2 inches. It is almost impossible to achieve that and carry more than 175 pounds.

"Not everyone should be judged the same way. Sometimes acceptance takes awhile, but if we believe in a guy, we keep experimenting and pushing him," says Dan Deely, who scouts potential male models. "A man can wear lifts but he won't work with women. This is a question often asked by shorter men, who will tell the most bold-faced lies about their height. Height limits a male fashion model's income, but depending on the look it may not affect commercial print work at all. There is no end to the automobile, business machine, and illustrative work that can be done for corporate clients.

"Men's basic categories depend on age. A man who ages well can go from a young student through first employment, young married, junior executive, successful spouse and father, and, finally, contented retiree. A man can break in at any age if he fits comfortably into one of these categories. There is more longevity for a man than for a woman. Though women earn more at the top, a successful male model can eventually earn as much. It just takes more time."

It's great to be taken off the beach and put on the pages of *GQ, M, Esquire,* or any of the European men's fashion magazines, but a model must know what he's doing in order to sell clothes. Gay models used to predominate, but straight men have now also joined the ranks. Where modeling for men used to be fairly loose, it has gotten competitive and follows closely behind the women's divisions as very much a business. Ten-years-plus experience has taught Vicky Pribble, executive vice-president and head of the men's division at Zoli, what a male model needs to make it. "There once was a European look and an all-American look. Now anything goes. Clients still call and say they want a 'real'-looking man, but they don't mean anything as narrow as they once did. Models who have good, bright personalities added to their photogenic qualities are the ones that work best. It's no longer just types: All-American is always a winner, but agents don't let their models get pigeonholed anymore. The top people got there because they work hard to main-

tain themselves. This can be a fickle business; one minute you're the golden boy and a year later nobody knows your name. The market has moved drastically toward younger models. A Father's Day department-store insert, for instance, will now depict a twenty-five-year-old dad.

"In 1970, we had to push men to get them into this business. Female models were acceptable but males were seen as second class, as props for females to play off in a catalog or an advertising shot. There was no menswear business to speak of except for stiff-as-cardboard catalog shots and manufacturer ads. Department stores were always big clients in a male model's career, not only for daily newspaper ads but for monthly and seasonal work, which is the mainstay of the male model's world. It is up to each man to show as many different looks as he can on editorial pages. This is where a good model gets across a sense of himself. Editorial pages are good exposure and prestige; they are used to get catalog and advertising work. Advertising agencies take ideas directly from them.

"We start moving with new men right away. As soon as a model arrives in town, we send him over to the catalog studios, production houses, and photographers. A live male-model market flourishes during several critical week-long trade-association shows. We call the people responsible for booking models to set up special appointments for each man, depending on his look. Tall, dark, handsome, and sexy men work for advertising. These men are always stronger in look and usually a little older—in the thirty- to thirty-five-year-old range. Alcoholic beverages and cigarette advertising are big in terms of money. But where an agency will have five to ten women under contract for fragrances or makeup, they only have one man signed up for fragrance."

It took Zoli many years to validate male modeling and get the advertising rate for men and women to match. Now men are paid a rate per photography session and a bonus equal to that every three to six months, depending on usage and time. In commercials, male models are used more often as extras than as principals. Only principals are entitled to residuals. The extras, nonlead players, are paid a daily union wage, never the current $1,000 to $1,500 photographic day rate. Rates are calculated on the amount a model could command for a catalog booking; his editorial rate would be lower and his advertising rate considerably higher, perhaps as much as double or triple his day (catalog) rate.

HANDLING ROUNDS

Mark Ritter at Ford Men was discovered in Phoenix by Helen Rogers's Plaza Three. He represented the school and the agency in the yearly competition at the Waldorf-Astoria in New York before going to Los Angeles to try modeling. If he was serious about it, Mark soon realized, he would have to go to New York City. He was there for seven months. During that time his booker at Zoli sent him to see photographers with whom they thought the possibilities for good communication and rapport were greatest. "I thought to myself, 'That's too limited; there has to be a more efficient way.' The photographers were all in Manhattan, so I decided to contact them methodically, area by area. Starting with studios in the teens and twenties, I knocked on as many doors as I could each day. Next I hit the West Village, then the East Side, and so forth. When I finished covering the city, I would go back and start over again. My objective was to be relaxed and not to offend anyone. I presented my book and gave a little sample of my personality. I felt out each place and either talked or kept my mouth shut, whichever seemed best.

"With this method, there is an element of surprise. I was walking unexpected and unannounced into someone else's world. It was as if when I impressed them enough, I would be invited back. I was there to be judged by two criteria: Am I what they have in mind for what is being done? Second, and really most important, Do they want to work with my personality? It is easier to make someone you like look good through a lens. That's why it's not so much whether I have the right look that makes rounds intimidating. It's having to match a personality and do it with an outwardly 'throwaway' attitude. You can't be impolite; you have to be friendly and casual. If I give the impression that rounds are too important, it makes me look hungry, and that puts people off."

Charles Winslow watches for a reaction when he hands over his portfolio to be looked through on rounds. He was recruited by Elite after his university graduation. Being new at the game, he feels people more experienced than he is are better judges of his qualifications. He has learned that little can be done on a first interview if the person taking the Polaroids is looking for a particular type. "On a general go-see, with no definite purpose, it's best to have few preconceived notions and simply try to leave an impression before the meeting ends. For spot jobs, clients who book models only once a year or every six months, about all you can do is try to ingratiate yourself. It is unlikely, however, that you can do enough to swing a job in your favor until the call-back.

"For long-term clients like department stores or catalog houses, the ones who can make a career, the situation requires honesty: being yourself and selling who you are. I do not come in strong or weak. I say little before they look. I try a 'hello' and a smile as I hand over the pictures. I try to look them in the eye and seem intelligent, personable, and businesslike. If I am asked questions about the pictures, I respond politely and try to continue an exchange of pleasantries. Most of their comments are neutral remarks, compliments, questions about scheduling, or talk about a particular location. My type is simultaneously being sized up. Most of the time the photographer or client looks through the book and says, 'We'll get back to you.' If anything is going to happen, it will within a week."

FOREIGN LEGIONS

Europe is as rich a resource for men as for women. It is here that a man can build a portfolio while adding polish and clients to his credentials. It takes more initiative and self-assurance, and an adventuresome spirit and an entrepreneurial nature, to crisscross the continent seeking possible markets than it does to remain in the big fashion capitals, but it can be rewarding. Many men elect to move to Europe or stay there for extended periods. Because distances between many fashion capitals are comparatively short, there is the possibility of working all over. The independent model can build up a client roster while gaining the experience of working and playing far from his American counterparts.

George Weeks of David and Lee in Chicago had no intention of becoming a fashion model, but he made connections through friends at department stores in Washington, D.C., after college and modeled part-time. Washington's proximity to New York City made it practical for stores to show the top designers. Any company that sells via traveling shows gets to Washington eventually. George had just given up his federal job preparatory to going to New York to give modeling a try. "Just before the move, my agent in Washington stepped in and arranged for me to acquire some polish through Fashion Models in Milan. On my second day I got started for a solid week's booking. I was working for a Japanese company doing a TV commercial being produced by an Italian company. I got a genuine dose of clashing cultures.

"I worked between Milan and Zurich, a four-hour train ride, for seven months. In January I moved on to Paris—Milan is mainly a market for newcomers because there is so much editorial. But great editorial. Your tear sheets have real style. Through Milan, I worked other markets. The agency sent my card around to Hamburg, Munich, Spain, Austria, and London. Every agent has agreements that cover these situations.

"I learned from models I met which agencies and cities I should try and when. I worked all the capitals, and even little cities like Bologna. I did the rounds in each place and established myself so well in some markets that I would get fed into smaller ones nearby. They would call me back if there was some more work, or I would keep in touch with them. There is a different slant in each city. Germany is heavily into catalog. Italy is highly sophisticated, directed toward fashion advertising done directly by departments of the magazines. Paris is a center for fashion and the shows are terrific. Once you know your way around it is very easy to hit them all."

Jay Hemphill met a woman in a Seattle disco who was a successful working model, and she set up some tests for him. Jay followed through and started modeling for a department store. They felt he was wholesome and right for their image and were willing to book him from his home. Jay sat by a swimming pool waiting for the phone to ring. He worked that way for seven months, averaging eight hours a week at $30 an hour. After his reputation was known he was asked for by name and began to pull in $750 a day three days a week. "I was a little homegrown cottage industry; my mother was my answering service. Once I signed with Seattle Models Guild, things did go a lot smoother and less business fell through. Shortly after that, I went to New York for two and a half years and Europe for three and a half. I picked up a slew of agencies across central Europe: Amsterdam, Belgium, Paris, Italy, Austria, three in Spain, and three in Germany. In Paris, and Europe in general, one agent gives your services to another if he can't fill your time. The agencies booked my schedule three months in advance and I worked pretty much every day."

Jay recently returned to Seattle, but he has maintained his European clientele while building a domestic one. His theory is that he can acquire agents from a Seattle base as he once did from Paris and Milan. "The quality of work in Seattle is getting higher. I was booked six days a week in Europe, but taxes are very heavy. Europe has an enormous designer business. A model can have only a few clients because they all advertise at the same time and in similar places and therefore need an unspoken exclusivity on models photographed in their clothes. I got a few lucky breaks. One was a lot of photography for Nino Cerutti, including their one-hundredth anniversary. I do Christian Dior here and abroad. I've raked up six hundred thousand air miles, all paid by clients, over the past few years. If you photograph within a category and get known, you can branch out little by little. I am not alone; it is a growing practice. The key is availability. There is local talent, but professionals will always be flown into towns like San Francisco, Seattle, Chicago, Miami, and even into Europe and Japan. It widens your experience and does great things for your image at home."

Becoming Photogenic:
The Experts
Give Their Advice

During the testing phase of development a model learns to become part of a photograph. A model's most valuable assets, when it comes to being tested, are professional contacts and working relationships—connections not easy to develop and not guaranteed to work when you need them. Competition for a photographer's attention is intense, which is one reason why you want to show pictures. Scheduled appointments may be impossible to keep because of their tight deadlines or last-minute rush work. A good test requires the joint efforts of a lot of specialized talent; no element can safely be neglected, nor can any person's sensitivities. It is often a photographer's assistant who turns out to be influential and helpful later on because he is at the threshold of a career as well. On go-sees for tests, the agency does its best to get the model's foot in the proper doors, but the rest is essentially up to the model.

There are very few ways to shorten this process, but one possibility is something like Patti Hanson's Camp Mo-del or Giorgio Palazzio's scheduled workshop in Chestertown, Maryland. This experienced Milanese agent has brought to-gether on a three-hundred-acre farm all the nec-essary testing ingredients: clothes, makeup and hair stylists, photographers and assistants. His motive in creating this alternative was to cut not only the time but also the usual expenditures for mani-cures, hair and beauty maintenance, health-club membership fees, and such. The costs add up fast, and that's without considering living expenses in Paris, New York, London, or Milan, or money for transportation, makeup, and dressing simply but appropriately for rounds. Agencies give the best tips they can on money management, but few incomes can cover all that, let alone acting or drama classes and exercise or movement lessons—necessities too in their own way.

Some of these workshop programs are care-fully coordinated, take less than two weeks, and are well worth the considerable expense: The model comes away with a series of first-rate professional test shots. While all these workshops are quite ex-pensive, they may vary in quality and it is impor-tant to do some checking before deciding whether the one you're considering is worth its fee: Does the program accept only applicants who are qualified but need pictures to work? Would you get a chance—in a short period of time—to compensate for imperfection? What is the track record of graduates, and which markets are they working in? What direct agency experience has prepared the director and his staff for the job? Can they prove it? Before you decide, sit in on seminars and lectures. Look through any sample portfolios of currently enrolled models. Determine whether it would have to cost more money and take more time to accomplish the same thing in an urban center. Before entering any program, even when you're satisfied that it is good, ask for references and get promises in writing. Check out the organization thoroughly with the Better Business Bureau, local chamber of commerce, local magazines, and modeling agencies and schools, or, even better, ask department stores for information before signing up. With the rarest exceptions, don't pay for anything in advance without getting a receipt, and don't pay for more than a small portion of a program. You can't be too cautious.

There are special lessons to be learned from models like Kim Alexis and Nancy Donahue, who were whisked right to working situations. Each skipped in-agency training or workshop guidance and became photogenic through on-the-job experience only. These two women's physical attributes made them instantaneous successes. Kim Alexis is a top model who won the much-coveted modeling contract with Revlon. She went to modeling school in Buffalo, where she was discovered by John Casablancas. All Kim wanted was extra money while she studied to be a pharmacist, but, she says, "I came to New York two days before my eighteenth birthday. I got photos taken—Mike Reinhardt shot one roll of film. I sat down very self-consciously, not knowing what to do. He said, 'Relax, just sit there,' but you can tell from the look on my face in those pictures that I had no idea what was going on. John had a job for me three days later in Rome.

"My first job was editorial for the Italian collections. They'd ship the clothes over to the magazines as soon as the girls came off the runway. We'd shoot them real fast and get them back to the designers. It was a circus. European collections are always a madhouse. They are never on time, take hours to get ready, then work you to a frenzy until very late—and they don't pay overtime. I thought it was horrible. But you wind up with great tear sheets."

Even after this auspicious beginning, Kim Alexis, who now can ride a limousine to the cream of modeling jobs, came back to do the same dreary New York rounds as everyone else. "I remember myself as being very quiet. I still don't voice my opinion, I listen, largely because I meet so many people with opinions. I was shy and just took everything in. That was my way of learning what was right for me. I didn't want to be swung around in circles. Because I did not test before working, I had to rush to get to the point where all I did was my best, and I didn't worry. I learned to think that I was okay whether they wanted to work with me or not. An ego can take a terrible battering when you're young. When I first walked into Scavullo's, I didn't know whether it was really Francesco or his assistant. They were all sizing me up and giving me the once over. It can be disconcerting. Compliments can also be confusing. I tried to see through it all, good reactions and bad, and focus on reality. My instinct was to listen when I cared about someone. Otherwise, I let it go in one ear and out the other.

"When I go-see clients and it's not just at the photographer's convenience, there's a certain pressure. I know that there is something, some job to be had. Other models are sitting there and no one knows what to do. I usually thought they were all prettier than I was. I was never one to be overconfident and think I was going to walk away with the cover. I have done well, but I don't like being handled and poked or treated impersonally. Sometimes I see the pedestal as a butcher block and I am the piece of meat."

What creates superstar Nancy Donahue's energy is her innate desire to have a good time. It comes across as her photographic personality. "When we work together," says makeup artist George Newell, "we have laughs and carry on. Nancy, like most models, does her best work when the day goes fast. It is important to her to have friends around and to enjoy them. She's never in a bad mood on a set."

Nancy Donahue is from Lowell, Massachusetts. The summer before her senior year at La Salle College, she was a live-in babysitter and would go to the Cape Cod bars at night. She began seeing a bartender who had modeled for *Mademoiselle* the previous winter. When an editor asked if he knew any girls for their college issue, he suggested Nancy. The editor called to invite her for an interview, and she went—she, that is, and two hundred other scared girls. Nancy and ten others were chosen.

From that first issue, Nancy had enough pictures to start a portfolio: the cover and a dozen inside pages. "I signed a contract for ten more covers and was on my way, without ever testing at all. I was lucky and that part was very easy. Of course, I still had to trudge around on go-sees." Nancy tells how awkward she was at the start. "At the time of my first big money job, a catalog booking, I still had no idea of how to make myself up. We went to the location, in New Jersey, in a camper bus, and on the ride out I got a pep talk from one of the stylists. 'I want you to do your hair and makeup really well.' She got me so scared that when we got there I twisted my hair all tight in those pink rollers. It got completely stuck. I couldn't get those things out. Some had to be cut; it was such a mess. The other girls had to do my makeup; I was too nervous to manage it.

"I didn't know how to move either. For the *Mademoiselle* covers, the first photographer actually had to move my head and body himself. Some of those photographers were like fathers to me. They taught me everything, and they didn't try any moves on me. I had to learn by watching, and the more I modeled, the more I learned. I watched other models' facial expressions and how they placed their bodies. You can pick up almost anything if you're observant."

Once basic hair and makeup skills have been mastered, you're ready for the next necessity: learning how to move in front of a camera. First, how to look comfortable and natural; then, how to bring out the personality and animation that translates into the photogenic quality. That first projection is not the ultimate. The better a model becomes, the more facets of a personality can be beamed across to the camera. If a photographer is kind, patient, tolerant, and good at his trade, he may get a picture of a true "comer."

TESTING: DO YOU READ ME?

Listen to Alberta Tabertzi: "As a woman who photographs women, and also an ex-model, working with new models comes naturally to me. I start by explaining that you can't wear a bathing suit the same way you would wear a coat or a dressing gown. You have to dominate and control your body in front of a camera. That means, for instance, that if you raise part of your shoulders, you will look like a midget. If you thrust the shoulders out, it creates something different. I teach them to conceal the worst in themselves, to show what I call a musical side of life and the dress. A model can accomplish this only after learning the personality of the photographer. The more photographers you work with, the better you understand your own face, and that you must not let anyone do whatever they like with it. Also, you learn how to interact properly with light. In short, you learn control. The only way to do this, when you are young, is to look and listen. Study yourself; there is always the possibility of improvement. Or better care. The scrutiny of a camera demands that models take care of themselves."

A test will be good when the model is comfortable with the photographer. Only if communication is free and easy can something new and different come through. The photographer has to start things moving, and each one is different. Some take two rolls, some take two frames. On an organized test, the cost of film, processing, and contact sheets is more often than not complimentary, which is why photographers are selective about the people they will test. Time is money and testing photo sessions are not by their nature ever profitable. If a photographer asks to be paid for the testing above the printing expense, or perhaps to split the film and processing costs, proceed cautiously. Excellent black-and-white prints are reasonable if an assistant or beginning photographer can be found to do the work; however, color is always expensive. It is likely, even with extreme care, that hundreds of dollars will be spent on prints for your portfolio. Therefore, adding on extra and unnecessary photosession fees can make a portfolio prohibitive. Think before you pay. If it becomes your only choice, get bids and estimates from several photographers. Make a final decision only after careful inspection of a photographer's portfolio. Look through that book for exactly the kind of pictures you want taken. Make clear what you expect and that you will pay only on delivery of satisfactory prints or chromes.

Tom Holdrof, Bert Stern's assistant, frequently

tests models who meet his requirements. "Makeup is primary," Tom says. "To do a beauty test with an endless variety of possible shots, such as a head with an earring, a hat with a finger, or a closely cropped wink, you must have a competent makeup artist. They have the full range of products, know how to use them, and are in touch with upcoming trends. Makeup for photography is an art in itself. Photographic lights require makeup totally unlike what anyone would wear on the street. If there's no one to do makeup, go on to another type of shot. If you have a stylist, work with props, accessories, jewelry, clothes, or create moods extemporaneously.

"Then there are body shots, location and product-related tests. As any test approaches becoming a reality, think through what you want to accomplish with this particular photographer, or what will make the pictures more worthwhile. The model's imagination means everything. There are plenty of plain-looking girls who can become extraordinary when the action starts. As a photographer, I take a model's lead, whether she's listening to a record or sitting in front of a mirror. The best test model is one who loves what she sees in her mirror. I don't mean vanity; that's for after work. I mean she *enjoys* the way she looks, and can get excited about it over and over again before a test."

How to work clothes for a catalog shot, or create a comic moment, are the two most exacting pictures. Start off with editorial pictures dependent more on mood; these will work well in a portfolio too. Take your cues from the photographer, listening intently to what he says whenever he goes for his camera and staying alert to his mood. He is your best barometer of what's happening.

"All the credit for discovering my photographic personality belongs to a good and varied group of photographers, from systematic to spontaneous," says John Sommi, one of the hottest young Zoli models. A former bank teller from a New York City suburb, John says, "I feel most at ease with photographers who work in natural light and shadows. I respond automatically to that style. But I've learned to pick up quickly on any style. If a photographer stops to tell me something looks good, I try to hold it or add to whatever he said until I get a signal that he is after something else. It's rhythm, and it helped in learning to adapt that I had had sports training—a team thing where you work together but try to bring in your individual strengths."

People who tell models too often how beautiful or handsome they are do them no favor. The models begin to believe it and think they don't have to put anything into a photograph. Not surprisingly, they get nothing out of it either. Novices, on the other hand, aren't complacent—they're uncomfortable, because it's an unusual situation to be in. That, says Dan Deely at Wilhelmina, has its own adverse effect, and precautions must be taken. "Initially, everybody is nervous and afraid. That's why they look so bad. Human nature reacts strangely to unnatural situations, sometimes very strangely. Beginners are apt to get into weird positions on the assumption that they look good. Changing positions on-camera must be very subtle. If a photographer directs a newcomer to move to the left, inevitably inexperience will motivate the person to do it too quickly. The camera picks up details not seen, or seen differently, by the naked eye. Relating to a camera means looking at it meaningfully, whether the intent is warm and sexy or threatening and domineering. The emotion comes through the eyes. If you just look away without focusing, the photograph will look dull. Find a point off-camera to focus on. If there is no energy or connection, as James Agee put it, 'Whatever is in front of the camera it doesn't like, it takes.' Part of the testing process is going over the bad ones to realize you should do this or be aware of that. When you do this, that happens, so don't do it. Take notes, keeping track of your improvements, and growth will come faster."

What's most important in front of a camera is coming across naturally. A novice has to learn to project appropriate facets of her personality yet not appear self-conscious. How fast an agent promotes a new model depends on how rapidly she gets used to being in the camera's presence. Sarah Foley tells the story of an untrained German model who one day walked into Wilhelmina. She didn't speak much English, but "we sent her off to have some pictures taken. She were all excited because she was so extraordinarily animated. The photographs came back, and she looked ghastly, she looked dead. So I asked another German model to translate to her: 'Think of the camera as alive and pretend it is a person. Move in front of it but don't act scared.' She thought that you had to pose in the old-fashioned way. The translator managed to get through to her that even though it was a still picture, the camera was capable of catching her in motion. When the next tests came back, they were magical. She had her legs in the air, arms outstretched, and was all smiles. She looked a little ungainly, but practice and minor movement instruction takes care of those things. The photographer saw what we saw. All she needed was to have it explained."

"The way I learned to grow in modeling," Valerie Hamerton confides, "was to create tests for myself and to watch other models test to see how they moved. I got valuable kernels of information, like which photographs should make it into a portfolio." Valerie works from San Diego to Alaska but is based in Seattle. Since her return from New York seven years ago, she has maintained her success by what she learned there. "The contacts that I set up when I returned carry on throughout my career, especially in smaller markets. I first learned what to watch out for in black and white before tackling color. Then I noticed nuances of facial expression and gesture and made them mine by practicing. Last comes learning to act or play to the camera. Practice is what made me professional, but it took years to get over the butterflies in front of a camera. I tested with new photographers who were also nervous. We have grown up together and still work for local department stores.

"I learned how pictures were done during my six months in New York. I looked at contact sheets, where you can see one shot right after another, and I began to be able to tell good from bad. When I saw Patti Hanson's contact sheets, the message hit home. Each shot was totally different. First she would be sexy, then mad, angry, shy, coy. All this standing on white no-seam paper wearing the very same clothes. That taught me I could be whatever I wanted to be even in jeans and a T-shirt."

Frank Dwyer is a male character model who photographs as a twenty-eight- to thirty-eight-year-old. He recalls realizing that after a whole year with Funny Face Brigade, "I didn't know enough about getting across the range of my personality. You have to learn to talk with your face, to bring out liveliness and portray realism with gestures. You do this by going into tests with a positive attitude, willing to be open and to listen. The instructions can pave the way to another reaction or a change of emphasis. Some photographers explain exactly what is needed. Others come in and shoot without so much

as a nod. Some are sticklers for precision. But every photographer expects a model to be able to act."

It is helpful to check your pictures periodically for improvement and growth. It takes objectivity to see and admit what is right and wrong, good and bad about yourself. This comes gradually and usually only from talking to or observing experienced people. It also requires a developing sense of clothes: how far a hand can go into a pocket before it creates a bulge, which collars can be rolled with a curled finger, when a sleeve looks best pushed up—and then how far up. Graceful movement takes confidence. Acting, dance, or movement classes help, but each individual must find a personal path to looking loose.

Try to start out your tests with a head shot—one of the hardest shots for a man, perhaps because it requires looking straight into the lens. Many men find such eye-to-eye, almost coquettish, contact with the camera unnatural and difficult to bring off. Frank Dwyer ties such uneasiness to the photographer's role: "The person behind the lens must help make it into a friendly, animate object. Once you like this 'person,' you can show one small aspect of personality or emotion. Toss away your ego; it won't get damaged."

The testing process takes an adventurous spirit and an iron will. And practical things, like enough rest, if possible, before the pictures are taken. Melanie B. Neal of David and Lee in Chicago recalls tiring days of working conventions to pay testing expenses. "It took stamina, an equable temperament, and looking good never mind what. Every chance I got I was out pounding the pavement, trying to build myself a portfolio. I went anywhere anyone would test me. As I made rounds, I started to get feedback—and some understanding of how I was being perceived."

□ Model and Camera: The Need for Mutual Attraction

Models can't begin to be good photographic subjects until they acquire a taste for the process. This can't be rushed or forced and, as in anything new, the initiation is crucial to how long it will take and to the results. Learning to act for the camera is an alternative, but that demands genuine acting tal-

All photographers see differently, so two pictures are never alike. Some shoot fast, some take forever. Professionals rarely waste time or film, so be willing to work hard, on a moment's notice, and to go with whatever direction a test is taking (making sure you get the shot you came for).

A good portfolio is a model's most prized asset. It has to be put together with skill and care. The pictures have to catch the client's attention immediately and then keep his interest whetted until the end. Do not try to use more pictures than necessary to accomplish that objective. The portfolio has to represent a model's facets and talents while convincing the client of her ability to sell his product. "The talent to be photogenic is a magical gift that can't be tampered with. It can't be pushed around, and when charisma is gone—it is gone," says Apollonia, a Zoli model for more than a decade, on being a photographic model. "It

IF ALL THE WORLD WERE

MORE FASHION THAN MONEY

then dressing's a picnic...

shouldn't be questioned or probed, nor intellectualized too much. It is infinitely precious and at a very young age it can be destroyed by the ego."

By having control over her body a model can create different personalities. Every model must learn to give life to a photograph by understanding herself, light, and what to conceal from a camera.

Iman of Elite believes Apollonia's success as a model is due to her "ease in relating to any sort of person and then treating the camera as just any other person but in a working environment." Knowledge about how to move is taught to every model by photographers, who are often like father figures to young models. "I learned by watching facial expressions . . . and even how models placed their bodies," says Nancy Donahue, also of Elite. "Then I'd imitate them." Iman is more direct: "I just faked my way, until I learned for myself."

In the photograph on p. 150, a very early charming yet controlled picture, Apollonia is the most charming element. She radiates carefree, youthful joy. She interacts beautifully with her companion, yet is pleasantly the focal point of the scene. The bottom photograph on p. 151 is in a similar nature setting, again with other people. But here she is more subdued, presenting a quiet and relaxed image. She manages to complement the natural shape of the tree with her own body. In spite of that,

Apollonia still sets the mood and dominates. In the top photograph on p. 151, another outdoor scene, Apollonia assumes an awkward position, holding it with grace and naturalness. Through her expression and in the movement of her right arm, the reader can sense her total concentration on painting a lip. In all three Apollonia is a virtual adolescent. The photograph on p. 152 is a full head shot reminiscent of the Mona Lisa. The drops of water and the pouting mouth suggest the ripe sensuality of youth.

Apollonia Van Ravenstein: "The camera is a cold, precise instrument that is like a voyeur. It is always scrutinizing and will discover anything that is wrong. Therefore it has to be turned into a likable object. A model has to get over this by ignoring the camera and by becoming an exhibitionist. It is difficult for shy people. I enjoy working away from the camera. I like to move, skipping the scrutinizing shots close in near the lens. And, I like the challenge of making a shot look good. I discovered I was good at repetition because of my patience. Also, I like to climb and to use the limits of my body in lively, jumping shots."

If a romance happens, a kind of love growing between model and camera, then projection can be learned. The two photographs on p. 153 are a spread of Apollonia's early European style (around 1969). The latter is schoolgirl sophistication and the former is French country maiden, a delightfully coy soubrette. Apollonia assumes the personality of her folklike outfit.

ent. A camera cannot be fooled. Frances Grill, of Click, discoverer of many superstars, talks about why one model blossoms and another wilts: "There is no big secret to standing in front of a camera. It is not difficult if a romance happens, and that takes time, because there are very few naturals. A kind of love grows between the great models and the camera. For others, this projection from within must be learned. Can love be learned? Yes, if bad experiences don't inhibit or destroy the capacity. It's like a girl who dates and dates and dates, then suddenly falls in love. If she experiences this feeling once, she will want it again and again. Once a model has found true love, the yearning is the same. It is an intangible, but it marks the difference between competent model and star."

Working with very good photographers is what teaches models their trade. Only from someone who understands light can a model learn to appreciate all its facets. After seeing each test's results, notice the choices made by yourself and the photographer. Ask the photographer why he made his. Next, look critically for a movement or gesture, expression or feature, that doesn't work or that looks vapid. Be patient. Professionalism won't happen overnight, only step by step. There will be periods of great growth, and you will see striking differences after a few tests. Watch out for one tremendous pitfall: getting too impressed with a little knowledge. Results must be measured over several weeks or after each month. Keep a record of all the tests, possibly a Polaroid from each shooting for reference. Jot down pointers learned or things to remember. Keep a list of frequent faults and corrective ideas to try. Polish only comes from practice and building a repertoire of solutions to a variety of problems.

Alberta Tabertzi never tried to be pretty, but to give photographers what they wanted. As a model, she worked with the great *Vogue* and *Bazaar* photographers of her day. "You cannot be the same model with Avedon, Hiro, Richardson, or Penn," Alberta emphasizes. "Of course, you are better with one photographer than with another. That is why so many young Americans come to Italy. The problem is that good photographers don't have to do tests. It may be good for the model but so what for the photographer. You must make a photographer want to photograph you. When I scout, if I'm interested, all I ask is 'What are you doing tomor-

row?' It is important to a young photographer's prestige to work with known models. These young photographers are now assistants at established studios. They are the best bet for good tests and a booker can help make contacts there. I know how arduous it is, what tenacity it takes, to be beautiful, fresh, and alive under hot lights. A model must be able too to command respect—never through capricious behavior, which is commanding attention, but by being on time, being serious, and keeping up with the work pace. Try to resist losing patience. The better the photographer, the more difficult we are apt to be. It is never easy, but the harder you try, the better the results will be. It is music to see a beautiful woman move well in a dress! It can't be done with a stupid expression no matter how beautiful the woman. Most of all, become sensitive to light. This is easier for men because they stand up better under any light."

Many models believe in continuous testing, even after they are working regularly. Their reasoning is that you never really know when you're going to get that incredible picture. Everyone can use a new dynamite head shot that will turn clients' heads. At a small job with a photographer, if there is a suitable opportunity, say, "Would you mind popping off a roll?" It takes a little subtlety to imply they shouldn't just knock it off. If the roll works out well, the photographer may see you as right for other jobs. It happens.

The best tests come when a photographer has an interest and specific ideas to suggest. Photographers rarely risk using an untested model on an assignment. If they have a possible job, they will probably want to test. Motivating a photographer to take a test can be trying, making choices can be even more so, and finally getting a suitable portfolio print can be the most exasperating experience of all. But if a photographer seems genuinely interested, control your impatience. Don't procrastinate or wait to see what develops with just one photographer or test. To cope with uneven tests and delays, keep pursuing all the likely photographers. No model can afford to waste time; you should be out testing until you have a client-ready portfolio. The best portfolio is one culled from a series of fifteen to twenty situations. That doesn't mean you must wait until you have the perfect portfolio to get a taste of work. Pick out a likely client for yourself. Direction your tests toward them. What every professional wants to see is that his peers, other professionals, have successfully used you, that it worked out well. Each test can easily say a great deal about you.

YOUR PORTFOLIO: BUILDING ONE THAT WORKS

The portfolio is every model's trustiest ammunition and most powerful armament. Its purpose is to show individual assets. The challenge is assembling a book that "reads," which means deciding what to include, what to leave out, what the total effect should be. There is no set number of necessary pictures. You need only enough for a well-directed impact that says, "Book that model." To capture and hold a prospective client's attention, a portfolio must, first of all, look professional. It must express a distinct photographic personality. Don't go in conflicting directions; rather, reflect different facets of one personality so that the book is smooth and seamless from beginning to end. This means testing for images that are true to yourself in their different ways, then juxtaposing them to establish an intriguing and cohesive flow. One day, to your surprise, you will find the task done. The portfolio will then be ready to catch the discerning eyes of modeling's decision-makers.

Professional means a book that is filled with publishable photographs. Anyone browsing through should assume that each picture has been used in an ad or fashion magazine, because the effect is the same. If you're asked, never lie. People will be more impressed that you have created something so close to the real thing that it has made them ask. Prints are best; those made from black-and-white negatives have better reproduction quality and are cheapest and easiest to obtain. They must be technically professional—no rough prints ever. Color Xerox copies can be effective but are tricky; the composition and mood of the photograph itself must work as a textured matt print. If the photographer or his assistant can't make top-quality prints, send the negative to a good custom darkroom.

Weed out any traces of amateurism. The earmarks of hasty tests are painfully easy to spot. The market dictates what is a good photograph and all models trying to enter it must abide by these standards. Remember that your judges are professional and they expect the same of you. When a book's thrust is hackneyed or nondescript, or the clothes, backgrounds, and situations lackluster, your whole presentation will be dismissed. This is not ruthless. These people are used to performing in an arena where perfection is a watchword. Therefore, to be safe a client must be reassured by seeing a commercial-looking track record—he can't afford to settle for less. You must be more than just another eager amateur looking for a break.

☐ *Showing Your Look Is Pertinent*

Above all, avoid repetition. Fifteen takes from the same session just raises the question, Is this the first and only time you ever modeled? Avoid experiments that aren't reasonably applicable to professional modeling. There are obvious things to get across: presence, versatility, consistency, the ability to sell, and the willingness to do it over again. Show the best you have done, make it look skilled but easy and as though you are having a good time.

Do not include examples of a skill you have not perfected (like illustrating a line of copy, demonstrating products, or improvising sight gags). Be highly critical of *each piece* of work selected, willing to decide against it at any stage. Remember that a picture must be relevant to the modeling category you aspire to. Leave out light studies of wildlife, sunsets, or abstractions if you're after fashion work. Ask yourself, now and again, whether the style you present in your portfolio, however applicable it may be to mass-market advertising, catalog, sales promotion, or retail, is really you. Would the effect on a total stranger be the same as it is on you?

Every photograph must sell something. Commercial print is in many ways the most demanding, because it must fulfill more expectations within a restricted frame. Advertising does not exist in a void; it always appears within the context of its product. Someone close to that context—art director, director, photographer—must respond, and feel that an audience will respond, to the subject of the picture—to you. Study ads and define your own likes and dislikes. Imitating ads helps a model learn to interpret the full scope of an assignment. But add your own touches to it. It is *your* ability that you are projecting.

Whatever a portfolio's aim or content may be, it must stand out. It must show that you are good at presenting merchandise, good enough to compete with other models for assignments. Keep it dignified but not dull. Projecting too bland an image will diminish the dramatic impact and limit the commercial application. A good portfolio hits stylists, casting agents, or editors immediately, for better or worse. Make sure that yours not only represents you, but is you.

□ *Selling Yourself By Portfolio*

The ability to communicate visual ideas is critical, often decisive, in model selection. Portfolios are an art director's means of selling models to a client. The first consideration is type, then technique in projecting that type. What interests a client is interpretative ability, the intelligence and imagination a model brings to an assignment. Models whose portfolios show that they can communicate a message directly, and make a statement creatively, are the chosen ones.

Consistency is another essential quality, but that does not mean monotony. Include work from areas of special interest—any sport or physical capabilities you have mastered, for instance—or areas of specialization, such as legs, hands, hair, or even nails. Take care that those do not detract from your unified impact. A book can show direction, and a range of aptitudes and attitudes as well, but it must be well planned to do so.

Desirability also depends on experience, on enough variety for you to seem eligible for several contexts. Bear in mind that the range clients see in your portfolio is the range they will consider you for. Test in one area until you have enough shots or enough competence to warrant taking on the next. If you think you are better at fashion reportage, or at a stylized studio approach, show this in your portfolio. Show as many sides of yourself, as much versatility, as you feel you can sustain. This makes for a marketable first impression—the impression that you can sell a product through any one of the several personalities your portfolio presents. Stay coherent, but don't stereotype or limit your capabilities. Do justice to each one so that they will add up to a balanced whole.

A great model leaves her ego in the dressing room. Ara Gallant, the renowned beauty expert, feels this ability allows Apollonia to be the versatile model that she is today. Beauty photography requires makeup unlike what anyone would wear on the street. Illustrating comic moments for advertising and catalog fashion shots is most exacting, which is why models start to build their portfolios with editorial-style pictures.

Apollonia's pleasant disposition with photographers, editors, and clients provided her with steady editorial exposure and gave her a deeper respect and understanding of her profession. The photograph above is an extraordinary image of beauty allowing itself to be caught, eager and rushing forward. Barry McKinley captures a cocked head, an open mouth, and raised shoulders, all movement and receptiveness. Throughout a second miniportfolio, Apollonia shows that her focus must be on the clothes she is wearing and making them look good, not making herself the subject of a fashion picture. At the outset of a shooting it is important

to pick up on the photographer's working style. It helps the rhythm to try and hold or replicate anything that a photographer says looks good to him. Learn to adapt.

Apollonia says: "The time, place, and category of assignment are crucial to preparation. I do fashion shots, face shots, body shots—and each in a different character, mood, or location around the world. I must know what I am expected to have 'camera-ready.' If it is a body shot, I have to be clean, with no marks, and legs, arms, and bikini line waxed." Each booking demands a different energy. Remember: The ultimate object is to look natural in the lens.

"If I know the photographer I have an idea of what he expects, his working personality traits. Some photographers always want to do more with a concept, some are concerned only in keeping an account, some of the great photographers are very scared, and then there are photographers who want to create and command the room to do that. First, we must understand each other's signals. Next, it is important to know if the photographer is going to use black and white or color. This will affect the pacing of the booking and the lighting. Inside a studio, if the light needs to be horribly harsh or bright, to search for a better angle will be in vain because movement is limited. Often the picture is not about me being beautifully lit. The subject of a picture [the product] automatically gets the best light. That is a limitation that must be worked around. This is when trust between model and photographer is of utmost importance." One last point Apollonia

explains: "I have found that on black-and-white film the deep contrasts can create a mystery of their own, while color pictures need a focused, simple drama because there are so many competing images in magazines and at stores."

Each shot that is included in the portfolio has to be placed in context to what has already been seen. Ultimately the portfolio should display versatility, aptitude, and range, whether in the studio or on location. Clients remember a portfolio as a whole, as well as individual shots. Every picture must work with and for the others. In the upper left photograph, David Bailey's British *Vogue* demonstrates the strain under which a model must work and another facet of Apollonia's photographic personality. The effect of repeated vertical lines is striking, but to Apollonia, reality is to hold that position under hot studio lights, yet to have a look that remains glamorous for the camera. In the upper right photograph, a location shot on desert sand, Apollonia has the opportunity to display clothes and a pensive mood, and also casually command camera attention.

Because modeling is a youth-oriented business, it happens very quickly. Don't take months to evolve; success for a model comes within six months to a year. During that time you can become an overnight success once you find your niche.

Apollonia, whose body is acknowledged to be unsurpassed, shows her versatility in the commanding photograph on p. 158.

□ *Creating Your Trademark*

A trademark in a portfolio is an attention getter: It could be athletic prowess, a winning smile, or radiant skin. It could also be a quality in each picture that inspires the viewer to want to put you to work. Don't make the mistake of aping what's in when you are getting started. Try to make a statement that hasn't been made often, or ever, before. Piquing someone's interest is easier if you force him to react. Show some wit, even be a bit strange. Models should inject a little of their own humor into their work. It is one of the few things that separates you from other beginners. That may sound presumptuous, but if you believe you can fly, you should make it evident in your portfolio. Casting directors for commercials want you to make a contribution, not merely duplicate what has already been done.

Never think of your portfolio as merely a collection of pictures. They must work together in quality and visual consistency. The effect must be cumulative; an impression can be created by pacing. Arrange your selected shots so that your very best work appears toward the end, creating a strong final impact. The first page, though this may sound contradictory, is also important. A hard-focus head shot, for example, could excite the viewer and move him to look further to see if the same power persists throughout. Many photographers are creative at taking pictures of a face. Go to one. If something dramatic happens when *you* look into *his* camera, that is an invaluable extra. Even if the photograph was an accident that worked, practice doing it again and put it in your portfolio.

If the viewer is going to turn the pages, your pictures must work with and for one another. Avoid complicated, trendy layouts or picture combinations that confuse and conflict. In general, avoid busyness on double-page spreads. Watch out also for distractions, such as overpowering clothing on facing pictures. This undermines you as the subject, and takes the viewer's eye away from the image.

Check the so-called finished product to see: (1) that double-page spreads work harmoniously; (2) that your book isn't overloaded with too many similar poses or shots from the same sitting (the photographs should reinforce, not duplicate, one another; if you can't choose between two almost identical pictures, ask someone whose judgment you trust); (3) most important, that you are not leaving out any images that could sell you into related fields.

It takes diligence and detachment to blend variety into a smooth, even flow. It requires staying long enough in one place to make a point—pictures should not jump aimlessly around from area to area.

Edit out and reposition spreads that jar continuity. Each new page should reinforce what went before and add more information about you. A good portfolio builds to its dramatic shots. Don't change direction abruptly, unless, of course, you wish to draw attention to a particular page. A trick here might be to duplicate an especially impressive picture—not just drop it in, but insert it subtly into the second half of the book. Never repeat any bold gesture—once is enough. Another stopper is a blank page, but be sure to use this device where it works best.

When it is really ready, your portfolio should look sleek, dynamic, and in control. It is never really finished—you change, and so does your book. Refine it in terms of scenarios, short simple stories that will tell new clients, in new categories, what you can do.

☐ *Your Book Is to Be Carried Around*

It is highly unlikely that your portfolio's reception will be affected by its case. Those who select models see so many books they rarely notice the covers. It's what's inside that counts. For your own sake, however, select something manageable and easy to clean. Beware of laminates; however easy their care may be, they are very heavy. Black-and-white photographs, eight by tens or eleven by fourteens, are generally presented and protected behind acetate sheets; color photographs are presented as chromes or as color prints. Don't walk in anywhere with a slide tray; nobody wants to mess with carousels. Slides can easily be seen in the clear sleeves sold at most art supply stores. Select slides carefully, considering them as you would any other pictures. It is tempting to fill up empty spaces, but don't put anything in unless it accomplishes something specific.

☐ *A Portfolio Displays Your Potential*

A model should arrange a portfolio so that it puts her in the maximum number of possible situations. Take a young woman in her early twenties, for example, who still photographs as a teenager, but also as a preppy college student, sophisticated young mother, vamp, and tramp. For every one of these, there should be a different face. If each one is given a bit of a twist, it will get across this model's animation. The range of possibilities is wider for women than for men. Men can't use makeup to get to extremes and create an illusion of change. A woman's portfolio can go from a *Town & Country* cover dripping with glamour to a ten-speed bike action-wear shot with sweatbands on head and wrist to a smiling young executive-mother. A man can't be so many people, but he can show a good smile and vary his attitude and his relationship to products. On the fashion side, a man can show a suit, athletic wear, and traditional sportswear. But those are technical limitations. Photographic ranges vary as widely as human personalities. Happy and carefree, or serious and sensual, the options are endless. Suit your portfolio to a buyer's needs. Naturally a client is impressed with tear sheets, but until you reach that stage, aim for the nicest, simplest, most graphic pictures. Examine tests in context to what has been included before deciding what should be printed and how.

☐ *Your Fashion Portfolio*

A runway model includes many more full-length shots and always has great ones from the shows. A client who opens a portfolio and sees that a model has done Bill Blass and Mary McFadden shows assumes she can probably sell clothes well. Luis Lopez at Mannequin says of the runway model's book: "It has to show versatility, point out any aptitude, whether it be sportswear, furs, swimwear, junior look, or couture. The portfolio has to be built intelligently, with each look selected to fit the model's personality, or age, or style. If a seventeen-year-old comes in with a book that shows her in a Halston evening gown and looking like she's dressed up in her mother's clothes—or the opposite, a look that is very severe—no matter how extraordinarily beautiful the shot is, it must work for the model. It is very difficult to make it come off just right.

"The main purpose of an elaborate fashion show, remember, is publicity, so the designer wants a model who helps to generate it. It comes down to how well models photograph, because the shows aren't being done only for an elite clientele, but for store buyers, magazine editors, and press photographers. Now, every great print model needn't be a

S aving the last dance, a serenade of scallops syncopated with bugle beads. The empire-bodiced gown and cape-
let is Alfred Bosand's extravagance in apricot or pale green, $1055. Exclusively ours, Evening Collections.

Maintaining a photographic modeling career takes choosing the right editorial assignments, developing skills for catalog, or creating a range of types for advertising and commercials. The physical and emotional preparation for editorial, catalog, and advertising are different. Each has its own pacing and stress factors. There is also a different energy required for each type of booking. This is one reason a booker mixes clients over each week or over a month. "On editorial sittings there are only going to be three or four pictures each day," Apollonia says. "I conserve myself because I will have to wait a long time between each picture. I will also need to give my all for fifteen to thirty minutes to get each shot right. The energy to do up to twenty shots in a day for catalog is intense; there will be no relaxing. I will also do my own makeup and hair. Unless an advertising booking is for cosmetics, I will arrive half an hour early with all the basics, including foundation on, eyes painted, hair ready to be combed out; in short, prepared. Then I have to transform myself throughout the day with hair tricks, makeup retouches, and lipstick colors, manufacturing continuous variety. When a professional beauty stylist will be on the set, then I come in with clean face and hair, but I must be prepared for the two- or three-hour process to be camera-ready."

Once her reputation is in place, Apollonia can open her third presentation with drama. In the photograph on the left, Deborah Turbeville, for Saks Fifth Avenue's fiftieth anniversary campaign in 1975, shows Apollonia as the grande dame acknowledging admiration—basking in the shaft of light. She lifts her palms to reflect the glow. This ad demonstrates a mood and style—the Belle Epoque.

Think of your portfolio as more than an assembled group of pictures. They must work together, even in quality and visual consistency. The effect must be cumulative, an impression created by pacing. Therefore, a facing shot that reaffirms the luxury of the Belle Epoque might make the attention-catching fur picture at the top of this page just right. The initial beat, though this may sound contradictory, is also important. It is possible by placing equal-size or equal-graphic shots together as well. In the Bali photograph, endorsements for the corporate world, the quintessential advertisement—here an ad for fashion magazines—she presents yet another facet of her photographic personality: the hot Polynesian-like look. The photograph on p. 162 confirms the versatility of Apollonia; while a hard-focus head shot, it excites the viewer and motivates him to look further to see if the same power persists throughout. Arrange your selected shots so that the final and most lasting impact is strong. The last photograph here certainly does that.

A portfolio need not be arranged in clusters—all the best ones together. Make your book flow evenly and tell a story about you. This will bring the reader to the end: Quickly start a beat, then three-quarters through have another beat. This way the last three or four pages can still pack a wallop. If all you have is four good pictures, that's enough. Don't fill up the pages just to have a book that is full.

vive l'ampleur!

great show model, but being able to get from one end of the runway to the other *and* look terrific for the camera—you can't beat that. Any runway model who follows a great print model had better be just as photogenic and famous in her own right. That's what makes a runway model's portfolio so important."

"The portfolio can be the ultimate sales instrument, more effective than the model," says Marjorie Graham, who got her job-training from Zoli himself. She worked by his side, as an art director, arranging and keeping portfolios in prime selling condition. Here is what she says about the importance of pictures: "There are models who sell themselves to a lot of clients but still don't have a dynamite portfolio. Catalog models, for instance, are in front of a camera all week long and never put pictures in a book. You get catalog work from reaction to a go-see and from a reputation. But you still need to tell an aesthetically appealing story. Models tend to arrange their pictures in clusters—all the best ones in the front and the rest of the book painful to look at. A book has to flow along evenly to tell a story. You need to make the art director look through the whole book, not blow him out in the first three pages. Then three quarters of the way through there has to be yet another beat. This way the last three or four pages can still pack a punch. Ten good pictures will do it. I never put any stock in the quantity theory. Too many models have an obsession: 'I'll put anything in my book until it's full.' If you have four really fab pix, that's all you need. That will make enough of an impression.

"For a salable fashion book it's axiomatic that you give the client as much information as possible. A portfolio should therefore open with a head shot. Then two great fashion shots, and it should continue with fashion. If you have six or eight magazine pages, pick the four best and place them after the head shot. This gives you pacing and gets a story going. Then another fashion spread or a single fashion shot from a different shoot. If a model has a great body, that may be next. A woman could have a double-page body, a man an off-beat moody editorial shot. If there are any casual shots, outdoor fashion or beauty, that comes next. Head shots should be used to break up the book throughout. Never go from a big figure to a little figure. Those things should be done gently. Never use a picture that shows you as a small part of the action. I'm

So little can say so much. Contrasting down-to-earth elegance with sultry exoticism leaves any prospective client with the assurance that Apollonia is the supreme mistress of her craft. The photograph on p. 162, and many like it, can be reemphasized with a blank sheet opposite to give its statement space.

Edit out or reposition pictures that interrupt continuity or are jarring in any way. Each new page should reinforce what went before and confirm the initial reaction. A good portfolio builds to its climax. Put yourself in the client's shoes. Would you prefer to see something stimulating and out of the ordinary? Give clients what they need and they might think about you seriously.

not high on doubles unless the person whose book it is is, without question, in front and flawless. Get clients to admit that they can't see anything wrong with the book, and therefore the model, for beauty, retail, catalog, or editorial. Accentuate the positive and use nothing that's in between."

Pacing pictures means having them complement one another. Some color photographs are so strong that nothing works next to them. Then leave the page opposite blank or try a black and white. You don't have to fill every consecutive page. The finesse of relating black and white and color photographs can be learned. It takes time to work everything in properly, but the golden rule is: If it works, use it.

☐ *The Composite: Capsule of Your Abilities*

Anybody salable can be sold photographically from a composite. It is an important instrument for conventions, commercial print work, and TV commercials, as well as for fashion modeling. Its object is always to present the model as photogenic. Clients and photographers know most of the top models, but composites introduce new ones all across the country.

A composite tries to give a clear and complete idea of what the model can do, so that whoever looks at it will know what they can expect. It is like buying from a catalog, except that the composite aims to get across a personalized view. A woman needs a body shot featuring legs or any other particularly good feature, including excellent hair, or fine feet for displaying shoes. It is also important to display range, from sophisticated beauty to young junior. A man's composite will have an alive, sparkling head shot and a three-quarter or full-length shot, and should demonstrate versatility and range. Obviously, drawbacks are to be downplayed. A composite consists of approximately five pictures.

In form, the composite is a card measuring approximately nine inches by six inches, usually printed on both sides in black and white, but it can be partly in color. Its purpose is to show a model's possibilities so that photographs can be chosen to show a variety of the looks and the abilities she has to offer, such as parallel bars, horseback riding, or even magazine covers. Easily and inexpensively distributed, it is the world wide working résumé.

Over a twenty-three-year period, Peter Marlowe has cornered the world market in composites. As a student he lived with a top London model, and it became his responsibility to go around to the photographers' studios to order copies from the assistants (they earned extra money selling prints). The models would write their names and measurements on the back and give them out, hoping to get bookings. "I got so tired of going around picking up prints that I decided I'd put them together and design a nice layout for a present. I got a printer to run it off so I would never have to look at that problem again. When all her girlfriends saw the reaction, I was in a reverse fix. Now I had a stream of models knocking at my door. They wanted me to design comps, discuss the photographs with them, and talk to the printers." Peter handles five thousand models' composites now. "The rule for fashion," he advises, "is to put in as many good pictures as you want, but not one bad one. It can go to a six-page pamphlet. But that is only necessary in special cases; otherwise it need not go beyond eight photographs and two sides."

Very often the composite is sent on picture submissions, a precasting step that ensures all the right potential models are seen during the go-see but inappropriate people don't waste their time. Or sometimes clients coming to town will ask to see composites of the agency's roster. When an out-of-town client is coming to New Orleans, Dolly-Dean Martinez of Artists Representatives sends composites of convention demonstrators for him to preview. "They select a few to interview and see the rest of their portfolios when they arrive in town. Actors mainly use head shots, but models have specially developed composites, a kind of synopsis of their book. The convention composite consists of a head shot, a body shot, and a product-demonstration picture with full view of the model's hands. At least one of the pictures has to show a serious facial expression."

In advertising jargon, *look* means type. The object of a commercial-print composite is to show as many looks as possible. Says Wally of Wallace Rogers, "Big-time national advertisers look for honest pictures, no surprises. The agencies want clients to feel confident that the person can do the job. If a man looks like Tyrone Power in some shots, Wallace Beery in others, and Jackie Cooper in some more, he would be eliminated. It's just too confus-

TWIGGY

The female model above has one of the best-remembered faces of the century. It took a mentor/boyfriend, Justine de Villenueve, to engineer the phenomenal rise of Twiggy. Notice that her height when she began was less than the normal five feet eight. Twiggy grew her last two inches after Barry Lategan took these memorable composite shots. Within its simple and pleasing design are all the elements a novice would want to show. A full-figure picture, one closeup head shot, and an arresting studio portrait demonstrating Twiggy's allure. Contrasting Twiggy is Bill Sanford, who sought out a local Florida photographer to take his composite pictures after a high-school acting teacher recommended modeling. As with Twiggy's composite, there is enough to interest the powers that be about this young novice. Bill was invited to give New York and Europe a try by Elite when they received this card from their Miami office. Bill's first composite, like Twiggy's, consists of three shots: a full-face head, a slight profile, and one full-length body shot. Any effective composite must subtly hint at an instinct to carry fashion well.

Bill Sanford

Height 6'1" Weight 165 Hair Blond Eyes Blue Suit 40 R

ing trying to figure out what he really looks like. What they want to see is the same recognizable person in different situations: for instance, the all-American guy with his child on his knee or at a restaurant having a candle-lit dinner with his wife. Or this same man canoeing or hiking in the woods, smoking a cigarette and wearing blue jeans, work boots, and a big plaid shirt. It is very easy to imagine this outdoorsy type in a business suit for insurance, computer, or office situations. Then the romantic thing or a shot in a bathing suit for an airline or some resort ad. Relating to a child is always a plus. The photographer will want to see this man because he knows who will walk in."

A look is also something clients can identify with strongly. It can personify what they want for their product, express trust, and relate comfortably to it. They want reassurance that the person can epitomize the general market as a consumer. Aim to give the client confidence, to show unmistakably that you'll fill the bill. Often idealized situations read best at a quick glance, which is mostly what a composite gets.

A great portfolio can be a ticket to TV commercials, but the head shot is the main reference when it comes time for consideration. Whenever an art director brings up a possible choice to a client for debate, a head shot or composite is the picture he'll be holding up. The right eight-by-ten glossy is a major step in the transition from still modeling to TV commercials. Aside from straight beauty or grooming accounts, a head shot must show, feature by feature, exactly how you look. It is your smile that gets across your look and persona. The sparkle or warmth or whatever is in it must be conveyed in that one all-important shot. Maureen Malone of Funny Face describes how it should be composed: "The head shot should be better than very good, and the back should function as a résumé of commercials. If a model is thirtyish, attractive, and all-American, I would suggest shots appropriate to portrayal of a doctor, businessman, or family man, and recommend him for these types. It shouldn't just be a blank head shot of someone in a suit with the impression of potential left in limbo."

Go-See:
Pros Get Called Back
or Auditioned

◆

*N*o matter how highly qualified the model, the best way to get a job is to walk through the doorway looking right for it. If the product is chocolate pudding or sportswear, don't come in looking sexy. Usually there will be someone among the first six candidates who meets the minimum basic requirements. That person sets the standard that others compete against: That's why it's smart to be early for general go-sees (called, with good reason, cattle-calls). Only experience can prepare a model to audition for specialty modeling, especially commercials and conventions. Fashion work very often means seeing the designer himself; in the large fashion houses it will be a showroom supervisor or, when runway shows travel across the country, a representative of the manufacturer. When it's a photographic assignment, the photographer, his assistant, or a stylist usually selects the models they want to see from agency promotion pictures (composites) and recommendations. For commercial print campaigns, the advertising agency is likely to request the photographer's studio to assemble a file. This is when it is valuable to have a good head shot to leave behind and imperative to shine in Pola-

roids. Help any interviewer to get a sense of your capabilities—don't leave it up to the imagination. A good photographer wants to find out, at the go-see, what you can deliver. This way he knows what to expect and whether he can count on rapport and teamwork. That knowledge is what interviewers want in advance in every field of modeling.

Free-lance modeling means consistently going out for go-sees. You have a portfolio as a résumé of your experience, but there's no sales substitute for yourself. Every adult working career is bound to involve several dozen job interviews. As a model when you get a job, it is only a brief reprieve from making more cold calls. A call-back, though encouraging, is just one more interview along the way to a booking. Acclimate yourself to a world of endless go-sees, where everyone there is after the same job. "Cattle calls are the pits," says Kim Coleman of the Kim Dawson Agency in Dallas. "But they do bring you together with your peers. Once you get over staring at your competition, you can relax and start to interact. It can be good to talk over common situations with other models. Every day has its gaps, where all you can do is wait your turn and catch up on things you've brought along, like letters or reading." Kim sees go-sees as chemistry. "If the chemistry isn't right, you could tie yourself in a knot and still not get the job. You can't be everything to everybody; all you can do is try to be right for the majority."

Screening by picture submissions is far easier on the model because it leads to more specific invitations to go-sees. Also, it increases your chances by narrowing the competition. But any model should welcome all opportunities to be seen, no matter how large a call. Whatever the situation, go in the proper attire; it is your best insurance for being thought right. Plan for the appointment by asking the booker whether it is a general go-see. Before you go, find out who you'll be speaking with and what their function or position is. Learn what you can about the product or assignment. Try to arrive early enough to prepare yourself calmly instead of hurriedly. Review any points you want to get across. Finally, make sure your portfolio and composite are in shape and at hand.

"We often go crazy with go-sees because of the constant changing and juggling of schedules," says Luis Lopez, booker at Mannequin. "As an agent, I go to the shows to keep abreast of the clothes. It gives me the best clues about who to send to each client. The fashion market is small enough, even in New York, for us to know the reason behind the go-sees. Also, they'll tell you exactly what they *don't* want—things like sizes, height, hair color. There are always last minute go-sees before a collection is shown, for the models coming back from Paris and Milan—people designers want to see again even if they have used them before. They may have changed their look or their hairstyle, perhaps gained weight so they won't fit the clothes exactly. Or a designer may be worried because he cut the clothes smaller or larger."

It can help a rank beginner, when she's first exposed to clients, to be armed with some information. But there is really no technique or formula that assures success or foretells the direction it may take. "Sometimes you can tell very quickly, though, by the response," says Gillis McGill, owner of Mannequin. "About seven years ago there was a Screen Actors Guild strike. We got many calls from local casting directors, and I sent Alana Davis out on three. She got call-backs on every one. Unfortunately, she couldn't go to the return calls because she was away on vacation. The moment she got back, I called her and said we had to have a talk—I thought I saw an entirely different career for her. It is most unusual to get three call-backs on three calls.

"It turned out that Alana was a natural at acting. She had never studied, but she was able to 'cold read' scripts beautifully. It came as a big surprise to her. She continued her fashion modeling for five more years—until she moved into a spot on the *Today* show."

Lynn Yeager is a Mannequin model who got so good at scheduling herself that she could line up future free-lance assignments while she was working on a current one. She has some good advice about accumulating clients along New York's Fashion Avenue: "I learned never to go-see designers in jeans and sneakers. They would worry that I looked too young to bring off a twenty-thousand-dollar dress. Also, the personality has to be strong but not overbearing—just enough so that they remember they liked you. It's not enough simply to go in looking the part. You have to project enough of a *sense* of the part that they don't forget you. It comes down to understanding what shouldn't be faked and what needs a little drama for the benefit of clothes. What's worse is being remembered as a blonde or a brunette and not as Lynn Yeager. Never mind that they've seen my book or me. Now I am selling myself; how well I do depends on how I strike that person. It is always different; I never know how until I am there. I try to establish a rapport, find some common ground with the client. Otherwise I am just sticking my face in the door and saying, 'What about me?' "

DISPLAYING ABILITY

It was at an International Modeling Association of America annual convention in New York's Waldorf-Astoria that Marjorie Graham met the over-all contest winner, Keith Mitchell. As she saw it, the eighteen-year-old won for the same reason that certain models land jobs. It's not how they look that does it; it's the way they make the room literally light up. "You are almost overwhelmed by the energy Keith projects," says Marjorie. "His magic was that he knew what to do in front of an audience. At the convention, which is like an overgrown go-see, he didn't do what was expected or what was taught at school. He walked right to the end of the runway and stared at those judges, and then he walked right back off. Helen Murray and I, both experienced judges . . . we'd never seen an audience captivated that way at one of these events.

"Next evening, at the commercial audition, Keith again went beyond the ordinary. In one task, thirty seconds of a jean commercial, he outdid the current Avedon campaign for Calvin Klein. An exhibition of bathing suits put him in first place. Faced with the 'active' competition of seventy-five muscle flexers, Keith decided his best play was to stand still, merely touching and caressing his body to the beat of the music. These gestures were sensuous, but discreet and underplayed, which allowed him to get away with it. Keith Mitchell took a chance and won." At a go-see, just as in a contest, a model has a moment in which to sparkle. Your best bet is to play it according to your own style.

David Rosenweig, of Perry Ellis's men's division, is always on the lookout around the country for male models he could use for informal and runway shows. "I try to duplicate the feeling Matt Norklun brings out in the national advertising campaign with the local talent that turns up on the go-see. If a man walks in knowing the name, that's a good sign that he may be able to handle Perry's line. Then I watch how he moves, notice the way a man puts on the jacket. Next comes the question of fitting the garments. Carriage is vitally important—it gives a sense of proportion and an air of style. All of it counts. I don't choreograph a fitting. What I do is look for an attitude of support in displaying the Perry Ellis men's line. Here is a tip: I always look at a model's shoes. It doesn't matter so much what kind of clothes a man wears as long as he wears shoes that correspond with each look. When a model's shoes are right, I know he has a sense of clothes. A small point maybe, but it makes an impression."

FIRST AND FOREMOST, SELL YOURSELF

Ultimately, a model's job is to sell the product, but that is only the last link in a long selling chain. Your immediate aim is to make the photographer look

always had an edge the competition.

He knows how to wear his diamonds.

Your jeweler can show you other exciting trends in men's diamonds starting at about $600. The ring shown is available for about $950. Prices may var

A diamond is forever. De Bee

Accessories make pictures more interesting when used right. Every client must be sure that you are the best person suited to his needs in order to book you for his job. No matter how qualified the others are, the model who first walks through the door looking right has the best chance. It's smart to be early. That person will set the standard to which everyone after him is compared. A head shot, like the above, is valuable to leave behind, but a most important ability is to take good Polaroids at general cattle calls. Before each appointment, find out who you'll be speaking to, his or her position, and as much about the product or assignment as possible. Give yourself enough time to arrive and prepare calmly. Show what you could deliver for them. Try to stick in the interviewer's mind for being right and not for any wrong reasons. Before leaving, get across any last point to be remembered by. Finally, exit gracefully, making sure to leave a composite behind.

good. If *he* succeeds, it makes the art director look good, and he does the same for the client. If it's a small campaign, the photographer will choose the model. For a bigger assignment, he will select a half-dozen possibilities and submit them to the advertising agency for a decision by the art director. If there is a favorite, that will be discussed by phone or at a meeting. When the job is really big, the art director will put various agency people on it. If the model is to become a spokesperson for the product or on commercials, the client will more than likely be in on the selection.

Go-sees are nobody's idea of fun, but they have to be done because they get you where you want to be: in front of a photographer, on a one-to-one basis, where he can talk to you and study your features, your personality. Of all the possible results of that interview, immediate rapport is the most important. Sometimes there is more rapport than you realize, though not necessarily immediate. Take the experience of George Weeks, a model in Chicago, where the most famous photographer is Victor Skrebneski. When Skrebneski asks for one of his rare go-sees, it's by far the biggest catch in town. When his chance came, George thought, "I would rearrange my book, wear great clothes, do a real song and dance for Victor. It is tough to arrange a go-see because he is so busy, but my appointment finally arrived. I put on my best duds, got my face well scrubbed and hair slicked back. When I got to the reception area—which felt like an inner sanctum—out walked the studio manager. He takes your book into the studio—alone. I never even got a glimpse of Victor; all he sees is the portfolio. If you are right for him, Victor will come out to speak to you. I went through this process several times, and no Victor. Nothing but 'Thank you, we'll call if we are interested.'

"One day I was at the beach, unshaven and covered with suntan oil. For no special reason I stopped by the agency late in the afternoon, and what do you know? The greeting I got was, 'Where have you been, we've been looking all over for you! They would like to see you again over at Skrebneski's.' I said, 'Ye gads! I'll have to go home and shower, shave, wash my hair!' 'You don't have time, go just as you are!' I felt ridiculous, but I went. The studio manager took my book as usual, but this time, after ten minutes, Victor came out." George had laid the foundation on his previous visits.

A book can be an excellent selling tool *if* it's right for the purpose; very rarely does this happen in catalog. Bob Manella shoots every day as a free-lancer for New York catalog houses. As he sees it, "Too many models come in for a catalog go-see with a portfolio that shows great European fashions and locations. That's fine, but not for me." As photographer, he makes decisions, with the client coordinator, on modeling assignments. "I have to know that the model can sell clothes. Top editorial models work well because they project themselves in a natural way. Another thing: Catalog models have to know how to do their own hair and makeup. If a model's hair and makeup are not right at the go-see, I will ask her if she's willing to test to make sure she can do makeup properly for the camera. Catalog's demanding too. You have to go through up to twenty-three shots in a day. On the go-see show me you can keep up that energy level no matter what."

Attitudes matter a lot. Sometimes it's better to think, "I'm probably not going to get this job." Then when you do you can get genuinely excited. Never forget that the selection process is very impersonal and should be kept that way. Be positive but never overconfident about the possibilities. You won't get far projecting, "I am the only one you should choose for this job." You don't want to be too strong or too weak. If you've done editorial work, you'll be more recognizable on go-sees, which is an advantage. Even so, expect to be told to "stand here," "look right," "say this," and to settle for a "thank you" and "good-bye." If they like you, you'll get called back. The first time was just for a look; the second time around is when you speak to the client.

Vicky Pribble, vice-president and head of Zoli's men's division, has been a major force in transforming men's modeling into a high-powered business. "After a model has tested and has started his book, we set up five go-sees for each man each day. It is the bookers who set up the appointments for a photographer's rounds and client go-sees. We call photographers, magazines, advertising agencies and say we've got Mr. New-Guy-in-Town. Each agency knows who to call for their type. They trust us to send them the right talent. We know the market that models will be going to. I know our clients and respect their attitudes. Our job is to match client and model successfully. It's sales by telephone and a follow-up.

"There are request go-sees for specific models, and most calls are for specific assignments, say a liquor or hotel ad. The calls sound like this: 'I want a twenty-six- to thirty-year-old, all-American, macho, not ethnic.' We make our suggestions from there. That is why most models have at least two books. We will send a portfolio if the model is requested or right but unable to get to a go-see in person. It happens all the time when models travel a lot or are constantly booked."

Models have composites to drop off at the go-sees. These, Vicky says, are to reinforce their images. Clients and photographers get these composites in the agency book twice a year. When any of the models prepare new composites, they are sent to the five or six thousand clients on the agency's mailing list. On go-sees, models are asked to be on time and helpful, and to have the wardrobe that's asked for. A key word is flexible. "You never know what you will have to deal with, considering all the personalities in this business. If the photographer or someone is trying to be supportive, a smart model gives that back to him. Personality counts so heavily that nice, good-looking people do really well. Bright is a big point too; perception is constantly needed. Cooperation is fine, but mainly be nice, nice, nice! It is much more important for men than for women."

All this applies to every model, even those with established reputations and great portfolios. Each client needs, and deserves, a glimpse of a model's personality, energy level, and ability to perform. New models especially have to present their potential personally; a beginner's book can't possibly reflect all of his or her abilities. You want to exemplify the kind of individual the photographer will want to spend a couple of hours with. The model/photographer relationship will be intense during a shoot. The prospect has to appeal to the photographer.

SIMPLE DOS AND DON'TS

There are some hard-and-fast rules governing a model's behavior on a go-see. First, be polite, whether others seem to be or not. You must expect to be at a psychological disadvantage; after all, you are there to be judged. Be prepared to kick potentially annoying habits, like smoking, chewing gum, or biting your nails. Never brag, but do drop names at appropriate points if you have any to drop. Up to a point, photographers and clients like to know you're in demand. Photographers are particularly susceptible to such "in" references, but be cautious. Don't try to flatter anyone; it can lead to trouble. Be a good listener; use pauses to ask questions about the assignment. Don't say anything remotely negative about any aspect of the business or any person in it. If you can't be positive, say nothing; silence is negative enough.

People within the industry love fads and trends. Any new gadget or gimmick can be used to open or break up a conversation. But steer clear of politics or cheap gossip. Expect to be interrupted, and be gracious about it. Your aim is not to make points but to get across your potential and your ability to make a product look good. Listen for any final comments, take your leave without fanfare, and forget about that go-see unless and until you get a call-back.

Go-sees started with television auditions and have carried over into print work. Some clients trust the agent to send the right person, but don't assume that makes the job a sure thing. On go-sees, models are on their own. At any client meeting, the more you look like the layout, the better your chances of getting the job. In go-sees for commercial print or television, it may seem that they are casting for months for mid-American types of cereal products. Then suddenly they need older people for pharmaceutical trade ads. Don't get downhearted if you aren't getting immediate good responses on go-sees. You've got to be persistent to keep putting yourself in front of advertising and casting agents via promotions and photographs. Phone calls are not very productive. Every potential client gets a hundred a day and will forget your name the minute you hang up. Leave mentioning your name to your agent. He can, and will, do it at the right moment.

Whatever is or isn't going on, keep yourself in good shape. A reputation may get you to a go-see, but you won't book any jobs unless you look as good in person as you do in your portfolio, composite, or head shot. Casting people know exactly what they're doing, especially for commercials. They know what qualities they are looking for and whether they can get them from any given model. For commercials, learn the technique of being slated and of doing a scene on videotape. You will have to do this at audition after audition. Don't get impatient at all the repetitions. The more you audition, the more polished you become.

THE BIG PICTURE

Another nonlover of cattle calls is Roger Schermond, an artist and gallery manager in New York's Greenwich Village, who also models part-time for fashion-oriented print work through Wallace Rogers. As he views them, "Cattle calls are perfectly horrible because you're just a number. You fill out a card and they take a Polaroid to put together with your composite. Sometimes I think they're a colossal waste of time, but I always try to have positive energy—you have to. You've got to leave off the composites, even if you feel they'll never be looked at. You may be wrong for this particular job, but there may be one coming up that you are right for, and this way they have your statistics: suit size, eye and hair color, height, and weight. It takes a lot of time and money traveling all over town, often to do nothing more than leave a composite. But there's a percentage factor. If I go on one hundred go-sees I will get so many jobs; when my booker sends me out on the right calls the percentage increases. Bookings can come from promoting oneself or from a confluence of traits: being photogenic or easily sociable, making useful contacts, showing drive and ambition. You have to pursue jobs to the maximum of your ability. They won't just happen. I no longer feel anxious on go-sees; I've learned to take them in stride, almost as a game. I psych myself up for whatever they ask me to do—sometimes really preposterous things. If I depersonalize the situation, nervousness won't make me feel silly or foolish. I had to realize that they had no interest in seeing the real me unless I fit their image."

A model has to give the impression of feeling right for a job without seeming too pushy. On the other hand, a natural shyness mustn't come off as being too weak or uninterested. If you exhibit either extreme, you usually won't get the job. It can take time and effort to master this happy medium. Take the experience of Charles Glaser of Zoli. When he began at twenty-eight, Charles had two children and was waiting tables at night to supplement his in-

come. "It's when you're *not* in front of a camera that you do the really hard work. I go and see everybody on the same rounds list as when I started—no waiting for the phone to ring. To succeed, you've got to keep working. There are hundreds of new models making rounds all the time, but each job has different requirements. And you yourself change. I am now, at forty, starting to photograph as an all-American family man. This can be the most lucrative point in a man's career, if he leads up to it properly. Unless I have left a strong enough impression at a studio, and a recent one, they are not going to call me. You have to see potential clients again and again and again, at least once a year, better if it's twice a year or more."

PROS GET CALLED BACK

A model is most often asked to come in for a second interview, which is known as a call-back, for commercial print bookings. The ads are likely to be for banking, telephone services, or medical or grocery-store items. To be called back, you must have a face that will hold the attention of viewers long enough for them to get the point or read the copy of an ad. Lois Ross of Funny Face was an actress before her graduation from Syracuse University. "I wanted to be an ingenue but always found myself doing the male lead or a character part. A photographer came into my living room to do a Parliament campaign and told me I had the right face for commercial print work. The general public has no idea of the work that goes into a product advertisement. They look at it and say, 'Oh, I could have done that. It is just an ordinary-looking person and anyone could squeeze the Charmin.' The ad that 'anyone could do' takes five days of casting, with approximately fifteen hundred people shuffling through that go-see. Most of the candidates get little more than a cursory once-over and an even briefer 'Thank you, good.' The art director and photographer often don't even take a composite. They want to know what the model looks like that day. That is why they will take a Polaroid and cast from that. That's true of eighty percent of the commercial print jobs. You may never hear another word, so you walk away and forget about it.

"Of course, there are appointments where I have

spoken to the interviewer and gotten a call-back. Here, obviously, I have made more of an impression. Why, I don't know. Perhaps they saw a quality in the Polaroid. Whatever it was, I'll find out on the next appointment—and see if I can replicate it."

There's more to a call-back than just meeting people and making them like you. You have to learn to perform, and that takes a little confidence and a lot of practice. It demands, above all, letting your own personality shine through. Personality—and tenacity—worked for Andie McDowell, the Elite model who recently moved on to acting in *St. Elmo's Fire* and *Greystoke: The Legend of Tarzan, Lord of the Apes*. Andie went to modeling school in Columbia, South Carolina, and started modeling when she was twenty—just walked into a local department store one day and asked to model. She used a local school as a conduit (which, she says, "I recommend to any young small-town woman who wants to model") to come up to New York for a convention. She got pictures on her own after reading an article about John Casablancas. The article made her feel she would be well taken care of in New York. The first few weeks, Andie tested for photographers and developed a portfolio working for Italian *Bazaar* and *Women's Wear Daily*. "When I first came to New York I put everyone and everything on a pedestal. I felt like a nobody—I still find New York difficult in some ways. My experience has taught me two things: to stop making the same mistake over and over, and to think before you act. Attractive young girls, and boys for that matter, alone and starting to make some money of their own, are natural targets. So I grew up fast. I was nervous about going into clients' offices on go-sees—until I found out it was no big deal. You just do your best. I have wanted to tell girls starting out: Don't let it bother you if you're not chosen! It doesn't matter. That's how you have to look at it. The damned things are intimidating at the beginning because so many girls are after the same job. Finally you see that if you don't get the job, somebody else had their turn. The competition is there and that's that.

"I'm not too good at putting on my own makeup, but I think it's better anyway for casting people to see me as I am. They know what makeup can do. I have gotten good jobs even though the conventional wisdom is makeup for go-sees. Which is best depends on the person. I see models wearing too much makeup; I think I am more comfortable and that has to show through.

"The most exhaustive go-sees are for TV commercials like, for example, the ones for Calvin Klein jeans. I did five all together. On the call-back interview I began to suspect that copywriter Doon Arbus and photographer Richard Avedon wanted to hear something special. So when Avedon told me, 'Now, just get in front of the camera and talk about yourself,' I gave them what I thought they wanted and talked about my family and my dog that got run over when I was a child. 'I hear you're always funny,' Avedon said. So I told him about crank calls

Certain models sell themselves better than others at go-sees and therefore book a greater percentage of jobs. How you strike the interviewer is all that counts. Each category of modeling has its own system for model selection. For instance, catalog work is obtained as a result of go-sees and reputation, not just a portfolio. One cardinal rule is to be able to turn on the personality, to sparkle. In the Charmin ad above, the entire concept is to seem as though anyone could have been in it.

my sister and I used to make to the men who hung out in a bar called Firefly. I'd say, 'Hey Mike, how ya doin' sugar?' (There's always somebody named Mike at a small-town redneck bar.) 'Anyway, can we get together?' 'Sure can,' he'd say. 'I got me a white chev—roo—let and I'll be sittin' on the hood.' My sister and I weren't more than fourteen. I got the job by telling these stories about our hometown redneck bar. Understand I don't recommend saying things like this. That go-see was a most unusual go-see! It is very important to understand which, when, and where are the right appointments to go out on a limb for. Usually, they're straightforward and strictly business. You don't joke around or want to be perceived as immoral or indiscreet."

The selection process for each category of modeling has its own idiosyncracies, but the best shot at getting called back or auditioned for a job is to get there early, to come off as flexible, congenial, and cooperative, and, most important, to look right. It is wise to know what the job entails and who is the photographer, the director, and the client. To be the one selected often requires convincing a Polaroid SX-70 that you can get the client's message over. The first step is to sell yourself to the interviewer; if you can, refer to him by name. It's easier if you were asked to the appointment (through a head shot, composite, or an agency promotion book) rather than being at the appointment on a general go-see or cattle call. Always try to be memorable (as Andie McDowell's tale infers) for positive abilities and always leave a composite behind. The single best way to be perceived is as calm, cool, and collected, yet able to project a sparkling personality on cue.

Here Andie McDowell is captured at the water's edge for Bruce Weber's Calvin Klein Jeans billboard campaign. It is a long way from South Carolina to Times Square and Andie has mastered the art of keeping the city wolves from her door. She cautions: "When coming to New York, young girls (and boys too) must learn to be aware that there will be city slickers trying their maneuvers on every innocent young model who comes to town. At the beginning there were all those fabulous things I dreamed of doing. I had to get wise fast—there will be numbers done to get at either you, your money, or both."

PART THREE

Professional Modeling

Professionalism: The Consummate Professional

All you need is technical proficiency—and of course a client—to become a professional model, but you must bring a responsible attitude to the job if you are to be a success. *Responsible* means more than being sure you are physically prepared. Its more important sense is a willingness to work with other professionals as part of a team. Every professional has to accept job unknowns with grace and be flexible in finding solutions to conflicts and problems. Perhaps above all, professionalism requires a readiness to take direction from others—not always easy, especially not for independent people.

Cheryl Tiegs didn't simply wake up one morning on the cover of *Glamour*. She plugged away, taking half-steps, never giving up, going on twenty interviews to get maybe one postage-size shot published. "I had to start young," she explains, "because skills take a long time to perfect. It didn't occur to me to say no to anything either. It wasn't so much a concern with money as with getting things rolling. Actually, I had *some* rules and limitations—I wouldn't do lingerie, for example." Cheryl originally came East from California to see a boyfriend

at Dartmouth; it was his father, Robert McCloud, head of *Teen* magazine, who recommended that she see Stewart Models, a New York agency. Cheryl got an immediate yes at the appointment and was considered such a hot ticket that both Barbara Stone and Eileen Ford flew to California to do battle for her contract.

New York was a whole new world compared to little Pasadena. "I started out there in dead earnest at a high-school club. After one dinner, a local model agent was our guest speaker. He asked me and one other girl to come by and see him sometime; I took him up on it and gave him a call. He was the one who gave me my first break into modeling. He had a school of sorts—a woman would tell the class of aspiring would-bes such things as how to eat ice cream before it melts. This outfit was very small-town, and he put us through such ridiculous contests as Miss Army, Miss Air Force. Of course, I never won. What was amazing was that even though the contest had nothing to do with the army or air force, there it would be in the morning paper. He would come with a can of hair spray and have each of us ad lib a commercial. We were taken to old folks' homes to do fashion shows. We brought our own 'fashions'—a bathing suit, dress, and so on. Then we'd go around and talk to these elderly people, and they'd vote as to who they liked best. I was always shy, so I never won. None of it helped much but it was a start.

"My first work was fashion shows—for free, so I guess they weren't technically jobs. I traveled into Hollywood to have Polaroids taken for five dollars an hour; they were used as the basis for story illustrations in teen magazines. Also, I was an extra in those 'beach blanket bingo' movies, working from dawn to sunset for twenty-five dollars. I started slowly and just kept at it. I went on hundreds of interviews. Mostly photographers would say 'Thanks but no thanks' or 'You're too tall, your hair is too short, you're too something, but don't give up.' They all wished me good luck. The handful of times I was actually in one of the magazines, like *True Romance* or *True Story*, I'd bring my girlfriends down to the local drugstore magazine rack.

"At the start, you've got to get encouragement. My first agent happened to be small-town, but I did learn something of what went on in the real business world, so no one later on could take advantage of me. I did have one misconception: that I'd have to pay an agent a lot of money to accept me. That was because I paid that first agent three hundred dollars to attend his school. Therefore, by my logic, a good agent would cost thousands. I didn't know that all I had to do was bring a picture to the Nina Blanchard Agency. Nothing elaborate, time-consuming, or expensive. I spent months worrying: How can I do it . . . I don't have any money . . . where do I test? I put an entirely unnecessary mountain in front of me. It wasn't until I was seventeen that I realized a real career might be possible. Marion Smergen, who represented her husband Peter, a Los Angeles photographer, said to me after a shooting for a small client: 'Why don't you go see an agent like Nina Blanchard? That suggestion did it. Nina helped me. A proper agent knows immediately if a young girl might be right.

"Once I'd gone to Nina I started to get real jobs at reasonable rates. She raised my fee by five dollars an hour. I was just excited to be working. Nina gave me excellent advice and got me a double-page ad in *Seventeen* magazine for Cole of California. Julie Britt, an editor, gave me the first break at *Glamour*. She saw the Cole ad and booked me sight unseen for a one-week trip with Ali McGraw to St. Thomas.

"I was eighteen and so nervous and excited that I didn't even bring a bathing suit or sundress. I packed wool dresses for the Caribbean! But everyone was unbelievably kind. Ali McGraw had just come from Paraphernalia in New York; they were the first to have those little sixties minidresses. She would take a whole new world of clothes and accessories for me right out of her suitcase. I would giggle at everybody's jokes and go to sophisticated dinners, then be out till dawn dancing. I'll never forget how I felt—if I had died then and never modeled another day in my life I would have died happy. On that trip I got my first cover. We did the shot against a car in an alley with an assistant putting up a big white cardboard sheet behind my head. And that was it."

PROS ON PROFESSIONALISM

A client hiring a model has high expectations. There are a dozen surefire ways not to disappoint him. One is to be on time and never be the one to quit early. Also, a client has to be talked into rebooking models who cancel, and it's a rare client who does. There are a few taboos: no drinking or drugs or showing up without having had a good night's sleep. No client wants a model who wastes time or makes extra work, who is careless with the product, or who takes unnecessary chances with safety. No matter how perfectly cast, such models are not worth the cost or the risk. Clients don't like personality traits that grate on other people on the set, like gossiping, spreading rumors, or getting into arguments (who's right or wrong doesn't matter). Models must be able to adapt to the situation and place and to concentrate if they are to get the job done.

A sense of professionalism is something a model must develop. Without it, you won't last long. There's no time for leisurely development. You must exhibit professionalism immediately. It is not complicated, but it does take common sense and good manners. A new arrival in New York, the acme of professionalism, isn't going to find a pamphlet explaining how to behave. A few slips will be overlooked, but small inconsiderate actions are sure to be relayed to your agent. It will help to keep firmly in mind the result you're working to achieve, and aim resolutely toward it.

When the model appears on a set, she must have herself together from head to toe: hair clean but not set (until instructed otherwise), nails in close-up condition. Along with her groomed and gracious self, every model should carry the basic tools of her trade: a change of (neutral) underwear, including slip and stockings; two pairs of pumps, one high- and one low-heeled; a fully equipped makeup kit with a few nail polish colors; and all the brushes, combs, and rollers her hair might need, depending on the day.

Cheryl Tiegs is without doubt the single most successful model to date. She has sustained triumphs in every area of modeling for more than twenty years. By the time Cheryl reached eighteen, she was fast becoming the hottest model around—her lithe body gracing the pages of every magazine, that exquisite and expressive face on cover after cover both here and abroad. Association with her was like adrenaline to a product's performance in a market: not only for stores, designers, or cosmetics but also for cameras, sporting goods, communities, beverages, or anything. Cheryl's appeal transcended age, sex, race, or geographic area. Proof that it never faded was her return—after several pounds and years of retirement in Los Angeles—to New York and an even bigger and better career. This time Cheryl would make seven figures per year. A poster of Cheryl in a scanty golden swimsuit against a metallic background spurred sales of not just her posters but a slew of blond poster beauties, including Farrah Fawcett and Christie Brinkley. In the past five years, Cheryl Tiegs sportswear, exclusive with Sears, Roebuck, proved the profitability of her name, reaching unprecedented sales. A spectacular comeback, to say the least.

Cheryl Tiegs doesn't keep up that pace, and her standards, without effort. "Grooming maintenance is constant because I want to look my best and my best is being worn thinner throughout the day. Before I leave for a day's work, I go over my schedule, reviewing what products, attitudes, and age range I will have to project. The key here is to make whatever I am doing seem natural and easy for me. It helps the whole situation. Much of the atmosphere and attitude on the set has to do with the model. If the vibes are off, I can lighten things up or help the photographer bring them back on track. It is part of my job as the center of attention. Likewise, it is easy to take out or blame whatever is wrong on the model. There's no real way of fighting back except to be polite. I come in contact with hundreds of new people during most work weeks. I try to get along and have a word with everyone. I let the photographer or director in a commercial work directly with the client because they've had meetings together. I take *my* cues from the photographer or director.

"A model never gets to rest or be alone. As soon as I arrive, hair and makeup starts. Then it's the stylist's turn, and last, the photographer's. Everyone gets a breather, but not the model. All the tugging and pulling gets irritating, and it goes on all day long. I have to stand still for each person trying to do his job. This is the most tiring: Each one is eager to get going, and I have to be patient and appear fresh and chummy. It can take tact, especially if someone is doing a not too satisfactory job. I bear in mind that all they are after is a good photographic image for the client. I believe anger breeds more anger. If the hairdresser has gone too far, I give my hair a slight shake and let it fall into place naturally. You've got to work out the problem, not heighten the tension.

"During my twenty years in modeling, I have seen too many young, potentially successful models come and go very quickly. With their extraordinary beauty, they deserve to be at the top, and would be if unprofessional behavior didn't interfere. A little of that and they won't be around anymore, which is a shame because it is wonderful work. I pretend that every appointment or job is the only one of the week and that I am looking forward to it. Schedules are very difficult and will always be because models have four or five appointments each day and some will be short bookings. The possibilities of running over are enormous and fifteen minutes can mean a lot. Stress comes from all the changes that take me unawares and from trying to give as much as I can to each person. A rainy, busy day can be distressing and a frazzle. I have to gear myself up mentally. I don't get blisters on my feet now because that's part of maintenance and grooming, but I sure had them when I started."

Modeling has always been a financially rewarding business, but models' contracts have grown increasingly lucrative. This has elevated the standards required, demanding more professionalism. Modeling seems glamorous, but a lot of hard work goes on behind the scenes. That is a positive, not a negative. Discipline, responsibility, and professionalism build character. As in any job, there are mornings when anything sounds better than going to work. But a career is not a sometime thing. After a job has been done time and again, some of the luster wears off and only discipline will get the work finished. There is stress, but also strength, in finishing what you have committed yourself to.

The need for adaptability that Cheryl Tiegs emphasizes extends emphatically to clients. Your flexibility will be taxed, because each client has a different personality. "Be sensitive and cooperate," says Mannequin model Lynn Yeager. "I take stock of why I am there and what is going on. If a client is strict and precise, the model has to respond in kind. You bounce off the attitude that you sense from them. You can't be difficult or create a scene; a model has to make things easier for clients. If they are upset or nervous about whether *Women's Wear Daily* will like their line, it doesn't help to overhear a model say, 'I'm not wearing that,' or, 'You can see through it—I won't put it on!' "

At a booking for a national ad or on a huge location trip, there are sure to be lots of people around. And not always by necessity. The client may seem somewhat overrepresented merely to check on whether the proper eyeliner is being used. The advertising agency may bring in copywriters and art directors if the shot is important. Sometimes it seems to take a herculean effort to bring off something less than stupendous. Everyone, expert or not, has little clothing hints or touches to offer—as if there weren't enough details to cause commotion. Then, in the midst of everything, a studio manager or the photographer's rep may run around taking lunch orders. Get used to it; it will happen often.

THE COMMUNAL EFFORT

"People who work with you can make it horrendous or a pleasure," says Trish Webster of Wilhelmina. "There are too many pressures already, too much money being spent for incompetence to be put up with. Even where a job is a hard shot, it can be an easy day if there's a spirit of teamwork. In the last half of one all-day shoot, all I had left to do was clones. [Clones are identical tiny shots showing each color the pantyhose comes in.] It took fifty-three shots with my right leg exactly the same in each. I'd put on a pair, get into position, hold it—flash—take that pair off, on to the next. It took up the entire last hour of the booking."

Zoli model John Sommi's first big assignment was ten days' location in Honduras with photographer Albert Watson to do covers and inside fashion spreads for three Italian magazines. The party consisted of four models, an editor and her assistant, a photographer and his, and enough equipment, belongings, and fashions to keep the show going for ten days. John recalls, "We were scheduled to be in the capital first, then off to an ancient Mayan city, Copán, and finally, spend three days on a tropical island. The timetable was arranged so we could alternate men and women for each of the magazines: back and forth between singles and doubles; first men, then women, then couples, then mixed groups. I got deathly sick after the first morning, so bad that I couldn't stand up straight at the next day's shooting. And not only me. The other man, Matt Norklun, got sick too. The photographer asked me to sit on the top of a six-foot rock. Three or four steps and I got weak and dizzy. I had barely made it up when I heard him shout, 'Climb to the top of those steps!' I looked straight up the side of a pyramid to where Albert was pointing. It was nothing but professionalism that got me running when I felt too weak to move. I got my inspiration from the attitudes of other professionals at the location. It was unfair to the client to be sick at such a time. The editor expected my best. It is like a tennis match, where you work up to a better game when playing with other good players."

If one person starts complaining, it's contagious. It is all too easy to get something negative started, but harder to stop it. A model is there to help sell a product and make it look as effortless as possible—and it's easiest when you're looking happy. From a client's standpoint, if you're paying the salaries, you should get 100 percent enthusiasm. It is tough to reach a high energy level and even harder to sustain it after hanging around for hours getting bored and tired. Maybe so, but that's a model's job: to radiate and to sell.

ON THE SET

Cheryl Tiegs maintains that modeling has been a real character builder for her. Like any work it becomes routine after a while, and there are times when character is all that makes you get in there and do it. If a model starts early in the morning, at five that evening her hair and makeup have to be made to match the look of the morning. Her attitude changes, and it becomes necessary to try to look fresh. Self-esteem motivates Cheryl to forget for that one hour that all she wants is to go home. "It is simply mind over matter and willpower that gets a model to the top of her profession. I, for one, do not let myself get cranky. It is not what I want. Modeling has this in common with other service businesses: Professionals never want an outsider to see anything but their best side."

Cheryl has come to trust the professionalism of others to bring out her best at a photo session. "The client tries to figure out who Cheryl Tiegs is as a model. But the professionals around me try to interpret *me* and my ideas. So I surround myself with people who grasp the subtleties of my personality. They understand the importance to me of location, colors, naturalness, and light, all of which affect how confident, secure, and good I feel.

"Often I take a look at what is planned and think, 'How can I take this to a higher level?' These are the situations that require personality, and not standing like a mannequin. I try to make the result as natural as possible. If I'm holding up a product and feel stiff, a smile may save the shot. Some very small tricks can turn the key; it won't be the same for everyone. I try to give the impression that someone just happened to catch me holding this product instead of my being posed there. I am not very good at stylized, posed pictures, and I know it's because every part of the body must be in position. I prefer to move slightly, even if it is imperceptible, so there is a tiny bit of spontaneity. That to me is major. Every time the picture is about to be snapped, I jerk or move my head. I sort of settle in at the last second. It is important for the photographer to understand that. At the point when the picture is taken, our concentration is absolute. I believe there is a tunnel, an actual line, connecting me and the photographer at that moment. I zero in on him and how he is reacting. Some photographers work more slowly, so I set myself to that

pace. The hardest thing is to laugh and smile and to make it look natural. I try to think of something ridiculous or look at an object that can make me chuckle. Or I make up jokes. Sometimes I catch myself giggling at a funny story from a stockpile in the back of my head. A smile mostly comes from the eyes. I took me years to work out how to project a smiling look without having to grin. It should start in the eyes, but it takes concentration not to squint or try to twinkle your eyes. A smile is proof that beauty comes from within. It is coming from what you are thinking.

"In photography there is retouching, if necessary. But a sense of the model cannot be painted in. Some photographers are excellent; they pull me aside to tell me something about the attitude needed. If a photographer says, 'Just be yourself,' that's the lazy way. There are a lot of parts to myself. He's leaving it up to me. One photographer said to me, years ago, 'Just pretend you are Alice in Wonderland looking down from a tree.' He had created an entire scene in his mind, but it didn't make it the least bit clearer to me. But if a photographer says something positive and encouraging—something like 'That was terrific; let's try it a different way'—it builds confidence and makes it easier to respond. It comes down to tact. At that moment the ego is very fragile and the subtleties that I try to get onto film are difficult. The photographer has to be very careful in drawing it out.

"Lighting is extremely important. No matter how beautiful I feel, if it's wrong, I'll look awful. With great photographers the lighting is closely aligned to their statements, and the results will be consistent from picture to picture. Dietrich knew lighting very well. It is difficult to learn because, as the subject, you never actually get to see yourself in it. I have never gotten the knack of feeling light. It varies so much with the photographer, and then there are other criteria, such as which film is being used and how it will be developed, that also greatly affect the final picture. Polaroids are an advantage—they give immediate feedback.

"The studio is the most controlled situation. That makes conditions easier, but I happen to love locations. I like to work outdoors, as long as it is not below forty degrees and therefore difficult to get a good picture. I enjoy the spontaneity even if the wind is blowing a little dust. It is more to the point to me, and easier than trying to create a natural atmosphere indoors. I also like beauty shots outdoors, though it is more trying. The wind blowing hair in your face can be exasperating, but natural light works photographically. For my first *Glamour* cover, in that St. Thomas alley, we only used a white card behind my head because the lighting was just right. You can find an alleyway anywhere, but it's the light that makes the difference. And that shows up on the face. Light in spring sun is very different than in fall. Lighting is also very different on the East Coast, New York to Florida. And California is different again from Italy. It has to do with the angle of the sun's rays. It is very subtle. It goes unnoticed by most people. Models have to be aware of it and develop a working sense of light relative to their own tastes.

"I very much like going away on trips because everyone works together as a family; they'll eat dinner together and the camaraderie is good. Everyone is away from distractions, like the phone, that interfere with concentration. I find, for better or worse, it is always an adventure and the light creates situations for you to use. Also, everything around can be used as a prop. Often you don't even want the whole scene, only a sense of where the model is or an attitude that goes with the atmosphere you feel."

WORKING WITH PHOTOGRAPHERS

It is the photographer who sees how the picture is framed, a perspective entirely different from anyone else's. He gives direction based on what he sees through the lens and what is to be accomplished. A photographer should coach a model on emotion, but sometimes this comes the other way around: The model adds something, or experiments with a theme. As for the working conditions photographers prefer, the variety is endless. Some like absolute silence, others can't function without blaring music and tremendous commotion. Many photographers are encouraging—a blessing on the unavoidable days of tortuous positions to be endured in silence. Usually a photographer will let you know when he has gotten a shot. His primary job is to motivate the model; as he works, the assistants, or whoever happens to notice, will draw attention to details that would spoil the shot, such

as a label showing or a jacket buttoned wrong. All eyes are on the photographer and the model. They are like two people deep in conversation, to be interrupted only at a propitious moment.

As a rule, photographers can tell a model which angles are best relative to the lighting. Lighting makes a crucial difference in all photographs; it is everything. The best learning experience is working with good photographers who understand lighting. But looking at photographs over a long enough time can show you what light should be—in particular what it does to features. Black and white is the simplest starting point. From it you can learn the fundamentals, small motions like tilting the chin or lowering the head to eliminate puffs or bags.

George Newell, a renowned New York editorial and advertising makeup stylist and consultant, discusses the "it" that models seek to project: "At its base is inner peace and security, and not being intimidated by the possibility of failure. Models trust themselves and their desire to be in front of the camera, loving the whole idea. Freshness on-camera is an ability to be oneself, which can stem from naïveté or from self-awareness. Becoming too conscious of selling can cause stiffness. The professional can psych himself to deliver the relaxed attitude. Those who are photogenic can thank their parents and their lucky stars, but even if you are born with that inner spark, 'it' has to be found and developed. Once that is achieved, it becomes a question of reigniting that spark time after time."

Apollonia Van Ravenstein's career spanned fifteen years. She moved from European ingenue to international *Vogue* cover model, then into long relationships with designers, department stores, and commercial-print clients for every conceivable photographic need. Apollonia has achieved unique status on the runway for her effervescent style and in television commercials for her dialects and characterizations. All her accomplishments are based on an early understanding of photographers' methods and an appreciation of her own gifts.

"The talent to be photogenic is a magical gift that can't be tampered with. It is like the seasons, the sky, the dawn, anything of beauty. It shouldn't be questioned or probed, or intellectualized too much. It is not even mine; it is simple yet hard to explain. Some call it charisma; others talk about genes. One thing is sure: You recognize it immediately in others. It is infinitely precious and, when it is gone, it can't always be restored. It is genuine, innate, fruitful, yet so fragile that at a very young age it can be destroyed by the ego.

"A model must try to space out different categories of jobs because every type has its own pacing and stress," cautions Apollonia. "For example, on a *Town & Country* booking, there will be only two or three pictures per day. I save my energy, knowing I'll have to wait a long time before my picture is taken, then be expected to give my all for fifteen minutes to a half hour. Catalogs are another matter. There have always been two kinds: carriage trade and mass distribution. I call them editorial catalogs and catalogue-catalogs. The German type of catalog means eighteen pictures without a clue of where they'll appear. For these there is no direction and I work hard during every moment of the booking. It's paying-the-rent money, not really blood money. If there are three models booked on a catalog job, it will be easier. Jam-packed as they are, these jobs are often booked for several hours instead of an entire day."

Apollonia continues with firsthand tips about preparation: "The time, place, and category of assignment are crucial to the first steps in preparation. I do fashion, face, and body shots, and each one in any number of different characters, moods, or locations around the world. I must know what I am expected to have 'camera-ready.' If it is a body shot, I have to be clean, with no marks, and legs, arms, and bikini line waxed. I sometimes have to get booked the night before for false nails or special fittings so I can come into a studio prepared to start. Each booking demands a different energy. Advertising and catalog mean fifteen to twenty different setups a day. My energy must be at a special level because I'll be asked to do my own hair or makeup unless it's a cosmetic account. I come in half an hour early for that. It's enough because I do all the basics beforehand—foundation on, eyes painted, hair ready to be combed out. In short, I prepare at home. If there will be professional stylists, I come with clean face and hair. Doing twenty pictures for a catalog is intense work; there will be no relaxing. An advertisement will require the energy to transform myself a variety of ways through hair tricks and lipstick colors.

"If I know the photographer, I have some idea of what he expects, how he likes to work, and his working personality. We must catch each other's signals. Some photographers always want to do more with a concept; some are concerned only with keeping an account. Then there are the ones who want to create and command the room to do it. One very important thing to know is whether he will shoot in black and white or color. This affects the lighting, movement, and content of every picture. I know then if I can move or be dramatic. With black and white there are more and deeper contrasts. Also, mystery can be created. Color is more dispersed; drama in color has to do with simplicity. There is so much color around, especially in magazines, to compete with. Beautiful light is important: It sets a model free and establishes a reciprocal trust between model and photographer. In good light there are no limits to how I can stand or move my face. If the light is hard or bright, I usually have to restrict side-to-side face movements, but each situation, such as indoor versus outdoor, natural versus artificial light, and fast versus slow film will be different. You can work around horrible light, but it totally limits action. Often the focal point of an advertising picture will not be about me in beautiful light, so a search for it will be in vain. The emphasis must be on getting the product under the best light."

Peter Beard has been photographing models since the early sixties, mostly for himself but occasionally for clients, including *Playboy* magazine. He is best-known outside modeling circles for his four wildlife books. He discovered, near his home in Kenya, the glamorous Iman. "My hope, as a photographer," Peter confesses, "is that the model will do for me what all good models do: Isabella Rosselini, Apollonia, Verushka or Wilhelmina. They know how to come alive in front of that lens. When my eye is behind the viewfinder, I can see it. That, believe me, is a talent. Many others, even at the highest level, can't manage it and never will be able to. The least you hope for is that the model can echo back what the photographer wants. Unfortunately, I usually get rigid or clichéd attitudes and expressions. To get beyond that takes a psychological approach, an attempt at something true, authentic, genuine, which would be more akin to portraiture. The capacity to get across aliveness to the photographer is a rare thing, a rare combination of casualness, urgency, poignancy, and humor."

The photographer is in complete control of the shooting. Kim Alexis is an Elite model who is, in her own time, already legendary. She has been contracted to be the Ultima II woman. From her first test photographs, Kim has hurled her vibrant vitality unerringly toward the photographer. She has some suggestions about what a model can do when things aren't quite working: "Some photographers work so slowly that you have time between frames to think of shifts, adjustments, or changes to make in your facial expression. I get into his rhythm so I won't have to hold a smile—a smile gets dull and unreal very fast. I want to be changing my expressions at a beat the photographer can catch.

"Photographers sometimes send signals with body language they aren't aware of. I pick it up and play it back. If one of them scratches his shoulders and snuggles his chin, I'll snuggle too. Then I'll hear 'Great, good.' They think I've read their minds, when all I've done is seen that they're so involved with what they feel, I'll be right where they want me if I simply follow along.

"When I see a photographer struggling, I feel the picture isn't going right, and I try to think of as many things as I can to help. I have asked many photographers, 'What are you trying to get? I'm not understanding what you're saying to me.' If the shot is for lipstick, I will shout, 'How about a whole other flavor?' It gives him a chance to respond: 'I want it sort of smiling but not too . . .' Irving Penn's tendency is to sit across from me thinking. All of a sudden I will move in a new way, and he'll dive for his camera, saying 'That's it.' I know where my lights are. I position my body into a good photographic composition, and the shutter goes click . . . click . . . click."

MODELS WORKING WITH MODELS

Professional models can choose most of their work. They can, if they wish, turn down all assignments in which they don't work alone—a choice that can be lonely but does assure prominence in pictures and avoid the additional difficulties posed by multiple models. Of course, it is never easy for two people to look equally good in a single shot. Comparison—or competition—makes it probable that one will actually look bad. The working situation

with several models in one shot varies with the personalities and the goals. Bear in mind that the range is small for catalog, where group shots are most often needed. Some shots require precision, some a sense of genuine fun. Each person can affect the performance of others in the shot. For example, a model who works well can force the others to do more, but it doesn't always work out that way.

From the photographer's view, the more people, the tougher the shot. Three models on a set is hard on the photographer, and counterproductive if they don't know what they're doing. Beginners take a long time and some stretching out of the process. It can become tense when there is a group. George Weeks works in Chicago, Milan, and New York, and is experienced at the large production numbers formed by cigarette, liquor, and other big-ticket accounts. It can be rough, he concedes, but professionals manage in an intricate situation. "The push is to be rebooked, so everyone works together; nobody wants an unhappy client. Unfortunately, with subjects in a picture, someone is going to be out of step; a wise client knows that and is prepared for it. Getting eight men to walk exactly, symmetrically alike will be hard, but it can be done with enough rehearsal. Within any group, each man knows his strongest assets, and they all jockey for a spot to show their best sides. I've worked on many jobs where I get only a whisper—a nose or an arm—in a picture. It's easier for me to work with a partner, preferably a woman. Masculine interaction is limited to friendly smiles and serious rapport. It takes time to work well with another man and get beyond tightfisted stances."

When Cheryl Tiegs does a picture with several young girls, there is energy to spare. Tension too. It is hard for a novice to relax when she is working with a celebrity. If nobody knows anyone else, it is difficult to break the ice. When the pro is Cheryl, it becomes her responsibility to put the younger models at ease. She does this by nudging, tickling, even lifting one up as a surprise. It gets a group going. The photographer will take advantage of the spontaneity and chemistry and make it fit the demands of the layout. "Group work makes individual models shine and stand out," Cheryl says. "Aggression, on the other hand, shows even if it is subconscious. So each model needs confidence. When I work by myself, every four, five, six frames I'll make a face on purpose, stick out my tongue so the photographs don't work. Or once in a while I don't try, figuring that if some are bad, then the great can be greater. In a group shot that can't be done. There's a much greater chance that someone has her eyes closed or is looking in the wrong direction, so the number of usable pictures is already limited. In each one the pressure is on to look good.

"The working relationship with other models present is an individual thing. It requires extra everything: higher energy, more sensitivity to the photographer, greater productivity on the set, and special thought about the best approach with the personalities and temperaments involved. Some of the photographers I work with order a bottle of Dom Perignon for lunch. It is an expensive champagne, but worth it because it's shared, one glass each. Everyone feels better, and that has so much to do with the results. A small thoughtful gesture like that makes the work go better and faster. Another pointer is to be generous with praise. And don't grumble; that drags everyone down. I have not found model competitiveness obvious on the set. On the contrary, most models are helpful and look out for one another when they can. Sometimes working doubles is easier because you can laugh together or create a mood that helps you both to pull the load. One location trip to Hawaii proved extremely trying because of another model. She was crying all the time. One shot was to be of us dancing. If she wasn't getting enough attention, she managed to get everyone else upset—that seemed to be the only remedy for her crying. One picture was so close in on us that the tension she was creating showed. The picture had to be retouched. Fortunately, this has rarely happened to me in any form."

HANDLING THE INEVITABLE STRESS

Whatever its charms, modeling has its less appealing aspects. One is the many sources of stress in a typical working day. Some can be counteracted, others cannot. Most stressful of all is the monotony of repeated actions and waiting time and the boredom they produce. In the studio or on location, the tensions pile up just the same. To fill idle time, bring along reading or small tasks, such as letters to write. At a later point, when you've paid your dues, you can refuse bookings that you know mean stressful situations. Constantly changing groups, or exposure to abrasive conflicts, can cause anxiety.

Another modeling disadvantage is job insecurity and the tension caused by endlessly revised booking schedules. Emotional stress is inherent in the perpetual need to seek work on go-sees. There is the physical strain of long periods in uncomfortable positions, exacerbated by being the focal point all day long. Merely facing these situations daily builds up the pressure. The result is a rush of adrenaline that speeds up heart action and causes blood vessels to contract, so limbs become sore. All in all, a devastating combination for even the strongest to handle.

To photographer Peter Beard, "Recording beauty and wildlife is the most rewarding pursuit, but it creates extremities of its own. The commercial aspect is the most stress-producing. Beauty and truth don't always hit a photographer over the head, but rather must be sought out. The stress comes from the obsession and dedication it takes to track beauty to its lair, so to speak."

There is the weight too of producing a personality on demand—on the model and all concerned. The deadline pressures, combined with the time that details can take, mean that the model must sit and wait until everything is perfect. This is not a matter of choice. "If there are problems, they certainly will not be repeated. Photographers don't rebook models when problems arise." Understanding this, Dan Deely of Wilhelmina defends his models valiantly against the rigors that can make a model lose patience—for instance, the bathing suit in winter or winter coat in summer. "If the model gets upset, that affects performance. Experience has taught most photographers and clients to let the agency act as a mediator so there are no unpleasant outbursts. The endurance contest of hot and cold temperatures can be seen in professionals' books. In a picture, one of our men is sitting on a terrace in a bathing suit, and there is the Empire State Building covered in snow. It happens every year—spring and summer clothes shot in the middle of winter."

When a model is miscast for a shot, and it's the fault of the art director or photographer, there is nothing to do but persevere. Strain starts as a stomachache or sore feet. It is a model's job to stand, still and smiling, until each detail is worked out. It's when you let go that you know where the stress hit you. Many nights models go home and soak in the tub, their feet killing them from shoes a size too small, muscles aching from pants too tight or a shirt unbreathably small. George Weeks expects some pain each time a shot is taken or a fitting completed. "This goes on daily, and not for four minutes but for four hours. Each shot takes three to five rolls at thirty-six frames per roll. That is quite a bit of standing with pins, tape, and glue holding it all together. Fittings for clothes were never my idea of a good time when I was a child either. I never thought that, as an adult, I'd do so much standing for alterations."

Ford's Karen Bjornson relates some experiences that caused stress for her as a photographic model: "If the photographer comes in with an attitude, everyone tries to soothe him. You have to inspire the photographer by doing what he wants and then putting your personality into it. If you like him, it's *so* much easier. For some photographers I will do things that are physically painful. It was like that with Chris Von Waggenheim. I loved working with him and would go home aching, but I knew I had a great photograph. As an experienced model, I am careful not to grab an earring or accessories; I leave the choice to the stylist. I have to support their decisions. I learned a trick—I always try to keep the atmosphere light—even silly—clowning with accessories or cracking jokes. It makes everyone's job easier. The model can't put everyone on the spot or make them feel uneasy. You have to take it slowly and tactfully, to get what you feel is best."

But the physical stress experienced by models can be combatted, as it can be for dancers, acrobats, or actors. Carola Trier knows about body conditioning, stretching, limbering, and the value of being relaxed. Many of her students are professional models. "My first recommendation is to warm up before the day begins. Then again at home at the end of the day to relax the muscles. Warm baths and a swim can help relieve strain, but there is no substitute for being limber. Both men and women have to prepare so that positions are taken effortlessly. A twisted stance can be harmful, but can be performed successfully without muscular harm if proper exercises have been administered to increase and maintain flexibility. Assuming an unusual position for a long time is tiring. Awareness of muscular flexibility will help you improve performance with less fatigue. Second, you want your body strong *and* supple. Stamina also has to be built up slowly through exercise, and then constantly maintained. Stretching must be done correctly. It takes a limber limb to move properly without strain. Last, walking and breathing are actions everyone takes for granted but few do correctly. Carriage, posture, and body movement are all interconnected; a model needs to learn to stand tall and in an arched position if necessary without hurting the back. Mastery of breathing too can enable a model to hold a position longer and in greater comfort.

"A young model, twenty-five years old or less, should look in the mirror and say, 'This is how I want to look for the rest of my life.' Then work to keep it, because at thirty-five or forty-five there's no turning back. Think of your body as a building. The feet are the foundation. Your body rests on them but they were not meant to support the structure ten to sixteen hours every day. When taking a position, the feet should be planted as far apart as the hips, if possible. Then the knees are aligned over the feet and the ankles. The knees are the first story; the legs are like pillars. On top of these pillars are the abdominal and buttock muscles, a bridge holding the upper and lower parts together. The hips are the second story and the rib cage the third, and the head is a balancing mechanism that directs body movement."

Truisms:
Job-to-Job Variations

Beyond the personal and professional traits you need for all types of modeling, each category makes its own demands and has its own trade secrets. No one will sit you down and bestow every detail of this inside knowledge upon you. It will be passed along, often unconsciously, during the working day, or dropped as hints to be picked up and interpreted as best you can. When you possess such knowledge, you (and your client) will be more comfortable about any job and more sure of satisfying results. What follows is a look at how things work in individual markets—one that you would ordinarily get only on the spot.

SELLING FASHION

The success requisites in runway modeling are natural ability and awareness of design. Technique develops through exposure to clothes. *Great on a runway* means knowledgeable about which details to show, how, and when. Any garment has a feature to bring into focus: a collar to lift to show how sharp it looks up, a well-cut back to emphasize on the return with a shift of the shoulders. A good runway model instinctively places an arm or leg, or a hand or foot, to make a garment flow and move with the turn. Her body reshapes itself to each sample as it is tried on. Experience teaches the body when to cave in and when to expand.

Loving clothes leads to a yearning to know about them, not merely to show off the cape and the boa but to understand a pleated skirt, the shape of a hemline, the luxuriousness of a tissue-thin cashmere scarf. To show fashion you must make the clothes look meant for you, as though you had chosen them over thousands of others and wanted them for your own. Hairstyles and makeup help to project an attitude: classy, subtly sensual, natural, or mannered. Knowledge and experience teach you to capitalize on your best points and to develop an individual runway style. Then you have to make it look easy. To accomplish all this, you must get out and be part of it. Working, living, and traveling among the fashionable, exposing you as it does to taste and cultivation, changes you as a person. You develop a keener eye and a deeper appreciation of fashion's creative side. Models are closest to that

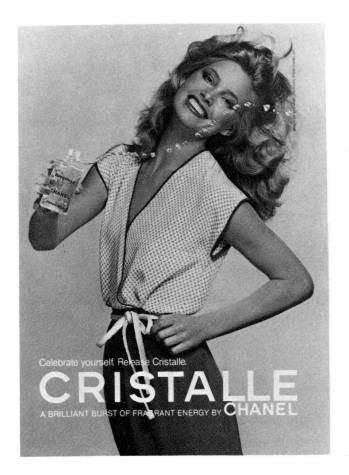

Fashion photography is pretend glamour. There are people rushing around and depending on you, so being a model feels very important. This involves pretending you lead a glamorous life. And a model spends all day with people who are also pretending. One reality is that technique develops through exposure to clothes. Each garment has a feature to bring to prominence. Experience makes knowing what it is instinctive; then it takes common sense added to practice and an affinity for style. By far, most modeling assignments are to promote clothing. It is hard work and requires a lot of energy. It takes skill to look graceful and relaxed. And it is very important to be in the right frame of mind, because timing is so crucial. A model has to get into clothes and onto the runway, then get into more clothes, each time riveting buyers to the garment. This applies to coats, sportswear, and daytime and evening dresses. To learn, a model watches professionals and then gets in front of a mirror to play with a garment. Next, she tries the same thing with another garment. Ultimately a model must feel comfortable enough to show and have one essential ingredient—the confidence to do so. It sounds simple—but it is not simple at all.

Men on the runway have become commonplace. They must show off the details while acting assured and prosperous. They walk to music, often at a quicker pace, and almost never stop. Men can learn the tools of their trade by jumping right onto the runway. There are signals for crossovers and turns, as there are for dancers. George Weeks of David and Lee in Chicago likens working a runway smoothly to driving a car. ''There are some basic rules everyone follows to prevent bumping into one another or falling off the raised platform. The first time I fell into a lady's lap she was more shocked than me, but I got right back up to applause.''

The three photographs shown here are archetypal fashion photography assignments. The first is a Chanel advertisement with Kelly Emberg of Elite standing and splashing herself with Cristalle. Kim Alexis (also of Elite) gives a sporty Jones of New York outfit a spirit of freedom. For Galanos, model and doctor Natalie Tirrell (Mannequin) adds a touch of class to a *WWD* reportage cover. The four pictures on p. 190 demonstrate variations on a fashion show. The tried and true hotel ballroom or showroom is no longer used exclusively. Sloped, even circular spaces have replaced the long, planked runways. Norma Kamali presents her collection, as she believes it should be seen, on the street (lower left); the two fashion models work right in front of her store. Very small paths often cramp the movement and gestures, but never the overall effect. It must look easy.

SLIM JIM

NEW YORK — James Galanos cuts fall into slivers in the collection he shows today, with the slimmest, most body-conscious shapes to surface this side of the Atlantic. Here, his short camel jacket in cashmere and alpaca and envelope-thin gray wool jersey skirt. More Slim Jim on page 20.

WWD

WOMEN'S WEAR DAILY   VOL. 148 NO. 38
THURSDAY, AUGUST 23, 1984   50 Cents

AAMA petition heats up push to delay origin rules

By MARK HOSENBALL

WASHINGTON — The American Apparel Manufacturers Association informed the Customs Service Wednesday it would like to see a "moratorium" placed on enforcement of the new country-of-origin regulations until Dec. 31.

With its strong constituency in domestic

A Hong Kong official expressed disappointment about lack of progress in getting the U.S. to withdraw its country-of-origin rules. Page 11.

The Chinese, meanwhile, canceled a wheat contract, apparently in retaliation against those rules. Page 19.

---

apparel manufacturing, the AAMA request is seen as a significant addition to the pressures on the administration to hold off on enforcing the controversial rules, scheduled to go into effect Sept. 7.

Since announced early this month, the rules have caused an uproar in U.S. importing circles, which the regulations will, under present

See AAMA, page 10

Stores seek spice to keep men's-look underwear fresh

By JOYCE WILSON

NEW YORK — A year after Calvin Klein's daring introduction of androgynous cotton knit briefs, bikinis, undershirts and woven boxer shorts, the look has settled in as virtually a basic for intimate apparel departments.

But as the look fades in newness, retailers are looking for other versions, new fabrics and additional items to keep excitement in an underwear classification that may be called status.

Furthermore, manufacturers are tending to discuss the look differently than they did six months ago. While executives then were quick to point out their prominent place in the androgynous underwear

See STORES, page 12

Photo by GEORGE CHINSEE

January 1982

ア
ン
ド
レ
・
レ
ザ
ー
の
結
構
な
内
輪
、
パ
リ
コ
レ
の
こ
の
秋
・
冬
の
発
表
会
は
注
目
を
集
め
て
い
る
。
デ
ザ
イ
ナ
ー
の
こ
の
秋
・
冬
の
コ
レ
ク
シ
ョ
ン
の
テ
ー
マ
は
、
柔
ら
か
い
ラ
イ
ン
と
ボ
リ
ュ
ー
ム
を
強
調
す
る
流
れ
と
な
っ
て
い
る
。
古
い
伝
統
を
表
現
す
る
、
セ
ン
ト
ラ
ル
ヨ
ー
ロ
ッ
パ
・
デ
ザ
イ
ン
・
コ
ー
ス
の
流
儀
に
よ
る
。

▶男女ともアース・カラーのミックス調カーディガン
にベルベッティーンのスラックスの組合わせ

process when they fit for a designer. During this creative process, the entire cycle, from paper or pinned muslin to finished garment, they see the development of a dress. Couture requires five or six fittings. Each step is deceptive; a perfect fit can take four or five tries, depending on the complexity of the design and the character of the fabric. Seeing the changes from one stage to another gives a marvelous overview as a model sees it: being cut, pinned, sewn, then presented formally, and again in the showroom. The ultimate in a model's world is to continue full cycle and wear it at the photography session, at a department-store charity function ball, then, last of all, to walk out of the store to see, lit up in a window display, a mannequin molded from her own face dressed in it.

"Learning how to wear clothes takes common sense, practice, and exposure to people who already know," says Karen Bjornson, who acquired her art working for Halston. "Being one more pretty face won't get you booked. To sell a coat on the runway you don't flap it around. Keep one hand in a pocket, and never spread the lining unless spread is what you're selling, as it is with a fur. If I'm going to take off a coat, I button it only partly, and I make sure I try it backstage. Pat Cleveland is great. She'll stand in front of the mirror as long as she has to, adjusting and pushing the garment and seeing everything it will do on her before she gets on the runway. That lets her concentrate on turns, twists, and watching her step. There are subtleties to making people appreciate what you're wearing without being conscious you're selling. I know exactly where to turn or stop. I recognize certain people, friends or supportive associates, and they smile or give me a wink to make me feel good in what I have on. Every time I go back out I am drawn to them instinctively."

The informal showing often is more ad-lib than a major show. Rarely are there rehearsals or instructions. Buyers simply want to look more closely at the garments; that's their reason for coming to the showroom. If the showing is for gowns, they must be made to look sophisticated. "In a fur I always pretend *I'm* rich, and I'm never, never, never nonchalant," says Lynn Yeager. "The rest of the day is easier if my schedule involves a more sophisticated look later that day. I just add more makeup. If later bookings are more casual, I may wash and reapply makeup half a dozen times. I have learned how to match my hairstyle to my makeup and redo it just as often. These are two powerful tools to changing my attitude to suit the dress."

MEN ON THE RUNWAY

Fitting requirements for men's clothing are equally exacting. A male fitting model is told to sit and stand up, and asked: How does it feel? Where does it grab? How is the pocket placement? The length? Every part of a garment must be assessed for fabric, fit, and function: shoulders, arms, chest, waist, hips, and pant legs. This applies across the board—for outercoats, tuxedos, suits, jackets or blazers, slacks, shirts, sweaters, underwear, socks, whatever is manufactured. Fittings are required first for samples and then on production garments for quality control. Buttons are placed and replaced; lapels are checked for width, shape, and lie (flat or rolled). To get the right proportions among size, flaps, length, and outline, each design must be tried on at many different stages.

The first necessity, for a man who wants to show, is the ability to carry himself and the clothes. The object is to look sensible, self-assured, and relaxed. Men, to do well, have to enjoy the excitement and appreciate flair. You can absorb a lot by observing people who have the knack. Eventually it becomes possible to give clothes a life, even *your* life. The casual smiles and authoritative looks appear natural. Above all, walk naturally, as you would down the street. Don't go spinning or pirouetting along. If the music is upbeat, walk to its rhythm. This is a performance, a piece of theater. Of course, scale any gesture to the setting—expansive for the grand ballroom of New York's Hotel Pierre, far less broad in a small showroom.

At a men's fashion show, women become props or accessories. Their role is to support the showing of the garment and what it was designed to do. If it is a cape, a big sweater, or a baggy pair of pants, the designer is interested in showing details and colors. Play your part by moving well, having fun, at times just being a ham. Larger shows are choreographed. Backstage, for a short runway, a starter will give directions, such as: On this double, you go right, you go left. For a choreographed show, each model is given a card with each change, for example: Enter, go to the left until the first pillar, pause, cross over. The next model's card might read: Go right, turn, join with model A. When it's a triple: Go center, halfway down turn, join with A and B before returning. If there are fifty models "running," all is precision and there's no room to be clumsy.

Runway has some fundamentals, not unlike those you're told when you learn to drive a car. Make any turn toward the audience. Never leave a blank runway. Always walk on the same side to avoid head-on collisions. Work out little signals between partners so that improvisations come off smoothly. Even so, everyone has made mistakes, usually more embarrassing than painful.

CHERYL TIEGS'S WEALTH OF EXPERIENCE SPEAKS FOR ITSELF

"The categories in my modeling career have been exceptional: catalog, advertising print, commercial, and editorial. The difference between catalog and editorial is the most extreme. Catalog is aimed at direct sales and requires exactness—showing the stitching, texture, and shape. I am always aware of showing the garment as clearly as I can. The picture is the customers' guide to what they are buying. In an editorial spread there is more freedom to accessorize and to inject a personal feeling. People aren't going to buy the merchandise right off a page, so a model needs to add an attitude. I would be asked by an editor which accessory I liked, how I would wear it, would I wear the collar up or down? I can sit, lie down, do whatever I would do in life. An editorial spread helps readers visualize how they might look and feel in those clothes. In a magazine, the designer is trying not only to sell merchandise but to create an image for his clothes. What I try to do for the Cheryl Tiegs line is blend the two: Show the clothes clearly while giving a catalog page more of the natural atmosphere of editorial. The clothes must be clear, since they will arrive unseen. But they cannot look stiff. The catalog pages I do are bringing in record orders. They don't have to be boring, perfect, and Kodak clean. Catalog work is challenging to me now, because I can bring in my personality and life-style—bring myself onto each catalog page.

"Retail advertising is well known as a big user of model talent. It requires maximizing the shape of a selling page. A pointer is always to relate positioning to the proposed copy. A model must be well versed in how clothes are worn because of all the designer clothes in today's stores. A real pro knows—and cares—if a blouse should be tucked in or not, how a bow is worn, and which shoes would be right. Commercial print and television for beauty products and consumer goods are the happiest mediums. There too the focus of attention has to be on what is being sold. That is, not on my personality directly, but on me relating to the object."

CATALOG AND EDITORIAL: MORE DIFFERENCES

For a model who wants to work in editorial rather than catalog, it is important to meet photographers who are good with newcomers. Editorial photographers can select a model simply because of a special quality. On a women's or men's fashion magazine, the editor selects fashion and makes the final choices among many pairs of assembled shoes, ties, bracelets, and so on. The photographer and editor collaborate on creating the situation in which the model will perform, from location to assorted professional experts. The sitting editor, as that person is called, is in charge of that fashion story. He or she explains layout requirements and picture specifications (horizontal or vertical, how many to a page) to the photographer and the model and is on hand for a final check of the outfit and to help the model put it on.

On catalog, the editor's place is taken by the fashion coordinator. Catalog shots are usually cropped to three quarters. There is rarely a sense of distance; details need to be shown closeup. Costs are carefully watched and economy requires more doubles and groups than on magazine pages. A makeup man is a rarity; almost never is there a hairdresser. The model must have a feel for the clothes and know how to show them to advantage. This is what separates the great catalog models from the mediocre. It takes sensitivity to the body and responsiveness to the space around it. Catalog modeling demands great concentration because

The catalog is fashion's most direct, most commercial application. The emphasis is strictly on the clothes, leaving little to the imagination. The clothes must be clear since they will be bought sight unseen. Usually the setting is stark, without distracting props, and the lighting is unsubtle. Every frame must be different, which creates a fast one-two pace. This makes a good working relationship between photographer and model essential. But basically it's up to the model: She must be able to bring out the quality of the clothes to their best advantage—known as working the merch.

The following photographs show Karen Bjornson of Ford in a series of *Vogue Patterns* catalog shots taken by Chris Van Wangenheim. Notice how she emphasizes the shortness of a jacket or the straight line of a skirt by folding her arms, creating a range from innocent to business executive. Karen also uses her arms and legs rhythmically to demonstrate a full skirt. By placing a hand on her hip or swinging a limb in the opposite direction from the hemline, Karen can show softness or suppleness.

VOGUE'S 22 LOOKS, EASY AS 1, 2, 3! All the silhouette news that makes for wardrobe versatility Today is in our BIG THREE! See how deftly you can switch from SLIMNESS to SOFT-NESS, all with the feeling of this CHANGING SEASON. From the SPENCER to the BIG TOPPER, from SlimDown skirts to dirndls, the Big Three is put together with vests, shirts and accessories the '78 way. Pay attention to COLORS and TEXTURES! Come on now and DO YOUR FASHION NUMBER!

The Big Three

Sew The Big Three for fashion versatility!

58

Photographed by Chris Von Wangenheim
Hair: Hamid

70

PARIS

PARIS IS DIOR & ST. LAURENT

DIOR

DIOR

Photographed by Chris Von Wangenheim

56

each frame must be made to work. Merchandising is the most important aspect of each shot. To be sold directly, clothes need something to light them up, to make them glamorous, desirable, and relevant to the reader's needs. It is up to the model to move in a way that accentuates any especially noticeable detail—a pocket flap, say, or a cuff. This is often done by creating a geometrical shape with the clothes and one's body. Then give the shot an air of confidence, vitality, fun, or serenity, depending on the situation. The worst response is to be overly self-conscious or afraid of spontaneity or experiment.

As each shot starts, the photographer or coordinator will tell the model whether it will run as a vertical, horizontal, or square. If it is tight, the shapes have to be held narrow. The layout may be no more than a description of the garments marked to be shot as a single, double, or group. Sometimes there is latitude for minor revision. If pants can't be found, for example, shorts can be used and the picture will be cropped differently. A model is responsible for keeping weak points out of the picture, and for getting a best feature into each frame: a good smile, a twinkle in the eye, or a sexy pout. There is no budget for retouching. Each shot must make its selling point but never "oversell"—a fine and difficult line to draw.

One more point concerns work load. Each day or hour will be scheduled for the maximum output, with fifteen to twenty minutes allowed per shot. That means you never waste time or disturb a rapport between the photographer and other models. Catalogs are shot in large studios—a small business within a business. If a model is good, people find out quickly. Unfortunately, the reverse is equally true.

CATALOG MAKEUP AND MOTION

Regarding makeup, the best advice is keep it simple, bearing in mind the difference of strobe versus natural light, filters, black and white, or color. Makeup and hair specifications are given to the model with the other booking information—wardrobe if any, nails a special color, hair clean, and the like. Understand and know how to compensate for any individual problems, such as fullness in the face,

or hollow or deep-set eyes. George Newell is a makeup stylist for *Vogue* and *Bazaar*. Hired by international cosmetic corporations for his knowledge of fashion trends and beauty treatments, George is one of those magicians who take a "stretched canvas" and turn it into a glamorous face. He is encouraging about what models can do for themselves: "With practice, you can apply your own makeup enough to model in the catalog studios of New York, Chicago, or Dallas. It is each model's responsibility to have her makeup look professional. The key is to play with the best features. I would work to even out the skin tone and soften the structure through contouring. I put in planes and bring up surfaces for the camera to catch. The lens picks up what is in the forefront, so if the forehead, nose, or cheekbones are lightened, everything else recedes. If the face is wide and flat, lightening the center 'ovals' the face and softens its contours. Contrasts between hair and skin have to be kept subtle and blended into the hairline.

"Lighting affects choices greatly. The light of a sunset, for example, is warm and makes the skin look warmer. Cooler light is harsher light. On even a blue-gray day, irritations and redness have to be covered. In natural light, generally speaking, use less makeup; more in high-voltage studio light, which causes a burnout. Luminousness alters skin qualities to the camera; there are places on a face where the pigment does not pick up light as well as on others. Women use cosmetic highlighting to equalize this. In most situations men do not wear makeup, but for black-and-white fashion shots, makeup is sometimes touched on to conceal blemishes, or an imperceptible hint of eyeliner is added for emphasis. A little sun brings oils to the skin's surface; within limits, these can add a nice glow to a man's face."

Clothes are not just pieces of fabric sewn together and thrown on without thought. Clothes affect a person's attitude. "If I'm in a very romantic mood, I don't wear dungarees and a T-shirt," says Joan Severance of Elite, one of the world's highly regarded catalog models. She is truly unique, having started in catalog and then been discovered by fashion editors. "In front of the camera something projects from me that comes from the clothes. It can't be false either. The camera is merciless on frauds. I always think an appropriate thought, dream up a little script. From the time I dress to

The Klein Shine!

In the rich, sophisticated depth of black velvet, Calvin Klein wraps up your nightlife like the shining pro that he is! Really an evening extension of his wrap blouse you love, we like the shawl lapel done in a shine of satin. Very Easy Vogue 1990, 6 to 16.

Aujard in the red

In the red, yes! But, this kind of nightlife pantsuiting is all on the good credit side of fashion! Credit Christian Aujard, too, with the kind of smashy tucked shirt and tapered pants that start fashion fires! Cool it in crepe de chine! 1954, 6 to 14.

69

The camera is merciless on frauds. For the male model to present appropriate wrinkle-free poses, there are dozens of small tricks, such as standing with a bent knee to have a crease fall straight or half-turning with pins stuck in the back like a voodoo doll. A female model is responsible for her makeup and hairdo. George Newell, a noted makeup artist, recommends: ''Playing with the best features works to even out the face and soften it through contouring.'' He cautions that lighting affects choices greatly.

In the accompanying photographs, Karen Bjornson, in evening wear, teams up with Eric Milon of Elite. She adjusts her makeup to underline the simple sophistication of a velvet dress, a deceptively casual evening pantsuit in crepe de chine, and, with a severely styled hairdo, in a masculine dinner suit with a matching partner. Both have an air that comes from a broad knowledge of current styles and clothes in general.

Shining Nightlife!

Give those stars that shine at night this kind of fashion competition. Vogue thinks you should put a special shine on your nightlife like this! Below: shine in a dazzle of heavenly blue crepe de chine! And, give a star to Very Easy Vogue for making glamour so drawstring-easy! 7073, P-S-M. Opposite, when the invitation reads Black Tie, shine in your tux! Put it together with his know-how! The jacket, bar Very Easy Vogue shawl shine in gabardine with shining satin shawl lapels, 7074, 6 to 16, matching satin-striped tapered pants, Vogue 10? PT 7215, 6 to 16. Classic plastron-tucked silk shirt, 7098, 8 to 16. See Backviews for lapel and pants shapings.

Photographed by Lynn Von Wengelowsm. Hair: Games of The Plaza

66

the stars are out tonig

the last frame in the camera, I go through different personalities in the same clothes. I don't even think of it anymore; I simply put on a new personality even if I just change earrings. This variation happens for every frame all through a thirty-five-millimeter roll.

"My clients know what I can do with clothes. They never worry that I will just stand there and waste their money. I will give variety to the clothes, which makes them salable. One good model is a better value than a mediocre stylist and mediocre model, but the cost is just the same. A good relationship between photographer and model is imperative if there is to be a choice every two rolls so the photographer doesn't go over budget. I put everything aside so I can become chic, elegant, whatever is called for. If necessary I could probably do it with jeans. It is a form of acting. Catalog shoots have a beat. 'Hip one, hip two, collar up, sit down, look left, look right.' Direction is *at* you. 'Don't do this, don't do that, put a hand on hip—watch out for wrinkles—stand up straight. Snap it up, we don't have all day, watch the budget, make each frame different.' This is not a documentary-style film where I simply keep moving and the director catches me. In life, I don't move and stop, move and stop, so catalog pacing is an acquired and difficult technique. I can't turn around because of the pins. I have to be alert to anything having to do with the dress, aware of every detail, including a stain on a sleeve so I don't show it."

Paris is the City of Light. Paris is a spectacular light-up of gaiety at all hours! Paris is Ungaro, Chloé, and Givenchy lighting up your life like this! Ungaro's romantic new flowering in a freedom loving dress for kicking up your heels, 1906, 8 to 16. Near Left: Chloé gives new youth and party verve to a bare camisole line, long-waisted, very sleek, 1903, 6 to 14. Right: Givenchy's blouson tunic rules the night in royal jersey. Very Easy Vogue 1909, 8 to 18.

Hair: Maury Hopson

GIVENCHY

WHAT CATALOG IS LIKE FOR MEN

Success in catalog work, for a male model, takes time and persistence. It depends on finely tuned relationships with stylists and photographers at the large urban catalog houses. Their clients scrutinize what goes onto every set as though it were under a microscope. If there is a better man for any job, he'll be hired. A fresh face will get a beginner a short booking if he has potential. A couple of months down the road he may try again, this time for half a day. Then a job comes from a stylist who once worked with him at another studio, maybe because of a cancellation. He is now working at two catalog studios, even if one is under special circumstances.

Karen Bjornson demonstrates in these classic catalog shots the ease and naturalness with which a model brings out the pleats and slit in a long skirt, the sporty blouson effect of an ensemble, and the charming practicality of a jacketed Chloé dress (helped by three distinct photographic personalities).

Cheryl Tiegs: "It took me years to work out how to project a smiling look without having to grin. It should start in the eyes. A smile is proof that beauty comes from within. It is coming from what you are thinking. I think of something ridiculous or look at an object that can make me chuckle. Or I make up jokes."

RENATA

58

Paris is soft.
Paris is easy.
Paris is Renata
and Givenchy
at a summer
dress best!
Renata turns
heads with
two-piecers
playing soft
skirts with
easy pullovers.
Left: overblow
belted blouso
1902, 6 to 14.
Right: scoopy
camisole, eas
skirt, 1901, 6
to 16. Far righ
Givenchy say
it with the
smock that
smacks of
Paris. Slit
leg show, tiny
tucks, a free
swinging line
1905, 8 to 16.

Chloé

40

The main thing is to make contacts, learn about the photographers, and not make any mistakes. Once a catalog house knows they can depend on you, the jobs will roll in regularly. A portfolio counts for very little; it is a model's reputation that brings in catalog work. Jamie Simpson says, "The bulk of a busy male catalog model's day will be one- and two-hour bookings. At the large catalog houses you always work with the same group of people. Like everyone else in the studio, you must be a positive element in the day, not just a model. Of course you must do your own professional part: Be prompt, be helpful when possible, be equipped with whatever you need. But most of all be ready to apply your knowledge of clothes." Jamie Simpson is a fashion stylist who also acts as fashion coordinator on catalog bookings. His experience spans three continents and thousands of catalog pages. "I think a model is booked according to how well people like him as well as how good he is at what he does. Time is always precious and can't be squandered. It can be a welcome relief to have someone joke around and ease the tension—as long as it's not too loud or distracting. Clowning works if it is kept impersonal or pointed toward the clown. Some days would be lost without it."

Pacing is necessary for long days with a steady stream of personalities. You learn to do even simple things at the right time, like getting that glass of water when you're sure it's safe. Many photographers respond to pressure very nicely, but there are some who turn into screamers. The atmosphere can become highly charged as the day wears on. Each new booking is a new situation. If a day isn't going well, seventeen people can be on edge and at him before he gets his coat off. It gets out of hand as people start coming in four, six, or ten minutes late from previous bookings. A rainy or snowy day can turn into a nightmare. Try to get people who are frazzled or angry to be respectful and polite.

It's hard to pin down what constitutes acceptability in catalog work. It goes beyond a certain look or size or type. It is a question of proportions, and a slightly broader shoulder is better. By far the majority of catalogs are for small regional stores, big interstate retailers, and specialty market books, like L. L. Bean for preppies and Fredericks for underwear freaks. The rate depends on the client. In the same catalog house the same model could work two hours for one client at $150 and then go to another studio and get $125 or $175. That's true for female models too.

A male figure in a catalog conforms to very straightforward rules of styling. It will rarely be high fashion. Everything has to be wrinkle-free and flat. Learn to help the stylist with tricks like making pants neat by tucking a shirt into your underwear. There are thousands of such tricks, all based on the principle that when a joint bends it creates a wrinkle. If a knee isn't twisted right, the crease will not fall straight; an outstretched arm makes the seam look unnatural. Become aware of how to raise a shoulder so the chest conforms without a bubble, or raise a foot slightly so the belt line is level, or eliminate excess bulk with a tuck behind the thigh, and smile while you hold it there. When a man wears a sports jacket and a pair of slacks, he isn't dressed as formally as when he is in a three-piece business suit; each could have an executive feel, but a sports jacket should look more relaxed and perhaps friendlier. A turtleneck sweater and slacks would be more casual still. Catalogs need models to understand and know how to project major differences in dress: aloof and mysterious for a dinner jacket, affable and affluent for a business suit, loose-limbed and vigorous for activewear.

WORKING ON COMMERCIAL PRINT

An advertising campaign relies on effective working relationships; these depend on good interpersonal communication—solving problems through negotiation or discussion among temporary work groups. Individuals within groups influence each other; the communal effort is successful to the extent that its members manage to cooperate. Accomplishment in the creative situation hinges on a more solitary endeavor: the model's openness in expressing feelings and emotions. A successful professional model has to rise to the occasion without photographic makeup, props, and set in order to function with them at a high level. We all have our bad days. For a model, these are shoots for which she is less than prepared, too nervous, or too much in need of sleep. The night before work a model should go to bed early; in the morning she should get up in time to eat breakfast. Never walk

In a commercial-print shot it is the communal effort that counts. For an ad requiring location work as well as a sizable cast of models, props, and crew, the coordination between the photographer, the stylist, and the hair and makeup people requires the teamwork found in a Broadway play. A great deal of what is expected is animated and improvisational, which is why a sense of acting is so helpful. The model has to be alert to pick up on what the advertiser wants. The product should be treated like a work of art: The client expects it to be handled with dignity. This is true whether the object is a pair of earrings or a glass of Scotch.

Everyone can look at the layout drawn by the art director to facsimile the shot. It is up to the model to understand what is expected. Everything else will be taken care of by the crew. Above are two examples. At the left, using two models, is a coupon for a rental car; at the right is a national ad that uses a visual play on the company's bar code, turning it into a comforting image and one to be trusted—a blanket. For both, the models had to create characters who would serve to endorse the products. It is the photographer's responsibility to draw out the image that a client thinks will help to sell his product.

on a set asking people to make allowances because you just got up. Anyone who's worked five hours getting the set prepared doesn't want to know about it. Top models are not necessarily top beauties; for the most part they are top personalities in that they *want* to get along with people.

Tommy Preston, a young Wilhelmina model, describes how he came to understand the team aspect of a commercial photography session. "On the first set I quickly learned to tell the crew members apart—the stylists from one another, the makeup artists, the hairdresser, et cetera. Then I noticed everyone dressed in attire that suited what they did. It was indicative of the way such a group works— each with a different personality and opinion, yet together, and so well orchestrated that everything simply melted together. There is a definite hierarchy but everyone is intertwined. While my hair was being trimmed someone started to put on my shoes. Simultaneously a shirt and tie were being fixed. Touches of makeup were applied. They hovered over me as if I were a statue, painting and straightening until I was ready. The photographer was called in for a final inspection. He gave me a few nothing-much instructions and then said, 'You really look great today.' It was mostly to be encouraging. Then everybody chimed in."

The stylist collects accessories and props for use on the set, often according to rules, as Candy Pratts informs us. "In shoes don't show the inside of the foot. The same goes for an inner thigh. A purse—today we call it a handbag—is held with the clasp on the outside if that is the way it opens. A scarf can be used in many ways but never with the label showing. A photographer and stylist expect the model to know these things.

"A model should hold a product like a work of art, lavish care and attention on a deodorant dispenser as if it were silver and glass. One learns, at a school for valets, that there is a way to handle objects. First, don't grab; that will leave fingerprints. Second, hold a glass by the stem, a perfume bottle from the bottom, neither like a pint of gin. If it's perfume it should be precious. You wouldn't hold a pearl with a clenched fist, so don't clutch that forty-dollar necklace. Hold it like it was an inlaid Indian sapphire that you always wanted. Every client expects the product or merchandise to be treated with dignity. A model should understand a product's use or beauty or uniqueness. Pick it up and practice holding it lovingly. This is crucial if you want to do advertising print or TV commercials."

Besides having a feeling for clothes, the model frequently has to show imagination with accessories. As fashion stylist Jamie Simpson points out, "An accessory can be highly beneficial to a shot. It can contribute believability *and* work as a prop. An accessory, looked at one way, is an umbrella, but it is also something to hold, to relax and work with. Certain models know how to play with an accessory to make a more interesting picture. A hat can be made more intriguing by tipping it or touching its brim. A barrette can be fondled by a fingertip, a necklace given a caress. If an accessory is attractive enough to be there, it should be 'milked' for whatever it's worth."

There is a constant demand for models who work well with objects: products, accessories, or props. Interestingly, many are Orientals, made desirable by their tones, proportions, and sizes. Hands are in greater demand than any other part—for accesso-

These pictures reveal only the tip of the iceberg as to the types used by advertisers for commercial-print assignments. Notice that in both the models express a sense of "up" with their smiles, and every eye is focused toward the camera. In the Amtrak ad, both models radiate a feeling of warmth with their smiles; they represent America's love of the train and all its traditions. Nuveen's model *is* the mature, self-assured, wealthy man who needs nothing more than an elegant dinner jacket to illustrate confidence in himself and his situation, and that confidence is then projected onto the product—Nuveen. At this stage in his career, the model knows exactly what is expected of him and how to deliver just the right expression. Elderly men are the one type of model where the supply is smaller than the demand.

"Tax-free income from Nuveen.
Now that's music to my ears."

BURROUGHS ANNOUNCES THE 80 HOUR WORKDAY.

© 1983 BURROUGHS CORPORATION

Thanks to an ingenious productivity tool from Burroughs called the Logic and Information Network Compiler, or LINC, computer programmers can now increase their productivity as much as 10 times! (In some cases, even more.)

It's like getting an extra 72 hours of work in a day.

How is this possible?

The LINC software system automatically writes virtually all the coding programmers would have to do manually, so it drastically reduces the time it takes to develop and implement even complex application systems. (It also simplifies program maintenance.)

Furthermore, LINC uses a new high-level language that defines problems in human terms, not computer terms, so important information can be easily created and managed.

And people can use LINC with very little training.

At Burroughs, productivity has always been a primary consideration, whether it's the technological innovation of our hardware or the advanced design of our software.

For more detailed information call 1-800-621-1776 Ext. 45.

It may be the most productive phone call you'll ever make.

Burroughs
THE QUESTION ISN'T WHO'S BIGGER. IT'S WHO'S BETTER.

Here are two ads where the coordination effort of each model is key. The models in the Burroughs ad form a much smaller, tighter group; their movements and expressions must be tightly interrelated. The alternating positions manage to give a positive emphasis to their surprise. Each model must create, hold, and repeat his expression, sometimes up to seventy-five times. The lucrative clients for males are cosmetic, liquor, and cigarette accounts. In commercial print situations, the model is first and foremost a sales representative of the brand's public image. No matter how carefully posed the group of men, as in this Kessler ad, each individual must radiate warmth and camaradarie in sharing a glass of whiskey, without touching. Each was cast to attract a portion of the brand's known market, and each in this case looks comfortable and at ease.

Earning a buck is hard. Enjoying it shouldn't be.

It's only a few hours on a Fall afternoon, but you looked forward to it all week. So it's only natural that Kessler's there, too. It's a smooth, easy whiskey–as smooth as silk. And Kessler's a smooth, easy whiskey on the pocketbook. That's easy to take, too.

Smooth as silk
KESSLER

layout indicates whether the shot is a tight vertical or wide, high or low. It is important to know if the picture will be on a right-hand page, so the product can be positioned to face onto the page and not into the gutter (the center point where left and right pages join).

Everyone gets a copy of the art director's layout or storyboard. Since everyone has agreed that this is the right model, it is up to the stylists—clothing, makeup, and hair—to bring out the qualities the client sought and saw. It is up to the model to find out what is expected. Models are never invited to preproduction meetings where decisions are made; their hourly rates would make it prohibitive. So these details are explained on the set. There should be plenty of conversation about them, especially among photographer, stylists, and model. "If I were cast in a Secret deodorant shot in a Central Park rowboat," says Candy Pratts, "I would want to know why I was in the boat and what I was expected to be selling. I see a model selling campus clothes in a Calvin Klein or Perry Ellis show and then that same model puts on a Halston for a department-store ad to sell a sophisticated shopper. That's a model who has her wits about her and asks the right questions."

MOVING FASHION AND BEAUTY ONTO TV

It's easy for a model to cross over from fashion and beauty commercial print to comparable TV commercials. The most requested type is Middle American, but very pretty or handsome. A model is booked in TV to project onto a product or garment the aspect of a photographic personality called characterization. In fashion TV commercials a model rarely delivers any lines, so models can know little about acting or product endorsement and still be successful. On the other hand, the false notion that modeling leads to acting grew out of commercials. An impressive list of actresses did start that way, Lauren Hutton for one. Commercials, not her Revlon contract, gave her the push. For models with the right look, it's as easy to be cast in TV as in commercial print. Vignette or scenario commercials lip-sync; the characters relate to a product visually and sound is added later. These two widely used TV commercial forms involve simple, basic

ries, cosmetics, even laundry products. The lights for such shots are extremely hot, and often the hand model is wedged between stroboscopic lights and their stands. Hitting a mark requires leaning into a shot. It's a true technique. A model never simply pours, steps, or touches. Handling objects professionally is no casual matter but a disciplined ability to predetermine and repeat motions precisely. Pouring shots are difficult because of finger marks left when the contents get repoured into a glass container. Some days a position has to be maintained so long that you're left with what seems a permanent aching in the elbow and shoulders.

Often the layout is drawn to accommodate the copy in the ad. Information of that visual kind is hard to picture unless it is laid out on paper. The movement. The commercial is shot in segments, the action repeated with slight variations until the director is satisfied. Each new start is called a take. The segments, perhaps five or six, are shot out of order but can be followed on the storyboard. The footage is assembled in proper order in an editing room using the best take from each segment. The five- to ten-second segments are then spliced together with sound.

Models assume a stance by setting the feet first and then other portions of the body—legs, torso, and shoulders. In commercials no one poses: Characters move more naturally than in stills. Men accustomed to taking a stance have to relearn presence and actions that are more lifelike. It doesn't work to look like a model from the neck down and have the head in character. You start from a neutral body position, putting your energy into the gestures. In this way movement expresses the character. Models whose movements were acquired on a runway, where position and carriage help to make clothes look good, must overcome some of these techniques for TV commercial work.

A photographic model also needs to learn to sustain a thirty-second scene instead of the single frame. Only when models can control themselves in front of a still camera are they ready to delve into more involved actions. One way to grow into this is by practicing movements that express extensions in attitudes about a product or garment—actually new aspects of a photographic personality. These then become character traits, which, like personality traits, can be projected. This does require imagination. An example would be projecting sex appeal into advertising—certainly the most constantly requested, so a good place to start. Sexuality in a still shot is necessarily abrupt and blatant. In TV, seduction is built up through the storyline, providing an opportunity to flirt. Models take what they know from still-camera work and utilize movement to create a beginning, middle, and end. Develop a characteristic to a workable point, then move on to the next.

Television commercials are harder work and take far more time to shoot. Days are scheduled more tightly and run longer because an entire set of movements, not just one split second, has to be captured. TV commercials too are very precise. There is no retouching, so if one of the thousands of possible details is wrong, the shot has to be re-

done. Hence, the necessity for several takes. The cost of setting up again and reshooting are enormous, so you shoot until it's in the can, so to speak. Now reshoots are rare because there are hookups between the motion-picture camera and a video monitor that allow the director to see on a video screen when a take is good enough to print (a perfect take).

A job that is complicated as a still is even more so as a TV commercial. Eric Milon of Elite did a shirt commercial for Damon Sportswear that he likens to a catalog job because of the director's insistence on impeccable detail. Not much has changed since Ronald Reagan did the Van Heusen campaign, except for the new emphasis on graphics. "The movement was to put on a shirt and sweater," recalls the director, Peter Tuttman. "The action was outlined on the storyboard point by point. There were close-ups of the shoulders and arms, the collar and the neck, as the garments were put on. Everything had to look natural and fluid. It required hours of dressing and undressing under hot lights and it was very tedious to capture. I had tested the concept and showed it to Eric before we started. The point where he pulled the sweater over his head, naturally, as if he were home, was the climax of the commercial. He appears to be a relaxed and natural character with sex appeal. But it was a setup because the viewer had to wonder, 'Who is that man with the sexy body?' "

As Eric Milon remembers it, "There was one movement after another and the camera angles kept changing. This meant partly putting the shirt on and off at different speeds and repeating specified turning motions. Sometimes Peter moved in on the arm, or the waistband. Each movement was choreographed. For a comparable still shot," Eric continues, "the photographer wouldn't need to know as precisely what he wanted. I would be asked to start putting on the shirt, perhaps slowly, and go all the way through, with the photographer shooting each stage. I could hold any position more easily than repeating an action. Sometimes I could complete the whole action before starting again. The photographer could zoom in or stop me to capture any peculiarity that appealed to him. The right frame would then be selected and retouched. A billboard, a magazine print ad, and a point-of-purchase placard with inserts would take half a day. For TV I was booked the full day."

Carrie Nygren at Elite has been doing commercials in New York for the past four years. Revlon originally brought her from Paris to shoot a Flex commercial in Dallas, one of the most memorable for its graphic desert, blue sky, and tall, spiny cactus. From off-camera jumps this spectacular blonde cocking a hair dryer like a gunfighter. "I had on a cowboy hat," Carrie (a Swede) reminisces in perfect midwestern diction. "The main action was that I took it off and masses of hair billowed out. A TV commercial is only a bit closer to acting—you still aren't living out a characterization. In TV the action is precisely set for focusing. I will be shown a small area in which I am to confine any movement. On my first day for Flex, I was fortunate because I could play around and do what I wanted as far as expression and movement were concerned. On the day of shooting, I was to swing my hair and jump. It was a slow-motion, stop-action shot of my hand. The gesture included running my fingers through my hair—a crucial part of every hair commercial because of the difficulty of getting it perfect. Repetition is exhausting because it takes so much concentration. In a TV commercial small differences can be critical. The aim is perfection and that comes from keeping at it until you hear 'Cut' or 'It's a wrap' at the end of the day."

The scenario for a recent foreign commercial called for Carrie to fall for "Mr. Barclay," the cigarette man with more than one woman in his life. Apollonia played the jealous girlfriend. Carrie Nygren and Mr. B were to meet at a big party. By the time the cast arrived, every movement had been drawn up. The models were told the situation, timing, and action, and shown to their places. This is called blocking. Obviously, the more people involved, the more chance of error. Carrie was to bump into Barclay when he was ready on the mark. But five other couples had to get set. And ten characters had to accomplish an action and go—right back to their spots. It was timed to a tenth of a second. Carrie says, "When a scene involves so many people, and is so precisely timed, many takes are required to get the timing right. It took us from early morning into the evening, but as professionals we hung in and got it finished."

The Model Child: Guiding While Guarding a Minor's Career

A child model's career is much like an adult's. It requires seeking out an agent, attending go-sees at photography studios and again for the client, and being persistent, conscientious, and professional. And it takes planning—an underlying career direction and reason for each move, and in particular for each passage into a different category or market. This does not imply tricks or deception, simply intelligent forethought and planning.

Most talent agencies that specialize in the handling of children aim toward the more lucrative modeling areas of TV commercials, television comedy or drama, and theater. As children mature, rapid changes in face or body size can make them, at times, difficult to book. An agent then has three choices: to exploit the changes, to wait and see what the next change might bring, or to move the marketing of a career toward acting. Few children are able to sustain a still career throughout the realities of growing up. Two who did, with the help of astute management, are Brooke Shields and Doug McKeon. Brooke, a sought-after model from infancy through her teens, went on to become an actress. Terry Shields, Brooke's mother, recalls, "It all started with *Pretty Baby*. A photographer, Maureen Lambrey, had done a portrait of Louis Malle for a book called *Directors*. She recommended that he see Brooke for the Baby lead." Something similar happened to Linda Blair, who was modeling when *The Exorcist* was being cast, and to Patty Mc-Cormick, who appeared in *The Bad Seed*. It is no accident when the right child is at the right place at the right time. Someone brought the youngster along to that crucial point. Doug McKeon, like Brooke, started very young. His moves were varied and rapid: from commercials to soaps to afternoon teen shows and ultimately to movies. One performance that he—and millions of fans—will long remember was in *On Golden Pond*, with Henry and Jane Fonda and Katharine Hepburn.

A SECOND BEGINNING

To start out as a model, the only "working pass" a child needs is a Social Security number. There is no association, guild, or union governing that field for adults or children, so every job and all rates are negotiable. Rates generally are, however, significantly lower than for adult models.

There are three ways to reach the attention of scouts: via parents of other models, child talent agents seeking potential actors, and direct inquiries to agencies (for these, check local industry directories or phone books). New York is the epicenter for child modeling. Youngsters who appear in commercials compete for the photographic work—most child agents handle print as a commercial training ground. In medium-size markets (Phoenix, Miami, Minneapolis), there is more print than commercial work. Opportunities for children are best in a minimarket because clients use local talent and TV commercial campaigns are not extensive. Every market has *some* potential modeling jobs for a child. Chances may be limited in your area, but don't let that tempt you into unwise arrangements. Beware of anyone who promises work in return for money paid down. With children, as with other models, the best sources for print work are retailers or catalog houses, advertising agencies, and photographers. You can probably get a list of likely agencies from the personnel office at any fairly large local retailer that employs young free-lance models.

A child must have constant adult supervision in any modeling area and at every stage of obtaining a booking and performing. Under the law, a guardian must conduct all aspects of a minor's business. A parent's role is best described as manager. An adult decides to model by choice, but parental initiative starts a child on that course. It may be best, in the beginning, to deal with several agents to see who works out most satisfactorily. As children get better known, one agent is ample—and practical: Casting agents always know where a model can be found. The better known a child becomes, the firmer his footing in the business.

This is a rough trade for children, and they need protection. People at work have their own interests, and they're not likely to match the child's. A parent must monitor photographers, stylists, clients, everyone around, on the child's behalf. Obviously, this includes any financial arrangements. A minor can't be expected to comprehend the need to put money aside for the future. Be it finances or bookings, the child's best interests should be the guiding consideration.

Just as grown-ups get fed up, children can go through periods where they don't want to model. Other things may become more important for their development. However, as long as the child is interested and motivated, the parent's job is to provide support, encouragement, and personal enthusiasm. Things go best when the parent is as willing as the child to forge ahead.

SUCCESS DEPENDS ON THE PARENT

For a child, entering the field of modeling can be easy, yet many parents approach it incorrectly. Agents get hundreds of inappropriate pictures every day. All that's really needed is one shot of a child with a good smile—and a simple Polaroid can accomplish that. If an agent sets up an interview after seeing a Polaroid, then you can discuss a professional composite. The entry pictures for a child are black-and-white, eight-by-ten head shots. Too many parents, anxious about getting representation for their children, spend a lot of money starting a portfolio that will be useless. A meaningful portfolio comes only as a child works with good photographers on assignments.

Hounding agents with pictures and calls isn't only a waste of time and money. Such frantic efforts can be counterproductive. Mickey Aquilera learned his trade at the Mary Ellen White Agency, the largest children's modeling agency. He offers this advice: "Be patient: the agent will call you. The mother who phones every day is interfering with a busy work schedule. The ideal mom is willing to wait for calls and able to get to the go-sees. She will have read some books about the business, and not be pushy or stagestruck. If a mother wants to do something constructive, she can get her child into theater workshops, or theater activity at school. This will put him in front of people."

Another parental role is preparing the child for what to him is a strange new world. He will naturally take cues from adults—first you and later the agent. If you're in control, the child won't get either defensive or inhibited on go-sees, when he's surrounded by many children wanting the same assignment. Often the best way to stand out is to remain calm. After the effort to show a positive feeling at the go-see, there may well be a letdown when it's over. You need to be ready to handle a day's schedule. Cramming a second go-see into an hour is stressful for an adult but more so for a child. An agent will give you specific information about a go-see: time, place, and purpose, and savvy parents, after they've been through it awhile, will know what to expect. "One of my moms," says Mickey, "brings along a small trunk of clothing. If it's a character part, she has the glasses. This is *positive* aggression. The kid is prepared and books the jobs."

Once the job is scheduled, the mother again sets the pace. Children need to be on their toes from the minute the studio door opens—animated, on, and as ready as possible. Make sure your child is introduced to everyone. Explain the type and length of an assignment to a child exactly as a booker would to an adult. This helps the child to develop pride in his work. For your own sake, have something with you to occupy yourself—crossword puzzles, reading, letter writing. You're less likely to volunteer comments, advice, or opinions, which is detrimental. Don't bring anyone with you—child, adult friend, or family member—unless it has been approved far in advance. Even then, double-check with the studio manager. On advertising assignments, it is often wise not to even ask; the studio or location gets hectic enough without extra people. Finally, leave politely when the job is done— no well-are-we-going-to-work-together-again? farewells.

HOW IT WORKED FOR ONE

"Brooke was born an achiever and a perfectionist," remembers her mother, Terry Shields. "Even when very young, her judgments were very adult. I never made demands on Brooke even when she was a child. I *would* tell her she was great. That may have made her feel she had to do better. I can't answer that, but I do know Brooke is happy and well adjusted. One sure sign: She is happiest making others happy. When she gets a reward, a good mark, for example, she is content until the next challenge—when she again expects to get the worst one! That's an insecurity in her. Also, she was always very serious, perhaps too serious. Brooke often takes silly little things too much to heart.

"As with most mothers, it was my love and re-lationship to Brooke that formed her. She and I were very close and we worked well together, so I had her around the house for an extra year or two. I saw to it that I could raise her. I had taught Brooke to read and write by age three. She loved learning—it came easily to her."

When the time came for grammar school, Terry's role really changed. "The teacher was there to teach and I was there to mommy. She preferred things that way then, and still does." At high-school time, Terry didn't want Brooke in a professional school. "She was always in great demand, and some schools give in to any request. I didn't want her out of school unnecessarily." They found a good, convenient school near the George Washington Bridge—perfect to prepare Brooke for Princeton and handy to photography studios.

Brooke started modeling unusually early—at age eleven months. That's why being in front of a camera was second nature to her. Modeling was part of the routine. When Brooke started school, photographers worked around her schedule. Clients have to do this all the time because of child-labor laws. Terry says she had never planned on Brooke being a model or going into the movies. "But once it started I made sure it became fun. My goal was to make the day pass without it ever seeming like work. Therefore wonderful things happened because of Brooke's career.

"Much of what made Brooke's career a natural could be cultivated in any child. She was well behaved and disciplined, so she could work fast—a saving for clients who couldn't otherwise afford the high modeling rates. She learned to hold poses, a godsend to a photographer. And she genuinely likes people, which is good on a set *and* comes through well in the pictures. She was fortunate in her looks and in being well spoken at a very early age." But it wasn't commercials that did it for Brooke; it was her physical aptitude for fashion. Along with being beautiful, she was tall, slender, animated, graceful. Eventually graceful, that is. Terry Shields recalls, "She did her first fashion show at three. She twirled down the ramp—so dizzy and so damn cute! She had no *idea* what was going on. All she knew was that she was having a great time, and she loved all those raves and claps. Later (but not much later; this happened in her early teens), a major fashion photographer, Peter Gert, made the first use of

Brooke as she is known today. Shortly after, at fourteen, Brooke became the youngest model ever to appear on a *Cosmopolitan* cover."

IS MODELING RIGHT FOR YOUR CHILD?

Modeling can be marvelous for a child, provided he likes it. But parents must be realistic about the possibilities. If you feel your child has innate talent, give it some exposure and see what happens. Terry Shields admits to losing count of the parents who have asked her advice about their children. "The truth is that ninety-nine out of a hundred kids who dance and sing happily around the living-room television will freeze when they're taken into another room. The successful child model is the one who would walk up to a stranger and say, 'My name is . . .' If yours is among the self-assured one percent, pursue it." But don't kid yourself. It will be harder than it should be on you, and worse for the child, if you're wrong.

A child of eleven or twelve can face some stiff competition. Also, friends at school will no longer see him as "one of the gang." Modeling can be especially alienating to little boys. They want to be Little Leaguers, not fashion plates. When a boy is used to making a buck delivering newspapers, how can he understand the value of a forty- or sixty-dollar hour? Another source of trouble is brothers and sisters. As an only child, Brooke's needs could be given top priority. Terry Shields remembers other mothers "dragging two other kids three hours by train from Atlantic City to a go-see. They couldn't have time to fix a decent meal for the kids, never mind their poor husbands."

The bulk of the work goes to children who fit the classic description of good-looking and wholesome. A pattern is emerging of more dark, black, Oriental, and ethnic models, but blond hair and blue eyes is still the norm, with a scattering of redheads and freckled faces.

Costs are a big consideration in building a modeling career—the inevitable outlays for transportation, an expanded wardrobe, dentistry, haircuts, minor cosmetics. There may be a bite plate for missing teeth, visits to dermatologists, and dancing, acting, and singing lessons. There will finally be an initial photographic fee, but this expense should be incurred only after acceptance by a legitimate agency—and never deal with anything else. When the time comes for those shots, invest in a very good photographer; you'll be repaid many times over. Before that, a snapshot or Polaroid will do—any smiling face shot at close range. If the child balks at that, maybe you should drop the whole thing for a few months. Another "wait" signal might be a lack of interest in going to a photographer's studio for a picture.

As for wardrobe sizes, those in greatest demand in stores are also the most popular in catalogs and national ads: sizes 3 to 6X and sizes 10 and 12. Photographers claim a slender and older size 6X is easier to work with than a child who is younger and larger.

CHILDREN AND PHOTOGRAPHY

Whereas adults can require several photographic sessions, you can tell in one whether a child is photogenic. Don't transfer onto a child any of your unfulfilled photographic fantasies. Many very pretty children don't photograph well; interesting-looking children can photograph wonderfully as types. Some children have a natural affinity with the camera and can easily take direction to move this way or that, put their head in their hands, do it again a little differently. Naturalness can be developed, but there must be some potential to work with. If likely traits are there, a photographer can spot them right away and teach an interested child to be better.

Layouts for still photographs are kept simple and the action down to bare essentials, but photography still involves some waiting, primping, and preparing. For fleeting attention spans, that spells boredom. Be ready with games, homework, or some other engrossing activity. It helps that print is booked for short periods, often only an hour or two; with so much to be accomplished, most of the time *must* be spent working, which minimizes waiting time. The child who succeeds is the one who learns to cope: He doesn't fidget while he waits, or get uptight when things don't go too well, or take the work so seriously it makes him nervous. It's up to

Quit
Smoking
Because...

I LOVE
MY BABY

AMERICAN ✚ LUNG ASSOCIATION
The Christmas Seal People ®

A child's composite is at best only a synopsis of a portfolio. A head shot of a child model has to reveal more than run-of-the-mill cuteness. The accounts want to see the physical makeup of each child. Types are cast according to shape (round face, thin face) or size (big eyes, small eyes). The portfolio, and/or composite, has to be reformulated as the child grows. The more a baby changes, the more recent the photographs should be. A good photographer knows that it's a question of how you handle a child, which is of course decided at the initial casting. The infant that is animated even while under lights and in a surrogate mother's arms is rare and hard to find. To test, an experienced photographer will separate the baby from his mother and watch the reaction to lights and unusual stimulation.

Most children who perform ·at home freeze in a studio situation. This was never true for Ryan Fitzpatrick (facing page), except of course if he was without his clothes.

At an early age it is not overpowering to be rejected for a still catalog shot. Therefore, it may be the best time to enter modeling. It is also easy to foster a nonchalant attitude about rejection based on looking right. Terry Shields: "Much of what made Brooke's career natural could be cultivated in any child. She was well behaved and disciplined, so she could work fast—a saving for clients who couldn't otherwise afford the high modeling rates. She learned to hold poses, a godsend to a photographer. And she genuinely liked people, which is good on a set *and* comes through well in the pictures. Once it started I made sure it was fun. My goal was to have the day pass without it ever seeming like work."

Joe Hunter points out that in all his years at Ford, Brooke Shields is the only child in this business who was a cute kid and turned into a beautiful, tall-enough adult to continue modeling. Therefore, child modeling is not necessarily a step toward modeling as an adult.

The 900 million dollar man.

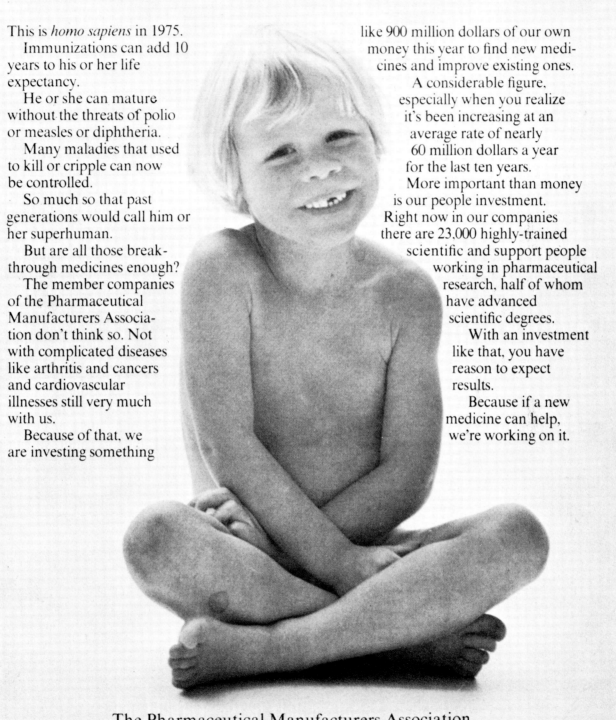

This is *homo sapiens* in 1975.

Immunizations can add 10 years to his or her life expectancy.

He or she can mature without the threats of polio or measles or diphtheria.

Many maladies that used to kill or cripple can now be controlled.

So much so that past generations would call him or her superhuman.

But are all those break-through medicines enough?

The member companies of the Pharmaceutical Manufacturers Association don't think so. Not with complicated diseases like arthritis and cancers and cardiovascular illnesses still very much with us.

Because of that, we are investing something like 900 million dollars of our own money this year to find new medicines and improve existing ones.

A considerable figure, especially when you realize it's been increasing at an average rate of nearly 60 million dollars a year for the last ten years.

More important than money is our people investment. Right now in our companies there are 23,000 highly-trained scientific and support people working in pharmaceutical research, half of whom have advanced scientific degrees.

With an investment like that, you have reason to expect results.

Because if a new medicine can help, we're working on it.

The Pharmaceutical Manufacturers Association.

We'd like to tell you more about pharmaceuticals. Send for our free booklet.
"When it Comes to Rx Medicines, There Are a Lot of Questions You Should Ask."
Write the Pharmaceutical Manufacturers Association, Dept. AT-506,
1155 Fifteenth St., N.W., Washington, D.C. 20005.

the parent to provide the right mix and help him keep his balance.

Josef Schneider, a photographer renowned for his portraits of children, learned to identify the photogenic child when he was a psychologist working with problem children in New York City schools. In his photographs for advertisers and private clients—and for children's portfolios, which especially need to show individual potential—Schneider says, "We try to capture the basic qualities of each child, to bring out the type no matter what type it is: round face, thin face, big eyes, small eyes, light hair, dark hair. The account wants to see the physiognomy of each child. A portfolio must not have a feeling of sameness: Each picture should contribute to a variety of mood and feeling. An adult head shot can tell quite a story. A head shot of a child has to go deeper, to reveal some things beyond mere run-of-the-mill."

The portfolio must be reformulated as a child grows. The ratio of body shots to head shots varies with the age. Action is important because it shows animation. Crawling, using a toy, interacting with any object—all these can work effectively. Younger children, up to, say, eleven months, can only work if asked for specific jobs, such as in parents' magazines and for baby products. Beyond that age, a proper portfolio—at least three or four pictures to show what range a child has—becomes vital.

Working with children, a photographer becomes astute at predicting their actions. With Josef Schneider, it's now almost instantaneous. "After fifteen minutes, I can tell what can be gotten. As the saying goes, there are no bad kids. Some are just better for your purpose than others. I can give an example in commercials. Thirty years ago, because of my photographs of children, I was called by a production house that was doing a job with kids and needed my model sources. The afternoon of the shoot I get a call. 'Joe, why did you recommend only monsters? We can't control them.' I said, 'No, they are only normal, healthy kids who are dynamic and vibrant!' The same child could be quiet and sensitive or active and playful—it's a question of how you handle them, and of course the initial casting. I have developed a keen sense of what can be expected from each age level. I look for behavior patterns, which kids can be brought out and which can't. During the casting I separate the wheat from the chaff. On average, about one in twenty-five can fill the bill."

Dani Cusson is a veteran child model whose first pictures were taken by Josef Schneider when she was two and a half, eight years ago. She has worked with Lauren Hutton for Ultima, as a spokeschild for Lipton tea, and in department-store catalogs. Her career took a new turn when she appeared with Meryl Streep and Roy Scheider in the movie *Still of the Night*. "I was given a toy and then Joe would take a picture of me," she says. "I would just play with it. I still remember his wall with all the toys on the hooks. He had everything. Joe made me feel really comfortable."

Modeling can be a fine starting point for children with talent. They can learn, with experience and time, not to mind if they don't get the pick of the modeling jobs, and to enjoy the new experiences, new challenges, and new people who they meet. If they do get the job, the on-set activity—taking direction, relating to other models, learning the professional ropes—will keep them too busy for many butterflies. Even the client running around might provide some diversion. A child works all the print areas at once—no waiting to learn from editorial before moving into commercial print or catalog, as men and women might do. Unless a child is very offbeat—which eliminates some from fashion—a child model can handle them all equally well.

Children, of course, are as they are. They can't put on makeup to look better. Few of them can handle themselves in front of the camera, work a look with style and charisma, or put on an act or a veneer. That comes with time. Children absorb it from the adults around them. They observe what works, find out about smiles and body language, and begin building the layers that characterize an adult personality.

A CHILD MODEL'S WORKING LIFE

A child model goes to school most of the day, and so is available from three-thirty to five-fifty; by law, children can only work part-time. A child's earnings—in their invariably lower range—vary as greatly as an adult's. In 1986, the catalog rate for a child is

GIMBELS
Spring
Shoe
Collection

Front cover
copy on page 15.

"A booker sends out a group of kids for go-sees for a toothpaste ad to be shot in several weeks," Joe Hunter begins a classic child modeling story. "The casting process will undoubtedly take a while since the client has to approve any choice. One seven-year-old receives a great response, so everyone waits for the necessary approvals. The photographer calls a short while later to book a go-see for the boy to meet the client. However, when the agent calls the boy's mom, she brings up the bad news. Sure enough, everything else is great except his two front teeth are missing." The successful child model, Joe points out, "has a bite plate."

To be successful as a child model means to be pushed toward commercials as a second step. Every child has modeling ability to some extent, but to make it in commercials requires something more. He or she has to be able to captivate a stranger by surpassing expectations. This is something that cannot be forced. Dani Cusson, left, had that ability, along with an uncanny adult awareness of catching attention. This came from experience on sets and at auditions at a young age. Dani went on to co-star opposite Meryl Streep and Roy Scheider in *Still of the Night*. Here and on the following page are two of her early shots that led to commercials. For a Gimbels shoe-catalog cover, Dani stepped into her mother's frocks. Dani's all-American, apple-pie looks help to land her many big national advertising campaigns for toiletries, foods and beverages, clothes, even vacations.

Modeling is a good place to begin a child's professional acting career. It is a mirror image of an adult model's career. A child must go to see clients, collect pictures by testing, and develop his or her skills. However, it also takes a unique parent/child relationship. Modeling requires letting a child get excited and making sure he is able to contain it.

For print work and TV spots, a child is asked to portray an everyday emotion or participate in common situations (usually related to school, play group, or home). As long as the child remains "in size," fashion-catalog work can be obtained. Be prepared for awkward stages, when perhaps other aspects of growing up should be stressed.

She has her daddy's eyes and *Johnson's* baby shampoo to protect them.

Some baby shampoos can irritate your baby's eyes. Not Johnson's Baby Shampoo. Its unique "no more tears"* formula keeps a smile in those little eyes while it gently cleans your baby's hair. More mothers trust Johnson's than any other baby shampoo.

We say "no more tears." We mean no more tears.

© J&J 1980 • Trademark

Johnson & Johnson

fifty to sixty dollars per hour; adults make three to four times as much. Though everything is negotiable, children's fees, like adults, are usually based on this catalog rate.

Occasionally a child gets a full day—$2,000 for a national-ad booking. A book cover or magazine may pay $100 to $125 a day, the normal adult rate. Bookings, as a rule, are for over one hour and rarely for more than three, the timing depending on age and medium (TV commercials would take longer than commercial print or catalog). Some jobs pay as high as $150 an hour (national ads with extensive usages), most middle-range jobs pay $75–$100 an hour, and some only pay $45 an hour (single catalog shots). Jobs like these add up at the end of the year and some are done just for a tear sheet at the beginning of a career. You must keep a record for such costs as coming into town, possible baby-sitters, paying for a snack, and deductions for commissions, which come "off the top" of the fee. Each is deductible for tax purposes. It is considered a good return if a child banks one third of the gross billing.

A ten- to twelve-year-old who has been in the business for seven years is considered a veteran. For infants of six months to a year, a tear sheet is valueless; babies change too fast and too much. A lost tooth or two and he looks entirely different. There is a concept called "in-size or out-of-size" that works very logically. At the size 7 stage, the teeth are out, limiting the child to offbeat bookings, such as a jack-o'lantern look. Size 6 is an active size because all the teeth are still in; sizes 8 or 10 get more action because the lost teeth are back.

"People have an image of kids making so much money that they're buying mink coats and Cadillacs for their parents," says Monica Stuart of Schuller Talent, Inc. Monica was herself a retail fashion model, working on staff with Jackie Rogers and Gillis McGill for Bergdorf Goodman before becoming a child talent scout and agent. She has developed many a child model into a seasoned performer. "All of the mothers I know are putting that money in the bank, in a trust, or in stock for their kids," she says. Monica explains what she looks for in a child: "Every child has some modeling ability. Like two people who meet in a crowded room and fall in love, you sense this, something connects. As an agent, you have to be able to feel the chemistry and, if you're to stay in the business, be right more often

than you're wrong. If a child appeals and captivates me, I have to say there is something more. It may be the child's response or his demeanor that interests me. Then, when I talk to them, I should surpass my expectation. What you look for in an interview isn't complicated. It's a child with potential or possibility, not one who can't be forced to do something. We ask questions to get a reaction. I'll ask: 'Do you like baseball? Are you married?' Whatever. John has his thumb in his mouth. He wishes he was in Red China. Mother says: 'John, I don't understand. When you're home you're talking all the time.' But I do understand. John does not want to answer. The opposite kind of kid has to be the center of attention. He's ready to go out there and grab what he can. The ideal is between those two: a child who is exuberant but can be controlled. That is what I want."

Monica Stuart likes to talk to children about TV commercials as soon as they reach reading age. For a print ad they don't have to do much—have a picture taken holding a box of cereal or drinking a glass of orange juice. For a vignette commercial, it may be something physical, like playing a game or cuddling a doll. Usually it is an action they would relate to normally because the products are things that come up in their daily lives. If the child has to react to what is happening, he is given direction: Run alongside your mommy, hold on to the cart like you do in the supermarket. If a child is verbal and outgoing, and reads well, he can do many commercials. There are limits though. Casting for commercials is much more competitive, so children can't get them every day. "Then," says Monica, "if they get the hang of it, the time might be right for something new—an off-Broadway show, a soap opera, a movie—though only if they are ready."

MODELING, ROAD TO MANY DESTINATIONS

Doug McKeon is a New Jersey high-school student with a dozen years of acting experience under his belt, most recently as summer replacement in Neil Simon's *Brighton Beach Memoirs*. Doug starred Off-Broadway in Ray Bradbury's *Dandelion Wine*, and from there was cast in a soap. He got his start indirectly, at five, when his sister was spotted by Monica Stuart and she asked to see the entire family. "Turned out I was the one signed, not any of the girls." Doug was too young to plan career-building strategies; Monica was the tactician. "She and Mom decided I'd have a trial-and-error period of six months, starting as a model. The second indirect step on the road to acting! I was very interested—contrary to what my mother initially expected. She had misgivings about whether I'd cooperate. Modeling was my stepping-stone into commercials."

Doug found himself matched up for size and color and look with the other kids at go-sees. Being a towhead, he always drew dark-haired girls. Catalog jobs went according to the clothes; that meant dressing up. If it was an ad, models had to bring a selection. "I met the same people over and over," Doug recalls. "There was friendly competition as I got to know the other guys. At a go-see a bunch of us would compare schedules and find out where we were going next. Sometimes we'd do two or three jobs together in one day.

"Photographers always wanted a nice expression. One picture will be forever in my mind: a child's face, mine, with a fixed smile. Standing very still—I remember that too. There was a child's game, playing statues, that photographers used to get the idea across.

"The photographers became my buddies. I learned to relate to a crew. Ever since, I've loved to meet people. I believe it was a plus for me. Also, growing up with a camera, a fear of the camera never entered my mind. A lens turned neutral while I was working, and I was always surprised to see myself months later in a magazine or on a billboard.

"Modeling started me toward acting, commercials made me able to do it. They were my transition into movies. I did Broadway and Off-Broadway, a soap-opera part out of New York (Timmy Farada on NBC) for a long run. I had to learn to control the vim and vigor needed for modeling and commercials. I enjoyed the change—it's not easy, always being happy. It's very draining to keep up that extra-high energy level of perpetual joy, actually tougher than serious acting."

Models are always living through periods of transition. Often, when things are slow, very little can be done about it. In Tracy Griefnow's case, she faced a major transition. And she was able to do something about it, something quite unusual. Her story began, however, in quite a conventional way. She went, at age eleven, from a school in Minneapolis to the modeling convention in New York. She won every category in her division two consecutive years. Encouraged by Claudia Black of Ford, who thought Tracy would do very well, that summer Tracy and her mother moved to New York and she signed with her first agent. "The best assignment I ever had was at Tavern on the Green for Bill Blass. All I had to do was mingle, eat, and drink in one Blass outfit after another." Tracy's first week in New York, she remembers, she and her mother would walk the streets, more often than not in the wrong direction. The agency soon started her off doing rounds. "The first Friday I got a department-store job. I fitted in well because in Minnesota I did mostly family things, not singles. Though of course I was ready to do fashion singles and doubles."

Tracy hit her first roadblock at fourteen, and the problem was her height. She began at five feet five, to be too short for many jobs. Of course, she would grow to the necessary five feet eight, but that takes time. Tracy used the intervening time to good advantage, partly through a lucky break. "I went with a friend to see a Japanese agent who was very interested in my going to Tokyo. It was a good move during a transition period because I could work there as an adult—the height requirement in Japan is less stringent. With the tear sheets from Japanese editorial jobs, I could go to *Seventeen* and *Mademoiselle*. I need to get all the experience I can while I'm growing to five feet eight. And besides, I want to keep in touch. I familiarize myself with the work of fashion photographers I want to be working for in the near future. As soon as I grow another inch, I am going to test with them." Meanwhile, Tracy continues her career with Petite Models in New York.

Adrienne Albert is a co-director of Kids & Co., a management organization that coaches talented children in singing jingles for commercials and teaches acting for commercials and for afternoon television. Adrienne helps with anything necessary to move a career along. From a small start, *Kids* has grown to a roster of diversified and capable talents. One agency service is the preparation of any qualified client for modeling. "Calls are limited mainly to all-American, beautiful blond midwesterners with a fresh look—usually a toddler two or size 6X. Age range is the only real variation in casting breakdowns. We occasionally get calls for black, Hispanic, or ethnic kids.

"We find that experience in front of a still camera develops poise and a sense of the work ethic. And, of course, it's a good springboard. At early childhood it is not overpowering to a child to be rejected for a still catalog shot. Therefore, it may be the best time to enter modeling. It's easy to foster a healthy its-no-big-deal attitude. Then, too, children and teens are used more and more, in a group or family situation, to sell virtually everything. The market is growing all the time—advertising, fashion runway, catalog, editorial, and TV. Clothing manufacturers and retailers are very large clients."

Most jobs are in a studio, but many take place on location around Manhattan or, for countrified scenes, in the immediate surrounding area. As a manager ("and that's different from an agent," Adrienne explains) she helps with the child's appearance for each go-see, seeing to hairstyles or appropriate clothes. To book to the maximum, a child has to remain flexible, be able to go from pigtail for mass appeal to *au courant* for fashion. Also, children, like adults, need to be prepared to meet casting people. "After all, a child gets very little time, and no second chance," Adrienne reminds us. "The response is based on the situation on that particular day. The child, like the rest of us, can get up on the wrong side of bed. Especially with the young, it is important that they know they went in well prepared and don't feel the insecurity of second thoughts about how they should have performed or looked. That's when you're happy, as a manager, to have a basically good-natured child."

A Teen's Dream: Turning the Key

*W*hether you start modeling as a teenager or bring to more adult work some experience as a child, you won't find concessions made to you that are made to the very young. You will be expected to perform as proficiently and professionally as an adult; people may be even more critical of some of your behavior and personality traits. Common sense, good manners, and respect for others will never fail you. Neither will attention to some dos and don'ts.

First of all, in the face of unaccustomed flattery and adulation, you need some balance and perspective about yourself. Never take to heart the hype being handed out on your behalf. So many egos are hopelessly inflated that any photographer, stylist, or art director will be relieved not to have to spend time massaging another one. You don't need to have a distorted perception of your abilities or display a lot of temperament to stay on top as a model. In fact, you're a lot likelier to survive if you don't.

Dedication to your profession is indispensable. So is eagerness to discover different facets within yourself. These can be difficult to sustain job after job; it will help if you develop detachment about yourself. Analyze, as objectively as you can, your knowledge and experience, your likes and dislikes, and what you can convey. Once you know these things, you're ready to react with sincerity to bring the desired interpretation to a product. It is important to remain a critic of your work and your attitude. Don't let yourself off easily; there's a challenge in pushing yourself further and further.

A FLAIR FOR FASHION

Those whose abilities point to fashion could start by working for a designer or manufacturer full-time or free-lance in the showroom. Many successful models have made their fashion connection in the fitting room or on the runway. It could be in Europe, but any fashionable city will do. You can't, however, be a high-fashion model straight off the main street of Dixon, Illinois. Kansas City maybe, but even then not for *Vogue* or *Harper's Bazaar*. You acquire a fashion sense through association with those who already have it, and nowhere else. This sounds so ordinary that many young models with their eyes on stardom think they can skip the step, or learn what they need from magazines. They are right to develop skills in *their* own hometown, or wherever they can acquire any degree of professionalism. After that, it's an easier move to New York, Tokyo, or London. The move can be even smoother if you develop a speciality that can be applied immediately—demonstrating skills useful to conventions, some understanding of activewear or skiwear, or the fundamentals of TV commercials.

Take care, when you plan that next move, that it won't overreach your capabilities. It is vital to be realistic. Better to be conservative than to find yourself in a strange city with hardly a prayer of attracting clients. Move from a medium-size market to a big city in stages, keeping your present clients intact. This will keep you and your tear sheets current. Nothing dates as fast as fashion.

Kim Alexis, like all of us, works in the present, but, she says, "I always think about the future, though I can't picture what I'll be doing." She does her best, however, to model the future to her tastes. "I write out what I want in fairly specific terms in three months, six months, or one year. Then I set down my longer-term hopes for three, five, and ten years. Setting goals helps me to know what should be happening along the way, to see different areas I could go off into. This way I work to some purpose, instead of floundering.

THE VALUE OF SMALLER MARKETS

It is not difficult to get some experience in fashion and discipline before coming to New York. In every United States market there are agencies with teen boards, or showrooms that hire for market week. In Tracy Nash's town, St. Louis, there is no fashion, but she got on a teen board in high school, mostly because people always said she should be a model. "It seemed pretty impossible to me. I was tall and thin, and wore glasses. And later on I became an engineer! But however it looked then, I ended up coming to New York to see five agencies—Ford, Wilhelmina, Zoli, Elite, and Click—and I signed with Wilhelmina."

Of course, a lot happened in between. During her freshman and sophomore years at Southern Meth-

odist University, Tracy worked at the fashion mart in downtown Dallas—sort of informal tearoom modeling. "I would walk, and the salespeople would sell. I sold too if they needed me after a few turns at showing. One time the owner of Esprit de Corp came to Dallas and took pictures of all the models. He showed them to Toscani, who said of me, 'Why don't you use her in your catalog?' I was plenty scared—I had never done a catalog before—but I flew out. Toscani was wonderful to work with. He jokes and kids around with you, but he knows a model has to be herself, not strike a lot of clichéd poses. I got the cover and worked on the next two catalogs with Toscani. When it was time, he told me to go to the New York agents.

"My junior and senior years I transferred to Atlanta, in many ways a good place to learn the ropes before coming to New York. I picked up some sound principles. People were sticklers for good work habits. And for a model it continues off the set. Actually, once you're inside the studio, Atlanta or Detroit or St. Louis or Dallas are very much the same. I am expected to smile, light up the product."

THE INTERCONNECTED WORLD OF MODELING

Modeling is a world of mutual acquaintances. Connections within the business are formed when people talk among themselves. Once a model has worked well with a photographer or a hair or makeup stylist, she will be mentioned. A chain reaction sets in, leading to requests for go-sees. The result is a network of people who relate comfortably and like working together. This needn't mean socializing after hours, but if that comes up and you are a social creature, feel free. The quickest route to modeling is a recommendation from the right person, one who feels genuinely able to tell a client, "I worked with that model last week. Real pro, nice person."

Something similar works in breaking the photographer/testing barrier. Except for the rare testing photographers, who are always testing new models, tests come about in several ways, depending on the photographer's circumstances. When an established photographer needs to revise or add to his portfolio, he will call the larger New York agents

One of the awkward periods for most adults is at the very beginning—as a teen. While waiting to attain full stature there are two choices: go to a market that demands smaller models, for example Japan, or sign up for the testing board in a local market. Tracy Nash (right) did move around during her teenage years. She was a transfer student in Atlanta, where she actually started her professional career. She had been on a testing board in St. Louis and had worked vacations and weekends in the Dallas showroom of Esprit de Corp. They used her for their catalog, after Toscani discovered Tracy from a snapshot taken in the showroom.

The *Hommes Vogue* photograph (facing page) by Stephan Lupino, was taken when Keith Mitchell, a modeling contest winner, arrived in New York and needed that difficult first composite. Armed with that composite, Keith never had to explain how he might look in a photograph. Fifteen months later, Keith and Stephan replicated the photo session (superimposed on the magazine photograph). The contact sheet exposes how under any circumstances a model must project a trademark, something of his personality, to the camera.

It is important never to apologize at an interview. If you have any photographs (either tear sheets or tests) that you expect soon, mention this; it will give you an opportunity to return when you have them in hand.

The best way to test with a photographer is to get off the subject at the initial go-see. The rule for photographing teens is to have a pleasant expression in a safe circumstance. The three photographs on p. 218 are of teens playing roles that are common. The top two are neutral male/female posturings. At the bottom is Tracy Griefnow, between the stages of child and teen.

about current talent. When an assistant to a known photographer is ready to test, the studio's portfolio will be taken to those agencies. When a photographer is new in town and needs to get established, he will call the agencies. Last, if an art director wants to spec test an idea, he calls a photographer who in turn calls an agent, and the request is put onto the testing board. Several models are sent out, but only a few can be tested by any one photographer. That makes the interview impression extremely crucial. Many first tests come out of these less-than-casual meetings of model and photographer or stylist.

Connections were no problem for Noelle Williams, the daughter of two celebrities, singer Andy Williams and actress Claudine Longet. What she faced was parental objections. She wanted, at age sixteen, to move to New York to model for Eileen Ford. They felt she should live the normal, wholesome life of an ordinary high-school girl and then go on to college. She was persuaded to do it their way, but as it turned out, she got a taste of modeling. While in college at Boulder, Colorado, she continued doing local advertising in Aspen, appearing in eight Mountain Dew commercials through Aspen Talent. Her agent submitted her picture to the New Faces of the Rocky Mountains contest and, as a semifinalist, Noelle met Helen Murray at that time a scout for Wilhelmina.

Noelle Williams recalls what happened after that:

SUPERFORME

la rentrée

Eh oui, l... existe, m... les homm... des lustr... rence, vo... soudain i... accomode... souci ser... jusqu'ici... seuls con... ticiens et... saltimban... victimes... de la ca... il est vra... prétexte... les rudes... de leurs... Mais, à... dermatologues et instituts, le taux des concernés aurait progressé de 25 % en un an, alors que jusqu'ici les griffures du temps les laissaient sans réaction.

...élioration (durable) ...vec, de surcroît, un ...au raffermie et la ...C'est un traitement ...ment idéal pour les ...prime le problème ...cicatrisation de la ...surgonflement des ...agène, ADN) qui, ...sont toutes à proscrire ...e que c'est une ...comble mais n'est ...ganisme, peut se ...leux) et rendre le ...t; le collagène (de ...i vous avez passé le ...squez de ne pas ...provoque parfois un ...re (petite boule ...très difficilement) ...ADN, prélevée sur ...mouton, est bien ...clat ne dure qu'une ...er, comme le dit le ...moyen le plus cher d'avoir encore plus de rides". A fuir...

Le traitement de Philippe Simonin existe depuis cinq ans déjà, ce qui permet une honnête vision historique. Il a dû à l'heure actuelle traiter plus de 2 000 patients, et des biopsies sont en cours à la Fondation Rothschild avec études des coupes histologiques semi-fines et ultra-fines pour la microscopie électronique. Qu'est-ce qui motive les hommes à aller voir Simonin, me direz-vous ? Eh bien, ce sont tout d'abord les cernes qui accusent l'air fatigué. Elles vont du jaune

STEPHAN LUPINO

COOK WITH CLASS

What better way to prepare savory Italian dishes than in your own *ATTENZIONE* apron! Choose from two styles: hip length (22" x 24") with pockets and knee length (26" x 33") without pockets. Both aprons (green only) are made of natural twill and have adjustable straps. A perfect match—delicious food and the *ATTENZIONE* apron.

Please send me: _____ apron(s) with pockets @ $9.95 each and/or _____ apron(s) without pockets @ $9.95 each plus $1.00 postage and handling (check or money order) to **ATTENZIONE APRON,** 55 E. 34 St., NY., NY 10016

Name

Address

City, State and Zip

New York residents please add sales tax. Allow 4 to 6 weeks for delivery.

SERO® and *Ms.* SERO

Matchmaker

The Purist® button-down and the Queen Anne collar — uniquely Sero. Profiles that blend the excitement of today with the elegance and quality of yesteryear. She takes pride in his soft, full-flared collar . . . the fit . . . and gentlemanly well-tailored appearance. He admires her portrait perfect blouse . . . the delicately ruffled collar and cuffs . . . and impeccable feminine styling. Sero and Ms. Sero — shirts made for each other.

Kodel®
polyester

KODEL is an Eastman Kodak Company reg. TM

Beach Blossoms from

Oscar de la Renta

Oscar de la Renta by **little dippers®**

"After I won the contest, I finished up my year in Boulder. I could hardly wait to get to New York! My parents were now all for it because I had an agent. The big town took some getting used to though. Coming to a New York agency, after Aspen, was a munch on a reality sandwich. I thought it would be just the same, but when I work in either place now, I can see the difference."

One big difference, in New York, was the importance of testing. Or, more precisely, why some interviews with photographers work and others don't. "Outside factors such as length of hair or coloring affect the decision to test," Noelle explains. "But mainly, when it doesn't click, it's because one of the two people decided against working together. I didn't have my first job for four months, and I was confused. All I heard was 'You're not this' or 'You're not that!' I found I *did* get jobs once a photographer and I had worked together during a test and the feeling was friendly when I left." Noelle's first job was a picture for *Interview* magazine, taken by Lynn Kohlman, an ex-Zoli model.

In the beginning, bookers gave Noelle one-on-one attention. "If I forgot to call in, they would call me. I could ask their advice. They were supportive because they knew, for a beginner, it's hard to recognize constructive criticism. Helen Murray kept in touch with me, cheering me up when I got discouraged. And she gave me some good advice: to stop eating and sleeping modeling—'Go to museums and beaches on the weekends. Give yourself a break!'

"When I relaxed and stopped wanting it so bad, it came to me: The best way to get results with photographers was to get off the subject of testing and onto something else of mutual interest. After talking to so many aspirants, it's a relief to discuss Colorado, fishing, whatever.

"I found too that the better the photographer, the less I had to talk. And if a photographer was as new and uncomfortable as I was, we'd just chat back and forth, and pretty soon we would both be at ease."

A teenager, just like a man, woman, or child, has to start to work on a composite with a closeup head shot, plus the different looks she can portray. The portfolio needs pace and variety to get across your attributes and versatility. Build your portfolio as an adult does, by testing until you're ready to go out for small jobs. Get in front of a camera at every opportunity. Learn all you can about advertising or fashion photography at the local retail stores. As you learn names and meet people, start to expand your rounds lists. Continually expand the areas of modeling in which you are proficient; such strategic moves as showroom or editorial to press kits, or convention trade shows to catalog, are tried and true, but they work.

A teen model's clients can be corporate giants or local retailers. Among the big product possibilities are soft drinks, grooming aids, music equipment and records, video games, clothing, and sporting goods. Their producers aim everything at the teenager: catalogs and brochures as well as magazine ads, billboards, and TV commercials. The field is almost as broad as for adult men and women. The larger corporations see their market as middle American, WASPY, preppy, and wholesome, or as an extension of the children's market. Record companies (producers of music videos included) and jean manufacturers, on the other hand, lean more toward the trendy types. Teenagers aren't often seen as characters, except for such safe generalizations as the greaser, bookworm, budding jock, or bike freak. Little is tried that doesn't relate directly to the American teenager's insulated world. Expect such locales as college classes and dorms, locker rooms and sports fields, disco dance floors and beach settings. Situations predominantly relate family, school, or peer groups through sports, education, leisure activities, or food. Advertisers never poke fun at embarrassing attributes, such as height or weight, rarely go in for extreme sophistication, and steer clear of sensitive or serious issues. With few exceptions, Madison Avenue likes teens who are upscale, well spoken, can carry themselves, and are conspicuously clean.

Keith Mitchell got the modeling bug when his girlfriend enrolled in a modeling school in Nashville. That summer, Keith got pictures taken by answering an ad in a local paper. In the hard lesson he learned, there's a message for aspiring young models. Keith was advised to attend a ten-dollar seminar. He sat through a slide presentation that purported to teach the poses for modeling. In fact, the presentation was a sales pitch for pictures, and their photographer: "You need pictures to be considered by big-time photographers." Keith was given a choice: one roll of black-and-white head shots for $100 as a commercial model, or two rolls of color for $250 for fashion modeling. He was promised prints and a portfolio. Feeling quite proud of himself, Keith negotiated a $150 charge for one roll of color.

"On a sunny afternoon, they strolled six of us down to the Mississippi. Everyone jumped in and out of clothes, bang, bang, done in three minutes flat. Next day at the office, boxes of slides awaited them, and that was that. I paid seven-fifty in film and processing, and ten dollars worth of photographer's time, to a company that, I found out later, also runs a contest that requires a two-hundred-fifty-dollar sponsor's fee!" Keith is wiser now, but then he swallowed the scam and believed that a prestigious New York scout would come to judge his pictures.

At a Tennessee University, Keith was asked to be in an all-male revue that led six months later to a bathing-suit calendar. That reawakened his interest in modeling. Armed with the calendar shots and two decent slides from the fiasco at the edge of the river, he approached local photographers. Some said they would test him, but nothing happened. "I did talk to one photographer who had an ad in a paper looking for free-lance models. He told me I needed better pictures and that he would do them cheap. It seems he made part of his living doing portfolios. This was his come-on, but he was sincere, and he did have his real clients. I made an agreement to do assisting work and to help rebuild his darkroom in exchange for an entire shooting. One booking actually did come out of it—a small show and the press kit for a shirt company that came into the exhibition hall."

Keith's girlfriend's modeling school said they would enroll him in a short course if he agreed to represent them in New York for an annual modeling convention. Besides a trophy, as an overall winner Keith got enough money to repay his dad for the plane ticket. He also took the opportunity, while in New York, to see a dozen agencies. "Some agencies were ready to sign me on and nearly all were interested in me for commercials." Keith got quite a reception when he got back to Nashville. "I had my moment in the limelight—I was a short-term near-celebrity! I had appeared on local talk shows, and an interview—along with my picture—appeared in the paper."

With these heady experiences Keith decided the time was right to branch out, and he headed for Key West with his brother. "The first stop along the way from Nashville was Atlanta, because I was given what I thought was a photographer's number to call. He turned out to be the art director of a department store. I walked in and said, 'I am a model. Just won a contest up there,' pointing north. The guy introduced me to an ad agency that hired me for two days at one hundred eighty dollars per!" The next stop was Jacksonville. This time Keith strolled directly into an agency, and the same thing happened. This was pretty encouraging, so he decided to explore the rest of the city's possibilities thoroughly. "All the way to Miami I stopped to talk to agents and left black-and-white glossies."

Miami was a wider, more varied market, and Keith could see he wasn't going to crack it overnight. He just gave each place a few days, starting back up to Nashville and eventually returning to New York. He got work through a few of the agents on the way north. "When I hit Tampa there was a cancellation at an agency—a half-day doing three ads for the Sunday supplement. In Philadelphia, at an athletic-equipment show, I got a day's work and the names of some California companies to contact later. In Washington, I did my first runway show in connection with a polyester product in a local department store. Even got my picture in the morning paper!"

Keith admits not making any money so far, but there were other payoffs. "As soon as I got composites, they went to where I had an agent. The tear sheets from the trip became a portfolio." Keith came to New York that fall and arranged to work through Mickey Aquilera, who was now handling teens for Gilla Roos. Initially he was after editorial tear sheets from the confession and romance magazines. "My first—illustrating a short fiction piece—was a romantic scene in front of a fire. In the story I get the young girl pregnant! Story illustrations led to a national deodorant ad." A long road, but, as Keith says, "All of it was enjoyable."

Strategy and Tactics:
Moving a Career Along

◆

The first principle in maintaining a career is to avoid overexposure in any single market. Aside from getting "worn out" in that place, you must work in more than one area to make a substantial, constant living, or not to be dependent on only a few clients. Strategy here means the method of moving from one area to another. It could literally mean branching out geographically, or applying your abilities to different modeling fields, or both. Either way timing is crucial, not only because most work is periodic but also because the periods vary with the geographic region. Never let yourself be caught on the "down side" of a cycle: in Milan or California during the slow season, or looking for runway work in New York from November through Christmas.

During a crossover period, from place to place or field to field, flexibility is a model's best asset. The one constant, as you stretch your horizons, must be fidelity to the standards and preferences at your client level, whether actual or hoped for. Giant corporations can be stuffy about hair length on men or makeup style for women, even about personal reputations.

In your search for new possibilities, be ingenious about extending your aptitudes—using live demonstration skills, for example, to solve photographic problems. Or devise a new approach to presenting a product or projecting for film. Experimentation is healthy, as long as you don't loose sight of the need for mass appeal. A model must have the capacity to reach a large audience, or settle for remaining obscure.

Addressing yourself to a new field demands unusual tenacity about making rounds and following up on initial contacts. You'll reach more new people faster by leaving printed self-promotional pieces—get those composites in circulation. You are your best PR rep. Of course, work out your plans with an agent, your invaluable ally in smoking out work. The right agent can minimize wasted and unwise moves when you take a new career direction. Behind every successful model is a good booker.

A reputation that took years to build can disintegrate in no time if you take inappropriate stabs toward a new goal. This is an image business. The path to success is a well-devised course of action backed by astute implementation. If the goal, for instance, is to work in the fashion area for such prestigious publications as *Elle* in Paris, *Honey* in London, or *Seventeen* in New York, a plan might be to meet and possibly test with the assistants of photographers who are regularly assigned pages in those magazines. If the aim is runway, and there are no showrooms available, you could model on the designer floor of a top department store.

MAN OFF THE STREET

No model can afford to pass up opportunities or ignore promising circumstances. Sometimes a chance experience or encounter can be the entrée you need into a whole new area. An example is what happened to unknown Tony London of Legends, via Andy Warhol's "on the streets" technique for *Interview* magazine, a publication Andy created and for which he now serves as publisher.

Interview is Andy's connection with the modeling business. Its major purpose is, he says, "to show the most glamorous clothes, makeup, and hairdos on the world's most beautiful faces and bodies." For the magazine's videos, Andy goes out on the streets to find obscure beautiful people and the occasional notables to appear together as a big informal group. "I told Tony to come down to the factory because he would photograph well. He is good-looking and with the Legends and Mannequin group, a perfect type for men's products or magazines like the revamped *M.*"

At the taping, Tony felt strange but decided cool was the way to handle the situation. He said hello to Andy and then sat back, watched, and waited. The room was filled with actors and actresses, art students, and a lot of bizarre types with names that were hard for Tony to pronounce and unthinkable to remember. Vincent, Andy's assistant cameraman, placed Tony and told him his part would be to smile and tell about his first trip to New York for one minute straight. The words "My name is Tony London. I'm from Nags Head, North Carolina" were Tony's first as a television model. He went on about coming to New York to model, and the fun it was for a small-town boy: "So many different people; all those subways and buses. It was almost a culture shock but now I honestly have to say I love it. I am grateful for the opportunity Andy's giving me here. Thanks, Andy." He finished his minute with his best smile; Andy told him he was great and wished him good luck with modeling.

Andy Warhol is a Zoli model for photography and runway. He began modeling in his more mature years, but was by no means an unknown in the fashion and art worlds. His avant-garde views and diversified career directions can be a lesson to us all. Andy Warhol has a unique look and admits that he has to wear two pair of pants to achieve the proper model size. "My motivation to get into modeling was to become less nervous being in front of a group. I get most nervous when I'm competing against beautiful young boys. I have to show what I'm doing there; they are there because they are right for the work."

Andy has his own theory as to why the competition is so fierce: "It is that good-looking boys don't go in the army. Remember, there is no war on so all those kids don't go to fight and the women don't have to go into factories. Instead they are becoming models. Almost everyone in New York could be a model. Last Saturday we were on location at the Bronx Zoo and all the young kids we saw could model. I think the best-looking go to Los Angeles and New York. When I am on go-sees and jobs, I realize the good-looking guys are no longer living upstate. They're right here being models.

"I started by reading *Glamour* and *Mademoiselle* to find out how to do those things for myself. They have the stories and features showing what to do. There is plenty to learn. I have finally gotten over my pimples. Clearasil works! I still use a lot of makeup; done in the right way it helps me look my best in front of the camera. Last week I did a Jordan Marsh catalog up in Boston—not as an artist but as a model. Someone even came up to me and asked if I was the model in the Barney's ad. I was thrilled to even wear the Missoni sweater, but to be recognized as a model! It was the highest point in my life. Working for photography involves standing around, so students should bring plenty of homework. Otherwise boredom can get to you.

"Modeling gets you around, and it is an interesting profession. I had to learn to pace myself and be organized. There is a lot of that to modeling; also, the constant meeting of new people. But it is runway work that has taught me how to walk, and how to work with the best people. Runway has gotten me in front of an audience and now I am much less nervous. There is no confusion and I have learned to enjoy doing the shows. At a department-store show, a model wears all the designers, not just his favorites. I have done six or seven shows, including one for Bill Blass. I can only sell clothes that I like, but a model who is really good can sell any product. The clothes are great to wear. Something special happens backstage; it is amazing to see. It is well choreographed—I recommend it as a good place to learn.

"If models are working their way toward being movie stars, runway is the ideal starting point. Apollonia, the co-star of *Purple Rain* got into commercials from there because she was seen—and because of the agency mailer that gets sent to everyone that matters. My agent has been sending me on auditions for movies and it seems to me that modeling is a perfect route."

TWO ROADS TO MALE MODELING SUCCESS

Wilhelmina's superstar Jon Weidemann's story is a classic example of a male model's career. It entailed intense effort by his agent at each transition point. At present, they are concentrating on commercials, knowing it will take time for steam to build. Jon has one for Calvin Klein in the can and another running for Cacherel. He noticed at several points along the way that coincidences were occurring. It was his agency that has made them happen.

Jon was finishing up his junior year at Harvard as a photography major when a girlfriend asked if he would do a modeling job. It would pay fifty to seventy-five dollars. After the shooting, Bruce Weber took Jon's Santa Fe summer address and called while on assignment in the Pecos Wilderness for British *Vogue*, wanting him to work again. Thinking back, Jon says, "I was embarrassed, so I told him no. Then I called him back and said, 'Yeah, I'll do it.' The crowd I ran with at the time were wilderness instructors and outdoorsy people—the direct opposite of the fashionable and urbane modeling world. The British *Vogue* job was shot at Georgia O'Keeffe's house. There was also a third job while I was working in Santa Fe. An East Coast assignment came up for redheads. Again it was British

Vogue and Bruce Weber. I hiked out about fifteen miles, drove my car to Albuquerque, hopped on a plane, did a shooting, and then jumped right back into the wilderness.

"I was beginning to drop my preconceptions about male modeling. At the end of the summer, the wilderness program closed, I was finished with college and thought I should decide what to do with myself. So I came up to New York to give modeling a shot.

"At first I was very aware who were the top ten or twenty male models. I was intimidated but I admired them. I didn't allow myself into a competition where I wanted to beat them; I wanted to be one of them. The shows and shootings for men generally involve the same group of male models. I have established friendships and find I work well with them. An important aspect in a man's career is how the agent initiates him. For me the next hurdle was a show. I did a big one at the Plaza. I was very scared and nervous, and to top it off the show was exclusively furs. For me there was a conflict: there I was wearing furs when it would have been more natural to be teaching environmental control. I was told to walk out and to smile like I always walked and smiled. Getting that show under my belt forced me to decide if I wanted the career to gather momentum. Meanwhile, my agents at Click were busy planning the next strategy.

"Next I learned to get along with the other men in the industry and to be part of a group: photographers, art directors, stylists for clothes, hair, and makeup. I now have a cumulative history with these people that results in each being helpful to the other. I had to learn everything about how to be a model. I picked it up from the friends I made. I learned how to talk myself up at go-sees and rounds. Though similar in some respects, it is not the same for a man as for a woman. They can improve modeling skills or bring knowledge and emotional qualities to wearing clothes. There are strict limits to a man's character allowed in a picture and that stunts creativity. We can only be happy, seductive, or manly. Women can be just about whatever they choose. Also, men are hung up about seeing other males projecting themselves. Men do perceive other men, but not in ways relevant to selling clothes or products to a large audience.

"I started to take care of myself and to make myself available and be at the important appointments being made for me. It was only after a composite was together that I appeared ready to tackle advertisements and catalogs. Once that card is assembled correctly, the tactic can be, on go-sees, to get those pictures seen. Again it was my agent who got me the introductions I needed. My first introduction was to people at the men's clothing manufacturers association. Working two or three shows a week got me acquainted with at least twenty designers; some of them called me for pictures they needed for publications or press kits. Second, I had been asked the previous year to see Avedon about a job as an assistant. He was starting a project on Working Men Throughout the American West. That had fallen through (for me, not for him), but I had another opportunity to speak to Avedon on a modeling go-see for redheads. I always felt it was having met him in another context that made Avedon book me for my first editorial job, an American *Vogue* assignment. The last piece to my composite came when Calvin Klein booked me for ten days—my first fully paid national advertising. Those Avedon pictures and the Bruce Weber series for Calvin Klein combined to give me exposure and credibility."

For a male model, the reward for editorial exposure is heavy demand while the issue is on the stands. It is prudent to prolong this demand by doing department-store and regional product advertising. New York editorial work will also create a demand in European markets, where financial rewards come in the form of German catalog work. Together these forces create two desirable effects: your not being available builds demand, and you secure a foothold in a second market. It's to a model's advantage not to be able to do every job. For one thing, he must be careful of the uses of his image on a printed page. Don't have pictures running for similar clients in the same issue. Watch out for clusters of pictures and overexposure in any market. This is the surest way to maintain control over a career. It comes from having a good marketing plan and an agent who understands how to implement it.

Here is one tale of a top model managed by MEN in New York: After graduation from a Big Ten school, Scott Connell went west to look for work. He took a job through a headhunter, who also suggested that an introduction to a modeling agent might be worthwhile. When Scott was told he could possibly make ten thousand dollars part-time, his eyes widened, but all that came of it was one mail-order catalog. He tried following that lead up by way of a few back doors, but he wasn't happy with that approach, and besides, there wasn't too much demand for a weight-lifting model. National Production Systems in Los Angeles became Scott's only interest as his job grew more and more challenging.

Then, at a party, a movie producer introduced Scott to Tom Hunn from Mary Webb Davis. Scott asked Tom, "Am I too large?" And the answer was yes. Tom sent Scott a list of test photographers to see if he ever dropped some of the weight. Shortly after, Scott underwent surgery. On doctor's orders, he gave up weight lifting for running. That took off inches from his neck, chest, torso, and limbs. Scott couldn't schedule a time with the recommended photographers, so he invested seventy-five dollars on pictures so that his chances could be accurately assessed. "Tom Hunn was thrilled. I went for a second test and those tickled him even pinker." With those two tests in a book, Scott went off to see Herb Ritts on his first go-see. "He offered me three hundred dollars for a day to do one shot for Gian Franco Ferre. I had never been offered that kind of money for a couple hours' extra weekend work.

"Whenever I could I went on go-sees, trying to fit them around work. One day I went on one in a rented room. When I drove up, I could see a huge crowd had gotten there before me. The line went down two flights, around the corner, and down the block. After two hours of waiting (there must have been five hundred people ahead of me), I was ushered in to see Donald Sturzient of *GQ* and Bruce Weber. They said they would be interested in using me up in Santa Barbara for a week—unfortunately during my workweek. I told them it was going to be difficult. They asked me to see what I could arrange. When the booking was confirmed, I went in to my boss and asked for the time. A compromise was easily worked out: I got off Friday and the first two days of the next week. *GQ* was satisfied with the arrangement. On Tuesday, Donald and Bruce asked me if I could get another day. It was after five and my boss had gone home, so I flew back to be on hand for work as promised. My boss asked me not to take off more time that week. When I called, Donald asked me to come up Saturday instead. I went up, and I thought that was that. Two weeks later I was booked for a *GQ* cover try in New York. It was on such short notice and we were facing a tough week completing a marketing project, so my boss asked me to turn it down. I took it upon myself to call and tell Donald I was flattered but I couldn't get off. He was irritated, having made all the arrangements. I remember him saying 'We don't fly many people around.' We went back and forth on it for ten minutes, and finally I went to my boss and told him I was going—provided he wouldn't fire me. I flew to New York but the cover was never used.

"I decided after the cover try (and thanks to Donald) that it would be worth quitting a secure job to model full-time provided I got four things. I would have to accumulate nine months cash reserve, in case making it took that long. I wanted a positive response from the East Coast and Europe as well—one market did not seem enough. My third proviso was a launching exposure that could be seen by a wide range of clients—a good kickoff. Last, I wanted a top New York agent. The last came first. I was contacted by Frances Grill of Click, and within a month I got a one-week booking with Aldo Fallai that brought me to New York. While there, I called Donald at *Gentlemen's Quarterly*'s offices, and he booked me for two weeks with Rico Puhlman. I got most of the August issue and the cover. That issue had more pictures of me than most men get editorially in a lifetime—and that took care of my other requirements."

CUTTING WOMEN ON THE INSIDE TRACK

Frances Grill, founder of Click in New York, has a reputation for producing phenomena. Her first top model at Click was Isabella Rosselini. From there, Frances, Isabella, and Click all went straight up. Frances describes how as an agent she can maneuver a career's course: "I would use the symbol of forks in the road and say that the turnoffs that can be taken are endless. Therefore, each model has endless possibilities. The process starts where the model is when she is what I call 'ready' to attach to a market. If a demand is created, the journey can be shorter. A model projects a particular personality that can be linked with a new photographer, magazine, or client. I determine what that next connector will be.

"A pitfall for one might prove a lucky break for another. The good agent is one who can predict most often what will be beneficial. When a model goes into the market, a chemistry must happen. Sometimes it doesn't happen immediately, sometimes not at all. To give you an example, if a client chooses a model the photographer doesn't like at the outset, there can be a turn-on between that model and the photographer during the shooting. The girl he thought he preferred might not be used at all. There are no rules, merely a great deal of educated guessing.

"An agent has the facts to go after and get a major assignment. One inside track is knowing who is right for a particular campaign. Certain accounts are more predictable than others. For instance, Noxzema uses all-American prettiness, and convincing them to change direction would be next to impossible. If a model has that kind of face, I would gear her up for that account. There is a pattern that will lead her there. To support the possibility, the account would expect to see her appear in *Glamour* or *Seventeen*. You'd also have to send her to any photographers, hairdressers, makeup artists, and other magazines that subscribe to that point of view. Image advertisements are almost always inspired by cover girls, so it is the editorial pages with that tendency that the agent is after. I try to complement and support her look and avoid assignments that might conflict with the goal.

"Women change. They go through stages with the influences that come into their lives, often through their careers. This alters expression and the way a model looks and communicates. A model can become sophisticated or chic; good health and a strong character help a model to stay fresh and young looking for many years. How a model evolves has much to do with her photographs. As their faces appear in magazines, models begin to look more and more like those photographs. One dream of every model is a big beauty contract. It is a nice thing to have. It gives the model a secure feeling and it is a big bow to take in the industry. Getting it takes covers from the *Vogues* of the world. That by itself is a dream, but beauty contracts can follow from those covers and many times have.

"You don't get there taking step one, two, three, four. It is more random—more like one to twelve, back to three, up to seven, way, way up to fortynine. You don't know, but it won't be pulled out of a hat, no matter how chic. One promising possibility is being sent to the photographers who are powerful in star-model creation. But there is no one path. In fact, those at the top are forever creating and re-creating the forks in their paths. Timing is a big factor, and how they enter in the first place. Changes are instantaneous in this business. What is considered beautiful at one point can be obsolete a year or two later. So the path to that beautiful look fades out of date as fast as the look does. It is like walking in social quicksand. Predicting the next look is no more than a guessing game. It helps that the market is reluctant to change but open to it. Expanding the beautiful is a very satisfying part of being an agent. The looks that I might present to the fashion industry help to bring about that expansion and to influence the direction fashion will take.

"At this point, certain accounts are, within themselves, the same as editorial exposure. They make a statement with a model. Creative commercial accounts, like Ralph Lauren, Calvin Klein, or Perry Ellis, understand what it means to support a look. The creative way they use models has overturned an old rule: that a model goes from editorial to advertising and never the other way. These accounts employ the most advanced creative people to make strong use of pages within a magazine. An art director usually selects or approves modeling talent, but they don't pull them off the streets: They find new faces on the editorial pages of European or American magazines. Anyone involved in a campaign can suggest a model. Clever booking agents will call these people if they feel they have someone appropriate. It is often a question of presenting the proper face, but not always. One of a model's big strengths is the agent's belief in him or her. If I believe in someone, I will get that person going. If I see her as a major star, I won't stop until she is one. Persistence and other elements have their place, but in the final analysis it is the agent who must present a model to the fashion powers that be. And who can take a fashion model on to the next stage.

"Each case is individual. Take Isabella Rosselini, the daughter of Ingrid Bergman. I did not permit her name to be used from the outset. I wanted her to be a *model*, to know she was wanted for her look and not for her name. This supported her ego. Her face has about it something of the classic, but that

One of the biggest pluses a model can have is an agent behind her, which is how Isabella Rosselini made her way to the cover of *Vogue*. "If I believe in someone, I will get that person going. If I see her as a major star, I won't stop until she is one. Persistence and other elements have their place, but in the final analysis it is the agent who must present a model to the fashion powers that be." Frances Grill at Click was the mentor behind Isabella Rosselini's rise. Likewise, there is a mentor behind every modeling superstar.

classicism is very modern. Hers is very much a look of women in our times. She has a perfect face—very even, with bones symmetrically the same on either side. That lack of imperfection is unusual. Her personality is expressed in her face. It is developed and strong. Fresh as she looks, she is not a very young girl. We had *just* gone through that very-young bit. The stars of the seventies had been teenagers, one of the brightest a fourteen-year-old. This lasted for over a decade. The sixties' gift to the seventies was an unprecedented youth boom, everywhere. Designer clothes and the leading magazines promoted adulation of youth. Brooke Shields represented the quintessential beauty. Youth meant beauty, success, sex appeal, money, and—dragging down the whole thing—a heavy drug problem. And youth wore itself thin. Whenever an element of disease appears, a phenomenon is on its way out. The smell ceases to be sweet as presented. So I knew something was about to change. All this happened as I was starting Click's women's division, and I wanted it to stand for change, for something more solid and mature. Isabella was no starry-eyed ingenue. She had worked and been successful in another career. She was clean and undesigned—never plucked her eyebrows, never wore makeup. Her hair, life-style, and manner of dress typified simplicity with quality. Everything about her said, 'This is the moment we are coming to.' She became that symbol. As it worked out, the powers that mattered supported my instinct, and the rest is history.

"It was four years ago that I asked Isabella to be a model, and I would do the same thing today. I sent her to see a number of photographers: Weber, King, Avedon. Bruce Weber had the first opportunity with Italian *Vogue*. Bill King wanted and got her for American *Vogue*. Of course there were questions about using a thirty-year-old, but the industry was ripe for the change. From Brooke Shields, no one knew where to go.

"Lancôme approached me after the second cover. The original pictures in Italian *Vogue* attracted their interest. By the time she signed a contract with them, she had more than two dozen covers—all that less than one year after she began to model. Her original American *Vogue* cover was their largest selling issue to that time. Everyone wanted to use her. Timing was important too, because Lancôme was in the market for a new image. It was a very good marriage. They are an international company and she is no all-American girl. Generally, beauty contracts are offered to women in their late twenties or early thirties. The assumption was that you worked up to a beauty contract. What you work up to is being thirty. Isabella had an advantage; she was a fresh image in the right age category. It struck everyone right because she has a perfect and timeless face. Isabella is a new idea that started a long time ago. She herself is tomorrow."

WOMAN OF LASTING LUSTER: APOLLONIA

Apollonia learned at the start of her modeling career to link her life with beauty and grace. Nothing about Apollonia is exhausted physically or emotionally, but she feels that in a youth-oriented field it would be a mistake to go on except for special bookings and TV commercials.

Apollonia has criss-crossed continents and delighted millions. Her uncanny ability to turn herself into virtually any kind of character became her signature, her stamp on each picture she is in. For the camera, she leaves her looks behind in the dressing room; personality is all. Another Apollonia trademark is a long and perfectly proportioned body that, in concert with her acting ability, gives dramatic impact to her photographs. As she moved from level to level, she removed any obstacle that might have impeded her access to the heights of her chosen profession. It was her evolving versatility that allowed her to remain at the top. The rise began with "discovery" by her older brother Teo. "He was always fashion-conscious and watched the magazines. When I was thirteen, he told me I could be a model. I told him he was off the wall." His wasn't an idle suggestion; they had been trying to leave their southern Holland village. "At age fifteen, right after my high-school graduation, Teo made an appointment for me with Model Planning in Amsterdam. The owner was a former Miss World. I went all gussied up with whatever makeup I could find. She liked me even with my pimples and started me on my way: first to a dermatologist, next to three test photographers. When the pictures came back, they were good."

Her career took off immediately, so she stayed in Amsterdam. Apollonia was invited all over Western

Europe. At eighteen she met Jean-François Jouvalle, an editorial photographer, and for the next two years she worked for French, Italian, and English *Vogue, Vingt Ans, Elle, de Peche Mode,* all of them his clients. Jean-François was ten years older and quite possessive. He never wanted her to work with other photographers. But he had so much work there was no need: She had a good book from those editorial tear sheets. Apollonia observes of photographers: "Each one wants to feel that while a model is booked she belongs to him. It can be a secure feeling but it puts on sexual pressure. That possessiveness must be transcended, made a component of pictures. It is a game of passion that must be played for the sake of the shot.

"I had my fair share of setbacks over those fifteen years, caused mainly by confusion between truth and fantasy. In modeling these can lead to growth, but they are difficult at the time. I had a hard time on two crucial occasions, so much so that both times I stopped working. I thought I knew about honesty, but I had to learn that people rarely said what they meant, especially when it concerned emotions. Nothing about modeling is real; in fact, everything is decidedly unreal. It is about creating illusions, not about having real feelings. It is ironic that only by showing real emotion to the camera can you make that illusion appear real. This requires an uncommon repertoire of emotional signals and languages. It was hard for me as a model to converse in these languages just for jobs. Jumping back and forth between truth and illusion can be treacherous. All too often balance is maintained with drugs, pills, and liquor, which only further distorts the picture. What is insidious about drugs or liquor is that they are such readily available crutches. Many people can only get high from stimulants. It takes discipline and emotional growth to stay away from these substances."

Another pitfall is being taken in by insincere compliments or being unduly affected by the reverse. You must accustom yourself to the exaggerated ups, downs, slips, and slides of a modeling career. The very saddest example is all the young models who have been lavishly exposed and given the "Darling, you're so grand" routine, then dropped by those very same magazines; and once they begin to believe they are no longer beautiful or desirable, they begin to look that way. A model must always be able to walk in and create an "up" aura

of freshness. If she feels like the proverbial yesterday's gardenia, she will start to look and act just as faded and jaded. Most models, at base, are insecure, and this about-to-be-rejected feeling can become a self-fulfilling prophecy, and a psychological hurdle increasingly hard to vault.

Apollonia says, "I have seen it over and over again. And it happened to me too. The solution is seeing modeling as work, something that cannot be treated superficially but is a business that requires skills to be performed. Just like any other. You must achieve some detachment, because to succeed, you must enjoy what you're doing. When a model doesn't like the work, it shows physically and immediately. It is harder to move, and everything can go stale.

"Staleness, boredom, ennui have to be tempered by an excitement from within. Without it, the most enviable location trip will be another part of the void; nor will the money or the photographer make the difference. My approach was to stay strong, and give the appearance of nonchalance. The difficulty is that the spark must come from private resources, not from modeling itself. It has to come with you. If a model doesn't replenish her inner strength with reality, the spirit empties and the work suffers. Early on, the temptations were huge: the parties, the drugs, the hot dates. But before too long, they started to turn me off. They were all too, too alike and did not create real energy. What would once have been glories turned to sadness. I didn't know where it all went or how to recapture it. Wherever I went it was the same. This is what causes models, after three or four successful years, to disappear and never be seen again."

But Apollonia was one of the lucky, or perhaps unusually plucky, ones. From this frequently lethal low, she emerged triumphant. Something more was happening; she wasn't sure what. She gained weight, stopped skipping meals. Everything began to feel right, and she knew that inside was now an integrated, adult woman. "It is human nature to postpone facing whoever we are," she says. "The longer I could procrastinate the better. But I couldn't really grow until I stopped avoiding who I was. Modeling depends so much on superficiality, or looks. It becomes tiring being concerned with your own perfection, but the camera scrutinizes so relentlessly, there is no time to concentrate on any aspect but the physical. No one realizes the strain of having to be perfect every day. Every flaw is a clunker and you can't come back until it is corrected. If you don't give that perfection, there are comments behind your back. With me, the feeling kept persisting that I should try inner growth and stop worrying about how the world perceived me.

"Every model who succeeds finds the necessary resources someplace other than modeling: right where they are or from their home. The people around me helped a great deal. Especially Zoli, my agent, who showed genuine affection and concern. He gave me a perspective by saying 'I love you, you are very beautiful.' I knew he was talking about what was inside. I stopped working. He helped me to find the energy again and to really accept things, because I did love to model and he knew it. I learned to express myself through my work and no longer depended on externals. This has permitted me to be fully self-actualizing as a model.

"The one external element that never dims in importance is the client: what he needs and what causes his tension. Sometimes relieving it is a matter of speeding up the shooting; the greatest relief is a good shot already in the camera. I find I get satisfaction and renewed confidence from fulfilling what is asked of me within the allotted time. Mutual confidence is the very best kind! If you get the client to relax, the booking can become fun and I will be rebooked.

"Keeping clients requires understanding what they expect and bringing with you the assurance of a good result. You can, by concentrating too much on the end result, squash the chance of something unexpected. You have to strike the right balance. A job has to be a big deal, but it can't be the same big deal all the time or it will spoil the picture. I often think that modeling in pictures is like making love. If it is too tense, with no atmosphere or mood, it can be a difficult thing. It is up to the model to relax things, make it not seem like an act."

Longevity as a model comes from unswerving integrity, at each stage of every level. It is this that gives a model an identity for which there is no substitute. Anyone can model for a while, but it takes a special quality to last. Apollonia mentions three surprising things in discussing her long span: ignoring the camera, moving like an athlete, and realizing that being small in a beautiful picture was okay. A small contribution was enough, as long as she had given the client what he counted on.

Apollonia's final advice about longevity concerns young models and money. "While the money is flowing freely, models must learn that not all of it is theirs. Forgetting about taxes has put many young models in a jam. To get out of it, they select beauty as a speciality, which seriously limits broader and longer-term exposure. This is because every beauty shot is a close-up." This is not the strategy that Apollonia or Zoli opted for. If exposure can be spaced out over many years, a career will last longer. Exposure is the basis of high rates. It's true that beauty accounts pay the most money fastest, but a beauty model can't conceivably last as long and has cause for concern about burning out.

In the Heavens
Among the Stars

JEAN SHRIMPTON

The first impression one gets from a Jean Shrimpton photograph is of an extroverted, confident, new woman—just what you'd expect from swinging London. She now dislikes hundreds of these pictures. Jean is remembered by the people she worked with for taking her knitting along when she went to put her extraordinary beauty on film. Hers was a mystery achieved through the magic of photography. No one ever saw Jean Shrimpton walk, talk, or move. This left her admirers wondering what she would sound like if she spoke and how she would behave. Jean herself believes much of it came from not having too high a regard for what the camera saw. "I wasn't that person. I now realize I was vacant, not waiflike but a true waif," she says. "Though others saw me as a style, I was always aware of temporariness, which arose from realizing how important yet totally unimportant I was." Jean is a very private person leading a very public life. Now twenty years past her period of celebrity, she and her husband run a country inn in Penzance, on the Cornwall coast of England. She sees herself as having been pushed into modeling because she was such a viable commodity. "There will never be a shortage of people willing to take advantage of a model. In that respect, the modeling world today is not different from the one I was in. It is, however, much more commercially oriented. I don't remember my contemporaries as mercenary. I actually felt guilty about making so much money endorsing products, and it was relatively little compared to what women earn now. They were a different time, the sixties.

"I don't feel there is a natural transition from modeling to becoming an actress. With me it was more a lack of identity and of the self-knowledge and confidence to think I should pursue acting. It is hard to explain, but modeling is a question of remaining sound, sane, and centered. This way I always knew which side of my personality had to be in the forefront. It is easy to get pressured into acting by others." Jean Shrimpton also never saw herself as a model. Her walk was more of a shuffle and she was not a fashion freak, usually owning one dress at a time. She never looked in mirrors or got trapped into defining her talent, which was to metamorphose into something divine and doelike as her head went up and her innate grace captivated the camera. "Having little taste for the so-called luxuries of modeling, my greatest indulgence was to have success and fame but not care much about it. It would have been hard not to aspire to success if I'd never had it, but to have it and decide it doesn't suit me—that is one of life's true luxuries.

"I got picked up a time or two by people in the fashion world who thought I should do it. Knowing nothing about modeling, I went to a school for a month. I went on rounds like everyone else, but what I really did, fairly early on, was meet David Bailey. He was young and unknown; I was seventeen and David was in his early twenties. We did a small thing together called Shop Hounds, which attracted more than a bit of attention and got me moving. It all just took off as part of London 1961. Photography always had been an elite sort of medium, for upper-class, society people. Bailey was a very different person from Margret Camerron, Baron de Meyer, Patrick Leitchfield, or Cecil Beaton.

"His approach of using a thirty-five-millimeter camera was a total switch from large-format plate cameras. It allowed a model much more natural movement and freedom. Cleverly, Bailey portrayed my faults along with my assets or virtues. It made me much more accessible; I was ordinary. There lies the paradox of modeling. You must be ordinary yet extraordinary. Bailey was exceptional at showing those extremes. My vulnerability expressed itself physically. His was the right packaging to project that. During the three years I lived with Bailey I took his advice absolutely. He insisted that I do nothing else than my best and wouldn't let me do catalog. After that relationship, I got in with some people who saw good money in endorsing things.

"Except for my being young and pretty, down-to-earth, and hardworking, nothing about me explains my success. On the whole, my career had to do with close friendships. Feeling that the photographer loves you is surprisingly important, even when you know intellectually that he's pretending for your benefit. I distinctly remember five photographers: David Bailey, Richard Avedon, Ara Gallant, Irving Penn, and Melvin Sokolsky. Penn is like a business operation. I developed a respect for him but an infatuation for Avedon. I went on an assignment with Avedon for *Vogue* on Niarchos's yacht

through the Greek islands. I could lie and say it wasn't memorable, but it was unbelievably beautiful and restful. Ara was always there; even before he was a photographer, Ara knew how to listen, and he made me feel secure and beautiful. A photographer like Sokolsky always makes an impact, and no matter how wise you get later on, no model thinks at the time that it's rubbish."

DEBORAH TURBEVILLE

After many years around creative people, Deborah feels that "the most interesting and rewarding part of modeling is the aesthetic growth you gain through contact with creative points of view. Nobody forbids an intelligent young woman to enjoy going to art shows, read books, or listen to music. Fashion by definition is up to date and expressive. All the people you meet—photographers, designers, magazine editors, fashionable men and women—are well read, often self-educated (though of course not always), and vital participants in the arts. What an arena to be a part of and grow in! I began to be sensitive to texture, color, and shapes—who wouldn't in such an environment?"

Successful fashion model Deborah Turbeville went on to become a fashion editor at *Ladies' Home Journal*, special editor at *Harper's Bazaar*, and photography editor at *Mademoiselle*. She is now one of the most renowned of fashion photographers. Her entire varied career has been an expression of her personal style. She has been exhibited and has lectured around the world. Her second book, *Unseen Versailles*, won the coveted American Book Award in design. Daughter of a nonconforming Massachusetts mother, Deborah never dreamed of being anything else. When she finally got out on her own, she ended up, through a series of accidents, working for a woman who could have been her mother: Claire McCardell, considered one of a handful of great fashion designers. Whatever instinct toward style a women is born with needs to be nurtured. "Women are drawn toward the idea of having style, and if you're attracted to something, chances are you'll acquire it. My mother was very attracted to style, and not just to conventional possessions—expensive clothes, or furs, or gems. It was to have something different. She used to say, 'I always want something different for my daughter.' She would want me to be unique, which in a small middle-class community would cause a lot of comment. She loved beautiful things and she thought of them as special. She was the rebellious type, with a New Englander's individualistic sense, and believed it was better to grow up extraordinary.

"We would travel into Boston to shop, as young as I can remember. Often to the same little shop on Newberry Street that carried Claire McCardell's line. I was exposed to all this at a very young age because these clothes were something my mother valued. As I grew up I would buy a few McCardell pieces. One time I tried on a full dress, and the shop owner mentioned how much like her clothes I was as well. She suggested that if I was ever in New York I go and see Claire McCardell. 'I'm sure she would like you, you're just her type of girl, just as she likes women to be.' As it turned out, I came to New York to be a dancer but needed money to support my lessons, and it occurred to me to go and see Mrs. McCardell. Within two minutes I was in one of her dresses and in the office of Mr. Klein, her business manager, being asked, 'Do you want to come to work here?' For years after and even for the *Time* magazine cover story, I was asked how a small-town Massachusetts girl wound up the sample model for one of America's foremost designers. How I wound up there, I said, was 'just off the street.'

"I don't know if it is actually that simple. I was the kind of girl she liked: not a perfect beauty, but with an individual look. That way she would say, 'The thing all the models have in common is that they all are perfect in my clothes.' They made a statement in an authentic American idiom. A lot of American women must have agreed; the audience for Mrs. McCardell grew and grew. For that time, her women seemed to express what everyone wanted to be. I worked among Jean Patchin and Ivy Nicolson and Sonny Harnett and Dorian Leigh and Suzy Parker and thought they were the most beautiful creatures that ever lived. I was not a natural. The most notable event of my first runway show was getting lost in the Waldorf-Astoria kitchens. I followed a waiter back to the runway. I figured he had to be going my way. After my couture debut, I was looking in the mirror and talking to my mother, and I said, 'I was going to give it up because I couldn't look like them.' She said, 'You'd better get out of this business if it only makes you

want to look like everyone else.' My idea of beauty never again leaned toward the bland."

CRISTINA FERRARE

Brunette Cristina was born in Cleveland, Ohio, and moved to Los Angeles at thirteen. She started what would be a classic modeling career at fourteen, when her mother took her to Nina Blanchard's office. She wore a blue suit with a Peter Pan collar, her hair was down to her waist, and she was carrying the same ten superfluous pounds she still claims to be trying to lose. Nina Blanchard became Cristina's second mother and has always been there for her. In Los Angeles she works through Nina, in New York through Eileen Ford. Agents have negotiated every aspect of her career down to the most minute booking. They took the lead role in establishing long-term endorsements for her. Since 1962, Cristina's distinctive dark coloring and flaw-less features have made her the paradigm of so-phistication and American style. "Nina believed in field training, not in a class. After six months of trial and error, I got my first job, at age fifteen, on a Catalina swimwear shooting. Illa Anderson helped me with my makeup.

"I feel I am at home in front of a camera because I made all the mistakes at the start." At each job Cristina learned a little more: "It was a good method that helped to mold me." Continuing on Nina Blanchard's strategy, Cristina says, "Nina was very careful where she sent me and who I worked with. The people were all kind and helpful. I tried to be professional and courteous. I felt that if I arrived late, I should make up the time afterward, or if they said come at nine, I should be there at five to nine. I got to the point where I hardly noticed pins stuck in me. I loved modeling. Even today I'm the best two-minute backseat dresser there is. And I mean elaborate—from totally naked to ballgown with diamond earrings. I can do sportswear while driving, but that's another technique entirely.

"I never had a romantic interest in any beauty photographer, but I have always had a special affinity with these men. If a photographer does good work, I admire him and want him to believe I'm the most beautiful woman he has ever seen, even though all of them work all the time with glamorous models. A great photographer, like Avedon, Scavullo, or Skrebneski, makes me feel for that moment that I am the most fabulous. The feeling of admiration should be reciprocal. Without give and take, any shot, but especially smiling closeup, will look mechanical.

"I always pay close attention to art directors, because they are the ones who ultimately must make a layout work. It is necessary to get along with them. I can express what is wanted if I am attuned to their visual desires. They are the creators and the client, but very rarely will they be involved with the details of posing. Nevertheless, they are where the buck stops. I learned to bite my tongue when I had to put on the green, red, yellow, white, and then purple blouse to see which would work best. There comes a time when covering every base, no matter how many, becomes routine. My advice to others is to have something else in your life and on your mind. For me, it has been a decided advantage to have a family to think about. There are always checklists of kids' needs and a home to review while I stand there. The actual shot requires a combination of exhibitionism and voyeurism. As the people on the set stare at my every move, I feel the excitement; it gets me going. It is unlike anything in real life. And modeling, for me, is a release. I can let something of myself escape."

BARBARA FELDON

"It's pure luck when the aspiring model, with all ingredients intact, meets the professionals who can help bring out the potential. What the model cannot be given is the ingredients. We can do our professional best to develop her, but if she hasn't the desire or the wit, the potential withers on the vine." Those are the feelings of Gillis McGil, director of Mannequin and mentor to Barbara Feldon.

Barbara Feldon herself thinks back to before the beginning. "It was in a high-school play that I found out that I was funny. It had nothing to do with my perception of comedy or with my sense of humor; it is self-kidding sincerity." Speaking of her infamous commercial for Revlon's Top Brass, Barbara says, "It was a similar tongue-in-cheek quality that made the tiger commercial so funny. It was sexy but not quite real; everyone loved it because they

There is a paradox in modeling. You must be at once both ordinary and extraordinary. For instance, David Bailey presented Jean Shrimpton this way, placing her in the mind as swinging London itself. At the same time, halfway around the world, a sweet thirteen-year-old (Christina Ferrare, above) walked into a Los Angeles agency and walked out a signed talent. Each of these two models believes that a great photographer makes her feel, for the moment at least, that she is the most beautiful woman he ever saw, but neither really falls for the line.

On the other hand, Andy Warhol started to find out what to do for himself by reading fashion magazines. "Modeling gets you around. . . . But it is runway work that has taught me how to walk, and how to work with the best people. . . . Now I am much less nervous. . . . I can only sell clothes that I like, but a model who is really good can sell any product."

On the following page is Lauren Bacall, on the *Harper's Bazaar* cover that launched her career. This was photographed by Louise Dahl-Wolfe and styled by the present doyenne of fashion, Diana Vreeland.

knew it was a put on, a spoof." The same comedic quality came through in her memorable "Agent 99" role on Carl Reiner's TV series *Get Smart*.

This gifted comedienne arrived in New York a trained actress, but never got cast in commercials because she didn't look like a model. Barbara was a Carnegie Tech graduate in drama when she came to the big town to starve in Greenwich Village while she tried to break into the theater. She met Gillis McGil socially, through a friend of a friend, which is why Gillis's capricious generosity seemed so extraordinary. Gillis decided, just like that, to help Barbara become a professional model, and she did it with incredible efficiency, including getting Barbara to do all the right things. She was a 144-pound, amply proportioned showgirl who loved to eat—and she did, until she met Gillis. "When she said casually, 'If you want help I will help you,' I didn't know what to say. I had never thought of modeling. It was Gillis who suggested I lose fifteen pounds. Eventually, I lost a third of my weight, and before we began was down to one hundred ten. At five feet

nine I was a cadaver. Reed-thin comes nowhere near it.

"I was in awe of Gillis because she was a top New York model and she had such incredible elegance. She got me a hairdresser named Kenneth. He was her good buddy, as he did it for nothing. He was adorable to me. So there I was, slender, coiffed, and with my eyelashes in place, at the doorway to a career. Gillis next said, 'I think you need some experience modeling. My friend Pauline Trigere would be perfect.' Gillis picked out a white blouse and black skirt for me to wear on the interview. Pauline Trigere couldn't have been more wonderful. There was no question she was going to take me. After all, Gillis had sent me. I didn't fully comprehend Gillis's power. I worked at Trigere for five months— until Gillis decided I'd spent enough time doing that.

"At the time—it was by now the early sixties— one of the two agencies in New York was Plaza Five, owned by Natalie Paine. Natalie gave me a test list— again, not questioning Gillis's judgment that I should be a model. One of my first tests was with a young assistant to Irving Penn named Neal Barr. He did my first book. It was a sensation in Europe. I went to Paris during the collections to get some more experience and spent a month there. Everyone wanted to use that girl in those pictures. Meeting Neal Barr was a stroke of luck. The test portfolio had me modeling on top of a mosque in Tripoli. I loved being abroad, but my entire career only lasted a year. I came back to New York and for the next few months I worked continuously.

"I loathed being photographed. I never liked the static quality of a still camera. I never warmed to it; it never got easier and I had to act my way each time through an ordeal by fire. I pretended model was my role, and that it included poses for the camera. I learned as an actress would for a part which were my good angles, which poses the most becoming, and which would work. Being an actress was a plus because I brought a comedic sense to dramatic situations. I did the same for other aspects of modeling I didn't care for. I did love being manicured and immaculately coiffed. I had a daily appointment at a special hairdressing salon. And the photography studios were fascinating. Everything smelled good. I met interesting advertising executives at different shootings. I was sent on one commercial audition, for Five Day deodorant pads, and my modeling career ended abruptly thereafter. I did a very beautiful Lillian Bassman commercial in a big white towel. Based on that sixty seconds, Charles Revson picked me up for Top Brass tiger and put me under exclusive contract."

LAUREN BACALL

Destiny decreed that Lauren Bacall would be propelled to fame by a picture in a wartime issue of *Harper's Bazaar*. It was photographed by Louise Dahl-Wolfe and styled by Diana Vreeland, so the stars, as they say, were already smiling on Betty, as she is called by these and other good friends. "I didn't try to change Betty or any other model into what I wanted," insists Louise Dahl-Wolfe, the venerable (now eighty-eight) and world-famous fashion photographer. "Color was just starting to be used, so I looked for models with something other than pink-and-white complexions. Skin like that looks cheap and 'candy box' to me. Betty's skin had a lovely greenish-yellow cast, a toning I like better with other colors in a photograph. It is good for engraving also. Mrs. Vreeland and I both came to *Bazaar* in 1936. She always had her eye out for good models and never liked anything run-of-the-mill. She preferred a distinctive, interesting face, not young, with bones, never fat, puffy cheeks. Eyes had to have expression or a certain chic. It wasn't Betty's beauty so much that struck me when I saw here. It was the way she moved. Some people are graceful and some are not. She had built-in rhythm she could feel in every bone of her body; the camera saw it as grace. She could do anything; fabulously styled shots or natural, elegant ones. I could plant Betty in a background and she would move exactly as I wanted her to without artifice, by instinct. I was always drawn to models who moved well. That is the vital element. It was from studying anatomy in art school that I learned about movement: that a women is a triangle with the base at the bottom and a man just the opposite.

"Some people are pretty but have no sense of personal style. Betty had both, and movement completed the picture. A true style cannot be copied. There is a personal way of looking and acting peculiar to that model. Even if the quality is odd, she can look smart and chic. I tried to give Betty great latitude, a freedom to react that would help my composition and yet remain rhythmic. I told her to move and then to hold it whenever her actions and the background come together naturally. I had to have that relationship and she understood that. I used spotlights and soft overlight to give emphasis to patterns that Betty wouldn't necessarily have been conscious of, though she did have an uncanny sense of black-and-white values.

"To appreciate Betty, it took a Cecil Beaton or a George Huene. The average photographer wouldn't have liked working with her until after she got famous. She was very much a New York girl and a little on the tough side. She had a ton of ideas; Betty was always spicy and witty. She was terribly amusing and I liked to play; I still like to. Let me give you an example. On the St. Augustine trip for *Bazaar* during the war, Mrs. Vreeland was watching over this young girl. And rightly so. She had promised Betty's mother to take care of the girl, so she warned each of us against going out after dusk. My husband, Mike, loved to kid Betty along. And she enjoyed fun and teasing. Betty was always one for a good time. We had a very handsome naval press officer on hand to help and keep us away from trouble. We couldn't do any pictures without consulting him and having an official escort. At our hotel one night after the sitting, I saw Mike leaning across the front desk egging Betty on as she talked to someone on the phone in the lobby. The someone was this lieutenant, and she was looking up with her chin resting in her palm saying 'Aw gee, Lieutenant, you have to take me out. I'm not allowed to go out alone.' I almost died. Betty was always such a scream."

A young Lauren Bacall was ushered into Mrs. Vreeland's red office by Wendy Iglehart and presented with a cursory "This girl, I think she'd make a good model." Diana Vreeland, remembering their first meeting, says, "She had literally nothing to offer except her existence; she looked like she had blown in from Madison Avenue." Notwithstanding that unpromising introduction, Betty became quite wound up in the lives of the ladies at *Bazaar*, appearing on ten covers or more. It was during the war, but fashion had to go on. Only American models were available, and it was Vreeland who first said, "As soon as the war is over, let's open the door! Let's get in some fresh air! Let's bring on the Swedes, the Poles, the West Germans, the Italians . . . the Eurasians!"

Betty Bacall was American, but she was different. "I didn't think about Betty that way—I loved her. She was my special friend. She always kept her own thoughts and her own dreams. When we found her she didn't have a cent, but she had her high hopes. She dreamed of being Bette Davis. 'I can dance,' she said that first interview. 'I can sing. I can do anything Bette Davis can.'"

On her return after the St. Augustine sportswear shooting, Mrs. Vreeland found stack after stack of elastic-banded letters. They all wanted the same information: Who is the girl on the March cover? "Every single person from Hollywood, from the theater, from everywhere, wanted to know. As it happens in the movies, not long after, Betty got to meet Slim Hawks, who fixed her up in that wonderful movie, *To Have and Have Not*. They dressed her all up and she was divine!

Was it chance or a guardian angel that put Lauren Bacall into the hands of Louise Dahl-Wolfe and Diana Vreeland? For some there are preordained appointments, meetings with unavoidable results. Perhaps it doesn't matter what a Lauren Bacall wears, whether she's on time or if she says not a word. The die was cast for "our Betty," as Mrs. Vreeland fondly calls Lauren Bacall. It was her destiny to cause a sensation on that magazine cover. When celluloid and light met the energy of Lauren Bacall and the genius of Louise Dahl-Wolfe, a legend was set in motion.

"The pay for *Bazaar* was ten dollars per hour," remembers Lauren Bacall, "a small fortune next to the slave labor of suffocating in winter clothes in the August heat. This was pre-air-conditioning. I wasn't a successful Seventh Avenue model. My entrance and exit from that role went very much unnoticed. I worked for David Crystal, a sportswear house, for less than what you'd call a staggering sum, maybe thirty dollars. It was a fortune to me, even though it is peanuts to what is at stake now. I was having a lark—it was a kid's adventure. I would spend my lunch hour at Walgreen's drugstore trying to figure out how to get into producers' offices, or land an audition. Modeling then, to me anyway, had an aura. It has become something different. It was a means to an end. I don't know that showing clothes or being photographed is akin to acting. I had no idea that it could be my vehicle to an acting career.

"If it hadn't been for Diana Vreeland and Louise Dahl-Wolfe, no way would I have had a modeling career. The fact that I met Nicky de Ganzbourg was the purest chance. He was the one who arranged that appointment with Diana. Nicky was head of *Bazaar*, Diana was fashion editor under Carmel Snow. I came in under his wing, but it was Vreeland who took me to Louise Dahl-Wolfe. It was fate that it worked so well.

I never thought of modeling in terms of selling a product. I was put into a setting and photographed there. I never went the route of spending time with designers, but in terms of style I couldn't have had better exposure than the stylishness of Diana Vreeland and Louise Dahl-Wolfe. They were both unique, extraordinary people. Louise is an exceptional artist; she was not just a photographer. Everything about her showed a commitment to taste. She took each thing she photographed into another realm. Louise understood me, and her pictures for *Bazaar* were the way I looked. Neither Diana nor Louise tried to change or glamorize me. They saw something in me and they took the pictures they wanted. They gave me a point of view. Vreeland was the heavyweight, ahead of her time in every way. I remember distinctly the way she looked each time I saw her. Absolutely perfect, for then, for now. She was and is timeless. She always was the person to spend your time with if you wanted to be a model. You knew you couldn't fail to get something of value.

"The great thing about Louise was that she took pictures very quickly. I made her laugh, so she was snapping pictures all the time. Both Louise and Diana wanted my personality in the picture. I had learned in drama class not to be frightened. Louise let me fall into whatever positions felt natural and then she would snap away again. Louise put me where she wanted me and I did what I did. It was Diana Vreeland who put me and my name in a *Bazaar* story on three up-and-coming actresses. Slim Hawks saw me and my name—a wonderful break for me. I was on my way to what I wanted."

Maybe you won't become quite so big a star, but if you have the qualifications—an affinity for style, a natural photogenic spark ready to be ignited, and that right mix of tact and ambition—then fate may send you the mentor who'll make the magic difference. Maybe, if you really want to, you'll become a model. Good luck.

National Index
of Trade Publications, Directories, and Resource Books; Modeling Associations

TRADE PUBLICATIONS: NEW YORK

Ad Day–U.S.A., 919 Third Avenue	212-421-3713
Advertising Age, 708 Third Avenue	212-210-0100
Advertising Techniques, 10 East 39th Street	212-889-6500
Advertising World, 150 Fifth Avenue	212-807-1660
Art Direction, 10 East 39th Street	212-889-6500
Audio Visual Communications, 475 Park Avenue South	212-725-2300
Back Stage, 330 West 42nd Street	212-947-0020
Billboard, 1515 Broadway	212-764-7300
Clio Magazine, 336 East 59th Street	212-593-1900
Editor & Publisher, 575 Lexington Avenue	212-752-7060
Fashion Calendar, 185 East 85th Street	212-289-0420
Fashions Magazine, 71 West 35th Street	212-594-0880
Film Bill, 254 West 54th Street	212-977-4140
Gallagher Report, 230 Park Avenue	212-661-5000
Graphic Arts Monthly, 875 Third Avenue	212-605-9574
Graphics Design: U.S.A., 120 East 56th Street	212-759-8813
Hollywood Reporter, 1501 Broadway	212-354-1858
Industrial Photography, 475 Park Avenue South	212-825-2300
Madison Avenue Magazine, 369 Lexington Avenue	212-972-0600
Marketing & Media Decisions, 1140 Sixth Avenue	212-391-2155
Marketing Communications, 475 Park Avenue South	212-725-2300

Media Industry Newsletter,   212-751-2670
18 East 53rd Street
Media News Keys,   212-924-0320
150 Fifth Avenue
Men's Wear Magazine,   212-741-4000
7 East 12th Street
Merchandising Magazine,   212-869-1300
1515 Broadway
Millimeter Magazine,   212-477-4700
826 Broadway
Modern Jeweler,   212-755-5400
133 East 58th Street
Modern Photography,   212-265-8360
825 Seventh Avenue
Photo District News,   212-243-8664
156 Fifth Avenue
Photo Weekly, 1515 Broadway   212-764-7300
Print, 355 Lexington Avenue   212-682-0830
Public Relations News,   212-879-7090
127 East 80th Street
Sales & Marketing Management,   212-986-4800
633 Third Avenue
Shooting Commercials,   516-496-8000
101 Crossways Park West,
Woodbury, NY
Show Business, 1501 Broadway   212-354-7600
Teens & Boys Magazine,   212-594-0880
71 West 35th Street
Television/Radio Age,   212-757-8400
1270 Sixth Avenue
Theatrical Calendar,   212-757-7979
171 West 57th Street
Variety, 154 West 46th Street   212-869-5700
Video, 460 West 34th Street   212-947-6500
Videography,   212-725-2300
475 Park Avenue South

TRADE PUBLICATIONS: OTHER

Adweek, 514 Shatto Place,   213-384-7100
Los Angeles, CA
Communication Arts-CA,   415-326-6040
410 Sherman Avenue,
Palo Alto, CA
Magazine Age,   213-873-7600
6931 Van Nuys Blvd.,
Van Nuys, CA
Ocular, 159 Platte Street,   303-458-6064
Denver, CO

TRADE DIRECTORIES AND RESOURCE BOOKS: NEW YORK

ASMP Book,   212-889-9144
205 Lexington Avenue,
New York, NY
American Showcase,   212-245-0981
724 Fifth Avenue,
New York, NY
Audio-Visual Marketplace,   212-916-1600
205 East 42nd Street,
New York, NY
Back Stage Directory,   212-941-0200
320 West 42nd Street,
New York, NY
Billboard Directories,   212-764-7300
1 Astor Plaza, New York, NY
Contact Book,   212-757-7979
171 West 57th Street,
New York, NY
Creative Black Book,   212-684-4255
401 Park Avenue South,
New York, NY
Fine Arts Market Place,   212-764-5100
1180 Sixth Avenue,
New York, NY
International Directory of   212-688-6215
Talent/Modeling Agencies &
Schools,
17 East 48th Street,
New York, NY
Literary Market Place,   212-916-1600
205 East 42nd Street,
New York, NY
Madison Avenue Handbook,   800-223-1254
17 East 48th Street,
New York, NY
Magazine Market Place,   212-916-1600
205 East 42nd Street,
New York, NY
Media News Keys,   212-924-0320
150 Fifth Avenue,
New York, NY
Millimeter Directors' Directory,   212-477-4700
826 Broadway,
New York, NY
The New York Casting/Survival   212-688-7940
Guide . . . & Datebook,
17 East 48th Street,
New York, NY

North American Commercial   212-477-4700
    Production Directory,
    826 Broadway, New York, NY

O'Dwyer's Directory of PR Firms,   212-679-2471
    271 Madison Avenue,
    New York, NY

Photography Market Place,   212-916-1600
    205 East 42nd Street,
    New York, NY

The Producer's Masterguide,   212-777-4002
    611 Broadway, Suite 807,
    New York, NY

Ross Reports,   212-924-0320
    150 Fifth Avenue, New York, NY

Simons Directory of Theatrical   212-354-1840
    Materials, Service & Information,
    1501 Broadway, New York, NY

World Photography Sources,   212-348-0025
    436 East 88th Street,
    New York, NY

Women's Wear Daily,   212-741-4000
    7 East 12th Street,
    New York, NY

TRADE DIRECTORIES AND RESOURCE BOOKS: OTHER

Art Director's Index,   312-337-1901
    415 W Superior, Chicago, IL

The Book, P.O. Box 794,   203-226-4207
    Westport, CT

The Chicago Creative Director,   312-236-7337
    333 N. Michigan, Chicago, IL

Creative Directory of the Sun Belt,   713-532-0506
    1103 S. Shepard, Houston, TX

The Golden Pages,   305-233-6510
    P.O. Box 560696, Miami, FL

The L.A. Workbook,   213-856-0008
    6140 Lindenhurst Ave.,
    Los Angeles, CA

New York Publicity Outlets,   203-868-0200
    Box 327,
    Washington Depot, CT

On Location Directory,   213-467-1268
    6464 Sunset Boulevard,
    Hollywood, CA

The Reel Directory,   707-795-9367
    P.O. Box 866,
    Cotati, CA

RSPV, P.O. Box 314,   718-857-9267
    Brooklyn, NY

The Standard Directory of   213-651-5950
    Advertising Agencies and
    Advertisers,
    6300 Wilshire Blvd.,
    Los Angeles, CA

Talent & Booking,   213-871-2216
    6525 Sunset Blvd., Studio A,
    Hollywood, CA

Publicity Outlets-Nationwide,   203-868-0200
    Box 327 Washington Depot, CT

Whitmark Directory,   214-826-9400
    4120 Main Street, Suite 100,
    Dallas, TX

MODELING ASSOCIATIONS

ITMSA Association of   702-369-2556
    International Talent, Modeling
    Schools & Agencies,
    101 Convention Center Drive,
    Suite 660, Las Vegas, NV
    Attn: JNR   702-382-3245

MAAI, Modeling Association of   716-852-8000
    America International,
    310 Delaware, Buffalo, NY
    Also, % John W. Johnson,   212-691-2812
    210 Central Park South, Suite
    14C,
    New York, NY

WMA, World Modeling Assn.,   914-737-8512
    Box 100, Croton-on-Hudson, NY
    Contact: Ruth Tolman

Modelling Association of Canada,   807-344-5973
    176 Rupert Street,
    Thunder Bay, Ontario
    President: Pat Potts

PHOTOGRAPHY ACKNOWLEDGMENTS

To the owners and managers of the New York modeling agencies for allowing me unlimited access to pictures historical and current: It is their enthusiasm that allowed this book to come alive. For photographic information, I am forever indebted to Koko Hakim for magnanimously providing her vast knowledge of modeling fashion on a runway, and to Marjorie Graham for generously sharing her insights into arranging a portfolio. I would like to thank Taki Wise and Ethyline Staley of Staley-Wise Gallery for their guidance and encouragement in searching for pictures and releases, Diana Edkins Richardson at Condé Nast for never losing patience, Linda Cox at *Cosmopolitan* for her continuous support, and Oscar Reyes of Elite for taking those extra minutes to find the best example. My sincerest thanks to Joe Hunter of Ford, Caren Ostrow of Zoli, Muriel Watkins of Elite, Dorian Castonquay of Wilhelmina, Al Kolby of Perkins Models, and, especially, to Tim Oussey of Gilla Roos for their help in securing the hundreds of necessary picture releases. I wish to express my gratitude to three photo representatives, Nancy Connelly, John Turner, and Bruce Levin, for taking care of the necessary paperwork directly with their clients; to Marne Libby-Jones at *Sports Illus-*

trated for prodding me to ask again; to Marian Powers of Time, Inc.; to Anita Bethel at Fairchild Syndication for that extra effort in securing a *WWD* cover; and to Sally Ferguson of Butterick Promotion, the first and fastest to respond. My appreciation to the people at the fashion designers' and manufacturers' publicity departments and at the multinational organizations for granting permission to reproduce their corporate advertising or promotional artwork. Special thanks to Joanne Petruzzo of Andrew Fezza; also, to Pat Goldberg and Michele McGuire of Ralph Lauren/Polo. And my gratitude to the following individuals for granting their consent, assistance, and encouraging words: Amy Lumet, Vance Klein, Eve Cusson, and Connie Fitzpatrick; also, to Barry Lategan, Peter Marlowe, and Jean Shrimpton for doing it from England; to Veruschka from Germany; and to Chris Royer and Karen Bjornson from around the corner.

PAGE 16 *(Top):* Ina Belin; courtesy Elizabeth Arden.

PAGE 16 *(Left):* Berthe; courtesy the collection of Albert Newgarden/Staley-Wise Gallery.

PAGE 16 *(Bottom):* Unknown; courtesy *Vogue,* Dec. 15, 1918.

PAGES 22 and 23: Clotilde for the Ford agency; courtesy Polo/Ralph Lauren.

PAGE 24 *(Left):* Michael King (left) for the Zoli agency; courtesy Andrew Fezza. Michael Harder (right) for the Click agency; courtesy Andrew Fezza.

PAGE 24 *(Top):* Rashid for the Zoli agency; courtesy Andrew Fezza.

PAGE 24 *(Bottom):* Tony Addabbo for the Ford agency; courtesy Andrew Fezza.

PAGE 25 *(Left):* Michael Harder (left) for the Click agency; courtesy Andrew Fezza. Todd Bentley (right) for the Wilhelmina agency; courtesy Andrew Fezza.

PAGE 25 *(Top):* Duke Lyskin for the Zoli agency; courtesy Andrew Fezza.

PAGE 25 *(Bottom):* Marcus Abel for the Zoli agency; courtesy Andrew Fezza.

PAGE 26 *(Right):* Billy Gleason for the Zoli agency; courtesy Andrew Fezza.

PAGE 26 *(Left):* Thom Fleming for the Ford agency; courtesy Andrew Fezza.

PAGE 26 *(Bottom):* John Crain; courtesy Andrew Fezza.

PAGE 30 *(Left):* Susan Hess for the Ford agency; courtesy Here & There; design by Compliche.

PAGE 30 *(Top):* Cathryn Timmer (far left) for the Zoli agency; courtesy Here & There; design by Valentino. Robin Nord (left) for the Wilhelmina agency; courtesy Here & There; design by Valentino. Lisa Rutledge (center) for the Ford agency; courtesy Here & There; design by Valentino. Tracy Lee (right) for the Ford agency; courtesy Here & There; design by Valentino. Diane de Witt (far right) for the Ford agency; courtesy Here & There; design by Valentino.

PAGE 30 *(Bottom):* Gail Quarles (left) for the Legends agency; courtesy Here & There; design by Fendi. Mounia (right) for the Zoli agency; courtesy Here & There; design by Fendi.

PAGE 32 *(Left):* Sermonetta for the Zoli agency; courtesy Here & There; design by Mugler.

PAGE 33 *(Top):* Jane Pleasants (left); courtesy Here & There; design by Mugler. Mounia (right) for the Zoli agency; courtesy Here & there; design by Mugler. Alva Chin (center) for the Zoli agency; courtesy Here & There; design by Mugler.

PAGE 33 *(Bottom):* Dejanne; courtesy Here & There; design by Versaci.

PAGE 35: Kira (right) for the Zoli agency; courtesy Here & There; design by Karl Largerfeld. Sophie Billard (left) for the Elite agency; courtesy Here & There; design by Karl Largerfeld.

PAGE 36: Bonnie Berman (front center) for the Click agency; courtesy Here & There; design by Steven

Sprouse. Teri Toye (rear center) for the Click agency; courtesy Here & There; design by Steven Sprouse.

PAGE 37 *(Right):* Violette Sanchez (left) for the Delphine agency; courtesy Here & There; design by Mugler. Axcile Dove (right) for the Delphine agency; courtesy Here & There; design by Mugler.

PAGE 37 *(Left):* Hideka; courtesy Here & There; design by Issey Miyake.

PAGE 39: Pat Cleveland for the Zoli agency; courtesy Here & There; design by Touche.

PAGE 40 *(Left):* Carol Niles for the Delphine agency; courtesy Here & There; design by Mugler.

PAGE 40 *(Right):* Pat Cleveland for the Zoli agency; courtesy Here & There; design by Kenzo.

PAGE 41 *(Top left):* Anne Fione for the Elite agency; courtesy Here & There; design by Jean Paul Gaultier.

PAGE 41 *(Top right):* Charon for the Glamour agency; courtesy Here & There; design by Willi Smith—Willi Wear.

PAGE 41 *(Bottom left):* Lisa Rutledge for the Ford agency; courtesy Here & There; design by Yves Saint Laurent Rive Gauche.

PAGE 41 *(Bottom center):* Susan Hess for the Ford agency; courtesy Here & There; design by Armani.

PAGE 41 *(Bottom right):* Sara Kapp for the Zoli agency; courtesy Here & There; design by Carolina Herrera.

PAGE 43: Cheryl Stevens for the Riccardo Gai agency; courtesy Armani Boutique; design by Armani.

PAGE 44 *(Left):* Iman (right) for the Elite agency; courtesy Here & There; design by Calvin Klein. Karen Bjornson (left) for the Ford agency; courtesy Here & There; design by Calvin Klein.

PAGE 44 *(Right):* Isabella Townsend (right) for the Click agency; courtesy Here & There; design by Mugler. Charles Winslow (left) for the Elite agency; courtesy Here & There; design by Mugler.

PAGE 45 *(Right):* Anne Bizamat for the Elite agency; courtesy Here & There; design by Byblos.

PAGE 45 *(Left):* Jackie Adams for the Ford agency; courtesy Here & There; design by Perry Ellis.

PAGE 47: Pat Cleveland for the Zoli agency; courtesy Stan Papich; design by Halston.

PAGE 48: Amalia for the Elite agency; courtesy Here & There; design by Kenzo.

PAGE 49: Margret Donahoe for the Legends agency; courtesy Here & There; design by Bill Blass.

PAGE 50: Jack Alexander; courtesy Saks Fifth Avenue.

PAGE 51: Kim Alexis for the Elite agency; courtesy Saks-Jandel.

PAGE 52: Tom Tripodi for the Zoli agency; courtesy The May Co.

PAGE 57: Kathy Ireland for the Elite agency; courtesy *Cosmopolitan;* photograph by Francesco Scavullo.

PAGE 58 *(Top):* Arthur Brooks for the Funnyface agency; courtesy *New York;* photograph by Buddy Endress.

PAGE 58 *(Bottom):* Jack Krenic for the Zoli agency; courtesy *Esquire;* photograph by Jacques Houilles.

PAGE 61: Wanakee for the Elite agency; courtesy *Essence;* photograph by Michele Momy.

PAGE 62: Kim Coleman (left) for the Kim Dawson agency; courtesy *Town & Country;* photograph by Douglas Kirkland. Murray Rodgers (right); courtesy *Town & Country.*

PAGE 63: Amy Lumet for the Ford agency; courtesy *Seventeen;* photograph by Robin Saidman.

PAGE 65 *(Right):* Cheryl Tiegs for the Ford agency; courtesy Sears, Roebuck & Co.; photograph by Bill Connors.

PAGE 65 *(Left):* Doug Yates (left) for the Zoli agency; courtesy Bamberger's. Jay Humphreys (right) for the Zoli agency; courtesy Bamberger's.

PAGE 69: Cheryl Tiegs for the Ford agency; courtesy *Glamour;* photograph by Sante Forlano.

PAGE 70: Cheryl Tiegs for the Ford agency; courtesy Time, Inc.; photograph by Gordon Monroe.

PAGE 71: Cheryl Tiegs for the Ford agency; courtesy Noxell-Cover Girl; photograph by Les Goldberg.

PAGE 76: Jason Savin for the Wilhelmina agency; courtesy Berkley/Joven Publishing Group.

PAGE 77: Jason Savin for the Wilhelmina agency; courtesy Berkley/Joven Publishing Group.

PAGE 80 *(Left):* Unknown Hands; courtesy Remy Martin.

PAGE 80 *(Right):* Trish Webster for the Wilhelmina agency; courtesy Sheer Energy-L'Eggs/Dancer Fitzgerald Sample.

PAGE 82 *(Top):* Janice Dickenson for the Elite agency; courtesy Wells Rich Greene/Max Factor.

PAGE 82 *(Bottom):* Sheila Johnson for the Elite agency; courtesy Napier.

PAGE 82 *(Right):* Carrie Nygren for the Elite agency; courtesy Revlon/Grey Advertising.

PAGE 84: Joe Melendez for the Funnyface agency; courtesy R. J. Reynolds/William Este.

PAGE 85: Joseph Sweet for the Wallace Rogers agency; courtesy Teemtsma Tabaksorten Vogelsanger.

PAGE 88 *(Right):* Joan Severance for the Elite agency; courtesy E. I. Du Pont de Nemours & Co./BBDO.

PAGE 88 *(Left):* Mark Ritter (right) for the Ford agency; courtesy Basile-Milano/Krieger. Annette Stai (left) for the Ford agency; courtesy Basile-Milano/Krieger.

PAGE 90 *(Left):* Jerry Briggs (left) for the Joyce Conover agency; courtesy Nen E. I. Du Pont de Nemours & Co. Mike Stoddard (right) for the Perkins agency; courtesy Nen E. I. Du Pont de Nemours & Co.

PAGE 90 *(Right):* Merry Bruns (left) for the Perkins agency; courtesy Reliance/Perkin-Elmer. Michael Callen (right) for the Joyce Conover agency; courtesy Reliance/Perkin-Elmer.

PAGE 92 *(Left):* Dani Cusson for the Ford agency; courtesy Eve Cusson; photograph by Schneider.

PAGE 92 *(Right):* Robin Meyerhoff for the Wilhelmina agency; courtesy Robin Meyerhoff.

PAGE 93 *(Top):* Jeff Acquilone for the Ford agency; courtesy Bristol Meyers/Grey Advertising.

PAGE 93 *(Bottom):* Monique Pillard for the Elite agency; courtesy Monique Pillard; photograph by Tara Shannon.

PAGE 104 *(Left):* Carrie Nygren for the Elite agency; courtesy Mike Reinhardt/Carrie Nygren.

PAGE 104 *(Right):* Helen Lee for the Mannequin agency; courtesy Barry Lategan/Helen Lee.

PAGE 105: Mariana for the Click agency; courtesy Stephan Lupino.

PAGE 106 *(Left):* Teri Toye for the Click agency; courtesy Teri Toye/Click-*Elle*; photograph by Gilles Tapie.

PAGE 106 *(Right):* Farah Fawcett for the ICM agency; courtesy *Cosmopolitan*; photograph by Scavullo.

PAGE 116: Tommy Preston (left) for the Wilhelmina agency; courtesy Wilhelmina. Christina (center) for the Wilhelmina agency; courtesy Wilhelmina. Todd Bentley (right) for the Wilhelmina agency; courtesy Wilhelmina.

PAGE 128: Veruschka for the Zoli agency; courtesy *Vogue*/Bert Stern.

PAGE 130: Christie Brinkley for the Ford agency; courtesy *Sports Illustrated;* photograph by John Zimmerman.

PAGE 136: Colin Fox for the Wallace Rogers agency; courtesy Hathaway/Ogilvy Matter.

PAGE 140 *(Left):* Michael Holder for the Zoli agency; courtesy Vidal Sassoon Hair Care/Peter Rogers Assoc.

PAGE 140 *(Right):* Billy Gleason for the Zoli agency; courtesy Lord West.

PAGE 141 *(Top left):* Billy Gleason (right) for the Zoli agency; courtesy Joseph & Feist. Willa Russell (left) for the Wilhelmina agency; courtesy Joseph & Feist.

PAGE 141 *(Top right):* Rick Spates for the Funnyface agency; courtesy Sony Corporation.

PAGE 141 *(Bottom):* Tom Orme for the Wallace Rogers agency; courtesy Control Data.

PAGE 150: Apollonia for the Zoli agency; courtesy AVR/Jean-François Jouvelle.

PAGE 151 *(Top):* Apollonia (right) for the Zoli agency; courtesy AVR/Jean-François Jouvelle for *British Vogue.*

PAGE 151 *(Bottom):* Apollonia (center) for the Zoli agency; courtesy AVR/Jean-François Jouvelle for *British Vogue.*

PAGE 152: Apollonia for the Zoli agency; courtesy AVR/Parkinson for *British Vogue.*

PAGE 153 *(Left):* Apollonia for the Zoli agency; courtesy AVR/Christian Hermet for *Elle.*

PAGE 153 *(Right):* Apollonia (left) for the Zoli agency; courtesy AVR/Peter Knapp for *British Vogue.*

PAGE 156: Apollonia for the Zoli agency; courtesy AVR/Barry McKinely for *Italian Vogue.*

PAGE 157 *(Right):* Apollonia for the Zoli agency; courtesy AVR/Jost Wildbholt for *Elle.*

PAGE 157 *(Left):* Apollonia for the Zoli agency; courtesy AVR/David Bailey for *British Vogue.*

PAGE 158: Apollonia for the Zoli agency; courtesy AVR (private collection).

PAGE 160: Apollonia for the Zoli agency; courtesy AVR/Turbeville for Saks Fifth Avenue.

PAGE 161 *(Top):* Apollonia (center) for the Zoli agency; courtesy AVR/Sanchez/Castellano for Saga Furs. Tony Sanchez (left) for the Zoli agency; courtesy AVR/Sanchez/Castellano for Saga Furs. Michele Castellano (right); courtesy AVR/Sanchez/Castellano for Saga Furs.

PAGE 161 *(Bottom):* Apollonia for the Zoli agency; courtesy AVR for Bali Bra.

PAGE 162: Apollonia for the Zoli agency; courtesy AVR/Bart van Leuwen (private collection).

PAGE 163: Apollonia for the Zoli agency; courtesy AVR for *Elle.*

PAGE 165 *(Top):* Twiggy for the Twiggy Enterprises agency; courtesy Peter Marlowe Press/Lategan; photographs by Barry Lategan.

PAGE 165 *(Bottom):* Bill Sanford for the Elite agency; courtesy Sanford.

PAGE 169: Scott McKenzie for the Wilhelmina agency; courtesy De Beers/N. W. Ayer.

PAGE 173: Lois Ross for the Funnyface agency; courtesy Procter & Gamble.

PAGE 174: Andie McDowell for the Elite agency; courtesy CRK Advertising.

PAGE 188 *(Left):* Kelly Emberg for the Elite agency; courtesy Chanel.

PAGE 188 *(Right):* Kim Alexis for the Elite agency; courtesy Jones New York Sport.

PAGE 189: Natalie Tirrell for the Mannequin agency; courtesy *Women's Wear Daily*/Galanos.

PAGE 190 *(Top left):* Roger Schermond (left) for the Wallace Rogers agency; courtesy Here & There; design by Mugler. Yvette (center) for the Fashion Models agency; courtesy Here & There; design by Mugler.

PAGE 190 *(Bottom left):* Alison Vietor (left) for the Model Management agency; courtesy Here & There; design by Norma Kamali/OMO. Crosby (right) for the Wilhelmina agency; courtesy Here & There; design by Norma Kamali/OMO.

PAGE 190 *(Top right):* Susan Hess for the Ford agency; courtesy Here & There; design by John Anthony.

PAGE 190 *(Bottom right):* Lynn Yaeger (left) for the Mannequin agency; courtesy Jeffrey Banks. Michael Ives (right) for the Wilhelmina agency; courtesy Jeffrey Banks.

PAGES 193–97: Karen Bjornson for the Ford agency; courtesy *Vogue Patterns*/Butterick.

PAGE 195 *(Top and bottom):* Eric Milon for the Elite agency; courtesy *Vogue Patterns*/Butterick.

PAGE 199 *(Left):* Merry Bruns (right) for the Perkins agency; courtesy Avis/Bozell Jacobs. Richard Cain (left) for the Perkins agency; courtesy Avis/Bozell Jacobs.

PAGE 199 *(Right):* Murray Schigall for the Funnyface agency; courtesy Symbol Technologies, Inc.

PAGE 200: Pam Harrison for the Funnyface agency; courtesy Amtrak.

PAGE 201: Ben Short for the Nuveen agency; courtesy Nuveen/Della Femina Advertising.

PAGE 202: Barbara Reeder (top left) for the Funnyface agency; courtesy Burroughs/Penchina, Selkowitz, Inc. Kerry Ruff (center) for the Funnyface agency; courtesy Burroughs/Penchina, Selkowitz, Inc. Richard Bassett (lower left) for the Funnyface agency; courtesy Burroughs/Penchina, Selkowitz,

Inc. Jill Skaisi (lower right) for the Funnyface agency; courtesy Burroughs/Penchina, Selkowitz, Inc. Rick Opates (top right) for the Funnyface agency; courtesy Burroughs/Penchina, Selkowitz, Inc.

PAGE 203: Arthur Brooks (top) for the Funnyface agency; courtesy Kessler/Warwick Advertising. Rick Spates (center right) for the Funnyface agency; courtesy Kessler/Warwick Advertising. Michael Mcguire (center left) for the Funnyface agency; courtesy Kessler/Warwick Advertising. John Freeman (bottom) for the Funnyface agency; courtesy Kessler/Warwick Advertising. Michael McCullum (right) for the Funnyface agency; courtesy Kessler/Warwick Advertising.

PAGE 210: Merry Bruns for the Perkins agency; courtesy American Lung Assoc.

PAGE 211: Ryan Fitzpatrick for the Rascals, Unlimited agency; courtesy Connie Fitzpatrick/Rascals.

PAGE 213: Dani Cusson for the Ford agency; courtesy Eve Cusson/Gimbels.

PAGE 214: Dani Cusson (bottom) for the Ford agency; courtesy Johnson & Johnson. Melanie Cain (top left) for the My Fair Lady agency; courtesy Johnson & Johnson. Doug Bauer (top right) for the Ford agency; courtesy Johnson & Johnson.

PAGE 220: Tracey Nash for the Wilhelmina agency; courtesy *Seventeen*; photograph by Rudy Molacek.

PAGE 221: Keith Mitchell for the ICM agency; courtesy Stephan Lupino/Keith Mitchell for *Vogue Hommes.*

PAGE 222 *(Left):* Charles Miltite (right) for the Wilhelmina agency; courtesy Attenzione Publishing. Deborah King (left) for the Wallace Rogers agency; courtesy Attenzione Publishing.

PAGE 222 *(Top right):* Doug Yates (right) for the Zoli agency; courtesy Sero and Ms. Sero. Katie Kremmer (left) for the Wilhelmina agency; courtesy Sero and Ms. Sero.

PAGE 222 *(Bottom):* Tracy Griefnow for the Petite agency; courtesy Oscar de la Renta/Triton Advertising.

PAGE 230: Isabella Rossellini for the Click agency; courtesy Rossellini-Click/Condé Nast; photograph by King.

PAGE 237: Cristina Ferrare for the Ford agency; courtesy *Vogue Patterns*/Butterick; photograph by Chris Von Wangenheim.

PAGE 238: Lauren Bacall for the John Robert Powers agency; courtesy Bacall/*Harper's Bazaar*; photograph by Louise Dahl-Wolfe.

The cover shot for this book met its chief goal: to stand as a testament to some of the finest modeling talent of our day. For this accomplishment I would like to thank the entire Elite organization and especially Monique Pillard, for her belief in this book and her effort to provide the most extraordinary talent for the cover. Many thanks to Fernando Casablancas and the MMI staff of Elite Models/John Casablancas for their unique skill in accomplishing new and challenging tasks. I am forever grateful to Joanne Koenig and wish to thank her for aiding me and providing her tremendous organizational ability. This picture could not have been produced if it were not for the public relations genius of, not to mention the use of undisclosable resources from Ken Lerer.

Photograph: Bert Stern, represented by Pam Reid. *Stylist:* Tina Fagin. *Assistant Stylist:* Karen Straus. The vintage dresses were supplied by Gene London. All processing was done by L & I COLOR, New York, N.Y. My sincerest thanks to Beverley Abdo of the Diamond Information Center for *everything* she did, and to Suzanne Eagle of Condé Nast for making this picture well known.

COVER CREDITS

Top row, from left to right:

Julie Wolfe   *Dress:* Molyneux; *Diamonds:* Bulgari; *Makeup:* Paul Goebels; *Hair:* Yoshi Kosaka

Iman   *Dress:* Valentino; *Diamonds:* Tiffany; *Makeup:* Paul Goebels; *Hair:* Michael Weeks

Nancy Donahue   *Dress:* Ungaro; *Diamonds:* Fred Joaillier; *Makeup:* Joey Mills; *Hair:* Garren

Kelly Emberg   *Dress:* Gene London; *Diamonds:* F. Staal; *Makeup:* Joey Mills; *Hair:* Garren

Kim Alexis   *Dress:* Bill Blass; *Diamonds:* Bailey, Banks & Biddle; *Ultima II Makeup:* Joey Mills; *Hair:* Garren

Carol Alt   *Dress:* Bob Mackie; *Diamonds:* Cartier; *Makeup:* Jonathan Wallace; *Hair:* Stephane Lempire

Bottom row, from left to right:

Tara Shannon   *Dress:* Frank Tignino; *Diamonds:* H. Stern; *Makeup:* George Newell; *Hair:* Thom Priano

Deirdre Maguire   *Dress:* Hattie Carnegie; *Diamonds:* Harry Winston; *Makeup:* Mark Heyles; *Hair:* Thom Priano

Joan Severance   *Dress:* 1950s prom dress; *Diamonds:* Poiray; *Makeup:* George Newell; *Hair:* Stephan Lempire

Alexa Singer   *Dress:* Mary McFadden; *Diamonds:* Petochi & Gorevic; *Makeup:* George Newel; *Hair:* Yoshi Kosaka

Andie McDowell   *Dress:* Gene London; *Diamonds:* David Webb; *Makeup:* Mark Heyles; *Hair:* Thom Priano

Carrie Nygren   *Dress:* Vintage 1950s; *Diamonds:* Black, Starr & Frost; *Makeup:* Jonathan Wallace; *Hair:* Thom Priano

Index